Praise for the Author

"I like his perspective and agree with many of his points, but his writing style needs some work."

—A reader

"Hey. Thanks for contributing! Unfortunately your submission has been removed as per the community rules."

—An admin

"Yet he seem to have a basic problems with plural. [sic] Is this AI teaching itself?"

—A reader

"This [author] seems to miss the most obvious reason. That they found more money elsewhere. Of every developer I have seen leave [a company], their primary motivation was a higher pay."

—A reader

"This [work] is passive-aggressive behaviour—I call it out."

—A reader

"[Doug delivers] a concise and valuable post that all managers (or aspiring managers) should read. I appreciate Doug for putting 'The most important action of a manager is to hire' first, as without the talent you cannot build a strong team."

—Oren Ellenbogen, Software Lead Weekly

Also by Douglas W. Arcuri

Undercover Toy Stories: An Anthology of Real American Inventions

DECONSTRUCTIVE
SOFTWARE
RAMBLINGS

Essays from the Mind of an Engineering Manager

Douglas W. Arcuri

DEPENDENT
S T U D I O S

Deconstructive Software Ramblings

By Douglas W. Arcuri

For permission requests or inquiries, please address to:
douglaswarcuri@gmail.com

The author made this book with love [and frustration]† in Google
Docs. DSR is set in EB Garamond and code in Courier New.

ISBN: 979-8-9919267-0-6
Library of Congress Control Number: 2024923783
First Edition: December 2024; Reprint: November 2025

To Hazem, who encouraged me to write.

And to Dad, who emphasized a software career—recommended by a man of the past who denied him lunch in the future.

"There are no adults in this conference room. I'll prove it!"
[The author writes his opinions—later—on the Internet.]

Contents

Forward

IN THE EVER-EVOLVING WORLD of software engineering, it's uncommon to find a voice that cuts through the noise—someone who doesn't just observe the industry from afar but dives into its gritty realities. In *Deconstructive Software Ramblings*, Doug Arcuri has done just that. Through a collection of essays that blend the pragmatic with the personal, Doug gives readers a rare look into the mind of an engineering manager who has seen it all: the highs, the lows, and the occasional absurdities that come with building software.

Doug's reflections cover an impressive spectrum, from sharp critiques on modern app experiences and practical team dynamics, to thoughts on work-life balance, career growth, and even the philosophical intersections between programming and daily life. His wit and candor make each essay compelling, while his technical expertise ensures that readers walk away with insights that are both thought-provoking and applicable—especially valuable for those new to the industry.

What truly sets this book apart is Doug's focus on the human side of engineering, a perspective often overshadowed by the code itself. In a field where we are constantly driven by the next big innovation, it's easy to lose sight of the people behind the technology. Yet, in *Deconstructive*

Software Ramblings, Doug reminds us that it's these very quirks and complexities that make engineering both challenging and endlessly intriguing.

Whether you're a seasoned developer or just stepping into the field, you'll find something here that resonates. Doug captures the mindset of a developer navigating both the technical and human aspects of the profession. His essays are a celebration of the passion, resilience, and occasional frustrations that define software engineering—a field he loves, critiques, and champions.

Hazem Saleh

*Software Engineer at Meta, Renowned Speaker,
Published Author, and Advocate for Open Source*

Introduction

SOMEWHERE, ALONG MY JOURNEY, I sat beside a seasoned software engineer on a flight back from the West Coast. We were returning from one of those extravagant tech conferences with massive loot in tow.

The topic of writing "openly" arose. The engineer shared their online blogging experiences. Now, they were writing a book, explaining their disdain of an editor.

He said, "The editor told me that I write like a child. It was torture."

"Nah, man, you're an adult engineer. You write well," I said.

Secretly, I had already read their work. And right there, I decided to write because I was knee-deep in the digital sh*t without a relief valve. I wanted to be that child but without the adult editor.

Making software is a crazy process. It's a thinking marathon, an individual solo sport often concocted with others who bring their own game. Perfect code is its exhibition among them, and deciding to write "openly" is a signal of pending burnout; a once-green-lit software person on a trajectory of flaring out in time. "Writing" means the start of its long tail, a final stage of software—an eventual exit of cashing out to blue-collar pastures in farming, beekeeping, gardening, or, in my case, a lack of funds and a new career—a broke writer.

Whether they know it or not, this person mentioned changed my life in that conversation on the plane, squished in coach class together; the result is what you hold in your hands.

This book brings all my essays together and organizes them into distinct sections. I assure the reader that each piece was debated, painstakingly handcrafted, and abandoned in haste for the next.

Some of my writings within this book made it to the top of *Hacker News*, a news site for dissenting nerds and geeks alike, which became a badge of honor.

I arrived in writing, I thought. "All my essays are taking off, free to read online!"

Well, nothing happened.

Then, I published *How To Place on The Front Page of Hacker News*, which collected upvotes. But a loyal pathfinding admin removed the post.

They banned me.

I came full circle to understand that no one cared. But there was an immense value in public self-expression. Just perhaps someone would read, applying new found wisdom. And people privately agreed.

"The writing was worth the effort," I thought. Instead, I was punching above my weight.

● ● ●

THE SUMMATIVE YEARS I practiced software are those I wrote, and these essays confirmed my burnout. And so I rambled. Each scribble is a passionate cry, drafted while working in the industry.

And the writings followed a cycle. In each, there was a moment I had become overtly aggravated or delighted in publishing loudly on the Internet—for many to laugh, squawk, confuse, learn, or change a view.

In most cases, no one took the time to read. But, I kept going.

Regardless of engagement, these writings are a window to an imperfect soul of technicality. And the act remains addictive—I can no longer help myself from writing. Now, I challenge myself to write one piece monthly on something interesting. And my writing days in software "feels done."

Is it?

Ultimately, software development is an endless intellectual reductionist game of abstraction and patterning matching. In writing, I found a profound joy that connected these innate skills without software's precise bullsh*t, or the politics of corporate, instead forming an unrestrained artwork that was once "mine but is now yours" to read.

I'd seen and felt many things in the industry early and young, and I never thought I'd construct a book, but a life opportunity brought it together.

And what follows are muses in a digital time of change during the era of a pandemic. Some essays are thoughtful, expansive, instructive, myopic, brave, pedantic, insightful, or just utter hand-wavy "how to brush your teeth" crap.

But will you write "openly" next? I'd sure as hell read it.

Douglas W. Arcuri
Massapequa, New York
November 9, 2024

DSR

How to Use This Book

DECONSTRUCTIVE SOFTWARE RAMBLINGS is a book of instructive, insightful, and reflective essays. Its goal is neither a memoir nor a "buttoned up" professional presentation. Instead, it's a collection of compositions that fall short of being timeless.

To use this text, this author suggests reviewing the contents section, finding a few essays of interest, flipping to the starting page, and reading. Then, tell your friends you purchased a fascinating book. Encourage them to tell others about the book and to spend coin on it.

Seriously, DSR can be seen as a companion for those starting their software career. But park the book on a coffee table at the office [welcome back to five days a week in office, sorry] for another to peruse or "borrow." You may catch a staff or principal engineer investigating it.

Maybe even a manager, a director, and those "high ups."

One can read DSR alone at night in between the patches pushed to production on support rotation, while taking breaks creating last minute slides of an important presentation deck, or when seeking an internship.

Wherever DSR lands, it's likely in the hands of a software industry professional or aspiring to be one [you got this]. Maybe not.

Either way, there is no right way to read the book except as you wish.

And however you read, with a little leisure effort, this author guarantees an atomic transaction of information, with new connections of knowledge. Perhaps the viewpoint may spark a new idea [or ignite a debate].

All chapters contained within are annotated, with each item presented in the endnotes *at the end* of the book. Each essay is maintained online at github.com/solidi/writing.

Section One

Gripes on Software Experiences

gripe (/grīp/) *v.* complain about something in a persistent, irritating way.

DSR

Apps Doing Sh*t

EVERY SO OFTEN, I get caught in a thirst trap of a newly spun Twitter [now X] bot. Aptly titled "People Doing Sh*t," they sling catchy videos of humans doing heroic or moronic things. I'll click on each video, clap at their success, close my eyes in horror, or be amazed at how people act in befuddling ways.

My consumer app experiences can feel the same. Imagine a continuing thread of five-second head-slapping experiences where reality is amiss. Apps are doing sh*t, either for good or bad, as I clap for joy or scream into the ether to those who make my life easier at a small price of WTF.

It Happens from Time to Time

You see, apps doing sh*t *are not* slow to load or crash. No, it's more like when things are working well, maybe too well. Their experience rises above the competition—spectacularly failing the customer without intending to do so.

Let's assume everyone experiences degrees of apps doing sh*t. I aim to unearth a list of *"check out these awful/amazing things I experienced!"* Then maybe, after a long thread of examples, those who craft our complex experiences will mold the app world into a beautiful place.

So here are mine, in no particular order.

➔ **Memories with ex-partners.** My spouse and I share photos on the cloud, and often the provider autogenerates *moments with others*. Last week, I saw my beautiful ex's face, titled "*Amazing Memories,*" served to my *spouse's phone*. Being cheeky about it, I said to her, "*Save it!*" The good news is they both share the same name, so no slip-ups to date!

➔ **Kids learn adult language through the Assistant.** Pop music likes to dabble in adult language when we sling songs to our home assistant. Curses fly, and I'll jump on the live grenade—"*Hey, Assistant! Please play music without these curse words. My young kids are present! Uh... no explicit. Yeah! Clean version!?*" Then the response, "*I'm sorry, I don't understand.*" Lyrics will continue to play unabated. I'm left fumbling with unhelpful parental controls.

➔ **Dijkstra's pathing efforts with the highest risks.** Every so often, I'll have to triple-check the car navigation. Rarely am I set on a slower path when the main road is the way to go. Often, it's the fast track, requiring the intense mental effort of maneuvering through dangerous intersections. I'll reach the destination, but my head hurts, narrowly escaping injury from a heroic left-handed turn with family in tow.

➔ **Friend recommendations to the beloving deceased.** One of our immediate family members passed away. Weeks after her passing, I was recommended to *friend her*, as she had discovered the joys of social networks. Sighing deeply, I remember her humor, "*Oh, Douglas... you never call me.*" I started to laugh uncontrollably due to the twist of irony. I miss her, but I don't have the courage to decline her request, sitting idle *for years.*

→ **The private becomes public through screen share.** At the height of the pandemic, personal screen sharing caused pain within my team. A side conversation was shown, resulting in hurt feelings. I was saddled with giving private feedback to this individual, which was funny as it was horrible. Surely, I would not want to be in their shoes. Afterwards, I posted a plea on the Internet,[1] but time passed without an answer.

→ **Scrolling into spoilers.** I enjoy watching missed sporting events, movies, episodes, you name it! With sheer willpower, I'll avoid people in fear of revealing spoilers. On more than one occasion, I'll sit on my couch, having food ready. Without thinking, I'll have a virtual cigarette, opening social apps *before* I watch. Sure enough, something is revealed. I *completely ruined the experience* to satisfy my subconscious need to scroll. Sometimes I don't make it to the couch, as a well-placed personalized push notification or a trending feed short-circuits the fun. I'll ask myself—*what just happened?*

→ **The baby formula on discount, buy now.** It is without question what we say in our home is monitored for market favoritism, *with good intentions.* As I type this, we are searching for delicious food for our youngest. In our exhaustive search for baby formula, we are slung excellent ads with deep discounts. Well, we click through. Look at that, *out of stock.*

Context Matters

I'm sure I missed other examples of apps doing sh*t. My hunch is we are moving through an awkward age of tween personalized recommendation systems. Mature experiences require a higher resolution of related information, its correctness, and providing personal choice—raising questions of privacy.

Aiming for smooth app adventures requires tuning context. I think solving this complexity is possible in time—it's not a technological problem but a cooperative human one. As the saying goes, we criticize within a context. And when apps are doing sh*t, the lack of context is to blame.

What have you experienced?

A Growing List

I've maintained a running note of laugh-out-loud experiences, such as AI recommending sending roses to an ex-partner and an assistant delivering minute notes, including the post-meeting "secret" break-out session to all attendees.

My list continues to grow at github.com/solidi/writing.

Cancel This App Update, Dammit!

MY MORNING ROUTINE hasn't changed over the years. I'll scan serializer.io, get the kids,[1] work out, eat breakfast, shower, and flip open the work notebook. Then I'll be a few goddamned minutes late to the first team meeting of the day.

I'm the Sucker

Apps have little regard for my time. They like to do sh*t,[2] working as intended. I'm late because of a random dice roll from the updating gods. They decided it was my time to watch a slow-moving progress bar as my manager waited in silence. Or it's simply Monday. Then the app will crash. I'm stuck in a loop.

I'm late. It's a bad look.

When I arrive, I'll apologize for my tardiness, being infuriated by the snag. I was really a minute early, but I knew no one believed me. My reputation bank account has *lost coin.*

These apps enjoy finding random suckers like me at their morning launch. A long-tailed update isn't the first nor last that will steal my time. I'm dumb for taking the abuse.

Then I'll contemplate. As a person who develops software,[3] it doesn't need to be this way. What is the problem with updating the app after I leave a meeting? Or execute when the day is over? I ask you, *damn app*, stay outside my critical path, please.[4]

Update to Critically Frustrate All

I'm confident apps sap millions of hours from poor souls needing to perform *on time*. Everything is at stake when updates wag their finger—such as a critical presentation, meeting a customer, joining an interview, or failing to join a one-on-one where the manager is stressed-out.

As I type, an angel investor is tapping their fingers, tending to their boatloads of cash, as their high growth potential screams at the best-looking progress bar on the other side of a digital pipe.

My point is the scheme for updating apps remains broken, and nobody cares.

Yeah, today another app is doing sh*t by disrespecting my time and yours. We all have been in meetings where many people sit, blissfully waiting for a stuck colleague while being paid. Some people are okay with that. Not me.

Do you know who doesn't screw around? It's the people that demand mission-critical software experiences because they are always on the critical path. Do astronauts receive updates while their rocket escapes the atmosphere?

But we all can't be starchildren. It is at this moment my rocket ship leaves the tower, my VPN disconnects, and I am staring into this effing stalled app update. *Sigh.*[5]

SemVer is Dead. Long Live SemVer!

OFTEN, A SWELL VERSIONING SCHEME appears on a link aggregator. I mutter, *"yeah, that's great."* Then I'll add it to a collection that has become a shrine of excellent thinking. In between, an opinion will come along on approaching versioning. Of the posts I read, the "Cargo Cult of Versioning"[1] made me rise off the chair and clap—until the author recanted the phrase:

> *You could even remove the version altogether and use the commit hash on rare occasions when we need a version identifier.*

Sigh, *correctness*, but is there truth behind the author's words?

What's Versioned Out There?

Fast-forward years from the write-up, SemVer[2] 2.0.0 remains the standard. Things stay as they are—a journey to communicate the intention of a change in a tangle of dependencies. If a reader is a maintainer, one receives requests about improvements. If a manager, their game is to reduce risks. If one leads a passion project, eighty-four

Label	Depiction	Introduced	Reality
SemVer	The "Standard"	2013	Here to stay
BreakVer	Clear intentions	2014	Patches can break things
RomVer	Human in the highest	2015	To err is to break some APIs
CSemVer	Limits are good	2015	SQL statements in versions
SimVer	Clear statements	2015	Even closer to reality
MonoVer	Fewer placeholders	2016	The fewer numbers, the better
ComVer	Clear statements too	2016	Confused with simVer
CMSVer	Specific to content	2017	Only if dealing with a CMS!
WendtVer	Tens, tens, tens	2018	Odometer goes on and on
Zer0Ver	Cool, lots of zeros	2018	Defines the incomplete nature of software
PandenticVer	*Sigh*, no	2018	Politics, I guess
ChronVer	A life on a calendar	2019	What month is it?
CalVer	Make me remember the date	2019	Technology marches on
FibVer	Matches the agile thinking	2019	Too many flashbacks to interviews gone sideways
SentimentalVer	Become a stoic	2020	How I feel about my failed essays
HyVer	Good	2020	Closer to reality
HashVer	Not very clear	2020	A good choice for lots of commits
MakeVer	For the C/C++ crowd	2021	Headers for versioning
SemancatVer	Love those cats	2021	I'm allergic to cats
GitDateVer	Make me remember the date	2022	Makes me feel old
SetVer	Set patterns	2022	Wildly satisfying
LatestVer	The reality	2022	Cool, this one is mine

Table 3.1: A decade of version schemes.

versions have elapsed on a Saturday, with one hundred seventy-nine regressions, which no one will find.

And if an adopter updates a library, it's typically to the latest, knowing the risks—even with a suite of ten-thousand unit tests.

Since I am a consumer of someone else's work (like everyone else), I'll avoid bumping the library today or bump it slightly through constrained pinning until I must update it to the latest. I don't have time to decode the version numbers. A version is a linear function where risk *increases* with number. Each bump is a subjectively *more* perfect implementation enveloped with possible dreadful outcomes.

So with versioning stuff, it depends on the intent of the change. Numbers don't communicate intentions well. Even when Rich Hickey said, "change behavior, rename!" relabeling fails to express intent. Regardless, I'll *pin* versions in the hope no one will force me to update[3] until I don't have the option. Then I'll throw my hands up, declaring that nothing is final in software, even when someone else states it's complete.[4] Code expires because labor is consistently involved, costing scarce human, social, or monetary capital to keep it running.

We are all at the continuing mercy of becoming outdated.

But we, as a community, try to do better and I search for a clear version scheme. So this got me contemplating. What is out there? Table 3.1 is the result of my research, and none of the versions strategies are straightforward. So, why not create a new versioning scheme?

Introducing LatestVer

While having good intentions, many versioning schemes are at the fringes. I've rarely seen alternatives in the wild, maybe zer0Ver or calVer, smiling when I do. Creating a new versioning system requires creative thinking *and* invoking a community change which takes exponential marketing. SemVer surrounds our work, and I'll label my libraries like yours. And what I care about is one number, the major version.

As an adopter, I don't sweat over minor versions. It's always about the best, the latest, the major, and the now. If I am building something new, I shop for the latest. Since dependencies are a land of extreme abundance, it is unlikely I will pin my hopes on an out-of-date library. So, while I construct a "shiny thing," perhaps what is happening in my trenches is occurring elsewhere. As a consumer, I choose the latest version while making a new thing. Otherwise, I place myself, the team, and the project in explicit protection until the pinned forcefield depletes, and I must do something. There is rarely an in-between. SemVer is correct thinking, and anything that increments on the far side is what matters to me.

So what is this pattern? Let's call my realistic library versioning scheme latestVer. LatestVer[5] is a simplistic approach to versioning. Choose whatever system—numbers, dates, or hashes. Let's call it a *LABEL*. Then ensure the adopters follow the latest version. The reality is that consumers will be looking elsewhere anyway, challenged by pull requests of technical superiors, or dealing with well-intended contributors. Whatever happens, the adopter must bump up to the latestVer in an ever-present dystopian cybersecurity vulnerability future. Implementers, including myself, will not have time to understand what has changed until getting into the weeds. When I unpack the work, the latest is what matters.

LatestVer is a shortsighted but truthful versioning scheme. As an author, it encourages "accretion"[6] as Rich Hickey said. As an adopter, it is my reality. Understandably I cannot speak for all since there are strict guidelines for implementing dependencies in different environments. But for those in my part of the world where philosophies are unrestricted, it's a general heave-ho, and `latestVer`'s motto captures the mood well.

> *If I'm not on* `latestVer`, *let me get there soon. Otherwise, I'll be forced to prioritize something out of my control. If my problem is not addressed, I'll drop the library for its alternative. And when building anything new, it's always the latest.*

Seldom do I have to cherry-pick a specific "in-between" version that will raise a project from a sinking hole. A feeling sets in while I do it, corresponding vaguely to purchasing something expensive but of little value. Feeling regret, I'll bootstrap my way to the latest, finding the courage to drive in the newest version of *their* shiny thing at the cost of *my* mental labor. In the end, it feels so good to have something new.

I love `latestVer` because it's my reality of working software. I wrote its specification at latestver.org.

DSR

Reply All Considered Harmful

Learning from Sending Thousands of Emails

LATELY, I'M WRITING FEWER EMAILS at work.[1] To me, authoring an email is torture. It's the time-sunk cost of carefully crafting the message. And when I do send an email, I avoid *Reply All*. If possible, I would like the conversation to be between just us.

Over the years, my perception of how to use *Reply All* has changed. Earlier on, my understanding of its intoxicating power invoked a sense of urgency to all those addressed. But after being scrutinized in these exchanges and me targeting others, it has soured. Mix this in with selectively adding in authoritative figures; I now *consider it harmful* for the long-term relationship for those involved.

You and I, but Rarely Anyone Else

While participating in *Reply All* threads over the years, I've learned the concept of a *directly responsible individual* who is accountable and owns the outcome. And when *Replying All*, the action muddles who is directly responsible. And suppose the message is poignantly addressed to a particular person. In business, the receiver may become anxious, find it combative, or downright ignore the ask while communicating to an *unfamiliar* audience. The perception of resistance is real when trust does not exist between them.

Reply All has the potential to *scorch-the-earth*. For select email clients, it is a dangerous default function. I've seen it become the *nuclear button* when context-sensitive information was released to an unattended audience. While I won't reveal the example to protect the innocent, exposure to sensitive information destroys trust between teams and leaders. The result: potential sales loss, team members distrust, and leadership perceived as evil. Yikes.

But it's not all bad. There are good points to *Reply All* that are helpful and effective. An essential function of *Reply All* is to broadcast information, directed at the group interested in the information. Where there is a call to action, *Reply All* is acceptable if all recipients are a trusting team.

Sometimes, job roles require the use of *Reply All* extensively, connecting disparate groups or gathering more *perfect* information that is useful for business outcomes. But in my opinion, these moments in time are rare. They are better served elsewhere, such as in physical proximity, a direct instant message, and thoughtfully crafting a *smaller* target audience for a higher percentage of success.

When I Use Reply All

I've summarized when I typically use *Reply All*. While it is a tool I avoid, there are moments where it's necessary.

→ When the information is vital to a broad audience without commitment to a call to action.

→ When a call to action is essential to a trusting group of individuals.

→ When a critical item requires urgent escalation—in good faith.

When I Avoid the Use of Reply All

Importantly, here are my reasons why I do not use *Reply All*.

→ Avoid detailed information being released to an unintended audience.

→ When the information is essential, a call to action is required, but the directed individual is not trusted.

→ When urgency is needed in an unjustified or repetitive matter.

→ Removing someone's voice by *prematurely* adding high-level authority to a fresh unresolved matter.

→ Replying to a long threaded email without value.

I've sent many emails in my career, and now *Reply All* is one of those tools reserved for exceptional cases. I prefer to defuse, whereas I understand *the individual* who can help me, my team, and the project and product. I continue that conversation *privately*. Once we have closure,[2] it's fused back into the *Reply All* as broadcasted information.

While privacy may seem like common sense, this was a long journey for me to understand. I've reflected on my abrasive *Reply All* exchanges. Whether it's a company of hundreds of thousands of people or just a startup between two, *it's always a conversation with another person*. To me, it's better to build a relationship and obtain results privately. And then give the other chances to do their work before the proverbial balloon is popped.

The people I partner with have come to respect this approach.

And for those in the past who have suffered from my nefarious *Reply All* dealings, I've learned to do better.

● ● ●

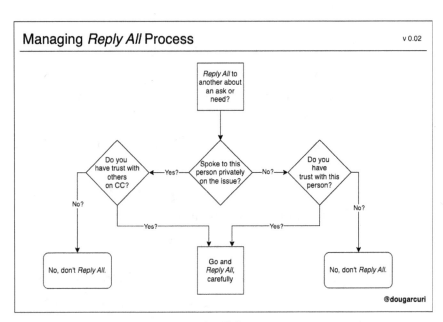

Figure 4.1: *Reply All* diagram process.

Applies to Every Medium

Whether it is instant messaging, email, or communicating in person in front of others, this conversation of "tact" can be applied anywhere—to build lasting trust with others.

5

Goodbye to Saccharine Feelings of Clean Code

A SURPRISING SOURED FEELING has come over me. Lately, the giddy feeling of sweeping up code is absent. As time accelerates hyperlinearly[1] within my text editor, the bursts of dopamine are no longer an assertion of *knowing*.

I'm middle-aged without its small pleasures.

I'm giving up on clean code, coming full circle in a game of sparking joy.[2] If I feel good about mopping up code, I'll remind myself that it's lost time, which steals from what needs doing [which is to ship].

Whatever I'm working on will be sullied over or thrown out,[3] anyway.

Editor's Note

Feel free to share this rant in your next code review. But if you wield this one as a peer or if I'm your manager, I promise you a promotion [as an appointed code reviewer for the next iteration].

DSR

6

Do Laundry During System Demos

WHEN I'M JAMMED ON A TECHNICAL PROBLEM, time evaporates. I'll bargain with myself on when to separate. After a lengthy back-and-forth in self-negotiation on "one more thing!" I'll go for a walk[1] to recover from mental despair. Walking helps my mind collect unexplored methods to attack a frustrating problem. I'll organize my bubbling ideas to rebuild hope that this intractable obstacle is solvable.

Moderate physical activity helps my mind focus, and studies have confirmed my experiences.[2] At least for me, doing something somatic unlocks new ways of thinking. A great example is showering. My likelihood of achieving the desired outcome increases proportionally to my number of showers. Showering is a time to navigate said problem. I just have to watch for an incoming instant message as my manager desperately awaits an answer.

My ritual of making tea or coffee, as a software build proceeds, helps me focus. Better yet, speaking out loud to a rubber duck helps me navigate logic. Sometimes writing,[3] typing, or talking to another human will separate me from a frustrating problem.

Yeah, there are many ways to unstick what is stuck. For me, it requires separation to refocus my approach. More importantly, I have to do something physical.

But what is my most productive activity? I look no further than doing laundry. Performing the folding, sorting, and stacking is a great way to organize my plan of attack in a frustrating situation. In my experience, it has dispatched all my technical and personal problems.

Funny as it sounds, there is no other place like speaking to my pile of warm linens as our system demo[4] proceeds on a videoconference. The best ideas have come from here.

7

Prefer Accommodating Over Accurate App Experiences

COMEDY CAPTURED THE MOMENT as I suggested a destination to the GPS app. "Navigate to such and such place," I said. [A five-second pause.] "Something went wrong." I tried again, *twice*. "You will arrive in three hours," said the assistant. Smirking, I said, "Hehe, yeah, right!" I've been through this rodeo. "No way it's three hours, more like four and a half!" An unneeded reply chimed, "Sorry, I don't understand."

We hurried above the speed limit, got fast food, and hit sporadic traffic. We arrived in *four and a half hours*.

For me, these experiences are typical, having not improved in years.

Apps Prefer Accuracy

Being involved in software[1] for a time, I've had the pleasure to work with brilliant product[2] people. And yeah, every team skewed toward the happy path, preferring *accurate over accommodating*.

Accuracy is demanded in our culture, driven by two points: the relentless pressure to release and moving on to the next thing. Failing gracefully is not on the incentive list.

Apps that are *accurate* perform discreetly, abandoning the user experience during errors, which drives odd customer behaviors. Consumers utilize unconventionality to get what they need, such as unduly force-closing apps, clearing cache, reinstalling, tapping numerous times to get the reward, or a secret action to perform the transaction, fiddling with settings to achieve it. Or, in my case, knowing how to deal with a familiar skew of results.

These behaviors have become common, a badge of honor. For customer service, there is a growing backlog of complaints, low user ratings, and rising churn.

The result is a consumer that acquires pessimism, frustration, the burden of remembering unique tricks, being overcome with doubt, and, in time, abandoning the product for something else.

Nonetheless, many experiences suck,[3] and there is room to improve.

Prefer Accommodating Over Accurate

If we reverse our thinking, preferring *accommodating over accurate*, it will positively change user experiences. For instance, choose to provide upfront rich information, being realistic of a flaky Internet connection, and give the consumer confidence when the transaction has yet to go through [but will,] as soon as possible. Mercilessly scrutinize the error paths, rooting out accuracy, and provide *accommodation* instead.

Yes, *accommodating* experiences costs development time and incurs intense technical complexity to achieve. There isn't an easy way around managing statefulness, and technological inventions are waiting to be found to blunt the digital trauma. But it's worth an inquiry within your team, especially if the app is in production and the rush to launch has eased.

I've seen it many times. When racing to get a product out, *accommodating* actions get cut out of scope[4] as teams repeat in chorus, "Nice to have!" Ask the question, "Why so?" If we don't ask, few experiences will become smooth, and cooperation in intra-app experiences will remain unexplored.

Fluid, *accommodating* interactions do not have to be something of science fiction in software. It is worth taking steps to improve the experience—starting now.

Human Effort Factor

Today's navigation apps select the fastest route to its programmed destination. However, their experiences do not optimize for minimizing human driving effort.

Would anyone want to arrive at their destination five minutes faster if it required three times the physical effort? Certainly not, but these apps forget "at what cost?"

This is a great example of accuracy versus accommodating.

So the next time "Similar ETA" appears on a route—take it! It will deliver a comfortable rate of return.

DSR

Section Two

Software Listicles

lis·ti·cle (/ˈlistək(ə)l/) *n.* a piece of writing or other content presented wholly or partly in the form of a list.

DSR

8

Read these Five Passionate Software Engineering Books

Recommendations that Inspire Building Something

WHILE WE SIT BY the holiday's proverbial fireplace, why not read what we love most? Classic stories that highlight human heat, passion, and the inner workings of software engineering projects. Here are my five *timeless* must-read books which capture the imagination.

The Soul of a New Machine by Tracy Kidder (1981)

No matter where you come from or what generation you're associated with, when a software project moves to a batsh*t crazy release, you're *flying upside down*. Tracy Kidder's story,[1] *The Soul of a New Machine*, covers the birth of the first 32-bit computer that pushes the register counts in a fantastic journey of human sweat, creativity, and the drive of Tom West (and his lieutenant Carl Alsing) to release Project Eagle at Data General Corporation in the late 1970s.

You want to read this for a gripping story with real people as if this was fiction. Along the way, technical jargon is explained not to alienate the reader. Learn about Tom's engineering management tactics to motivate the team (both good, bad, and frankly mushroomy!)[2] that ultimately delivers a project after a violent skunk-works development process with engineers who were none the wiser.

Sometimes it's okay to push the envelope. A triumph!

Code: The Hidden Language of Computer Hardware and Software by Charles Petzold (Second Edition, 2022)

Imagine *programming the machine is like eating from a toothpick*. In *Code: The Hidden Language of Computer Hardware and Software*,[3] travel through the inner workings of computers and their abstractions. *Code* takes the reader on a non-threatening technical adventure with the problem: how can two humans communicate through distance? Petzold's book is a fantastic walkthrough of the machine parts designed to *communicate*.

You want to read this book to have bite-size servings of hardware and software history on a platter. Go a level deeper into the workings of such machinery to see how humans invented abstractions in a fantastic multi-century dissection of its parts. In 2022, its Second Edition[4] added context by easing the ramp of understanding before going into microprocessors.

Code is all tweaked up for the twenty-first century!

Mythical Man-Month by Fred Brooks (Twentieth Anniversary Edition, 1995)

From machine to project focus, the late Fred Brooks' book, *Mythical Man-Month* (MM-M),[5] is an excellent self-analysis of challenging technical and management problems. He walks through lessons of the

IBM OS/360 project, which he managed. While everybody quotes MM-M, some people read it, and a few go by it. What remains is the most famous quote repeated by well-intentioned engineers:

Adding developers to a late project will only make it later.

Most technicians lose this battle to all well-meaning but silvered-tongued leaders with other ideas (really, it's their managers demanding the impossible!)

You want to read this for a fantastic write-up of how a technical lead directs their surgical team with a touch of religious context by Brooks' devout sensibility. While MM-M's technical breakout is now considered old-fashioned, it holds tested observations that have become fact, such as his thoughts on conceptual integrity.[6] His addendum paper included in the anniversary edition, *No Silver Bullet*,[7] is still raised in canonical conversations today. Please read it!

Hackers: Heroes of the Computer Revolution by Steve Levy (1984, Republished 2010)

While Fred was all corporate *inside* Big Blue, imagine a well-written book of the antiheroes *outside*. Steve Levy's book, *Hackers: Heroes of the Computer Revolution*,[8] captures the imagination of the hacker ethos in chapters logically ordered in a three-part series. Learn about the origins of hackers in the 1950s with the tech model railroad club, the room with the machine called PDP-1, and hacking the first video game, *Spacewar!* Move to the 1970s, go west to understand microcomputers with Ted Nelson, Homebrew, and social revolution via a bulletin board.[9] The book will take you to Bill Gates in the desert, Revolution at Stanford, and Woz and Steve forming Apple. Finally, move to the early 1980s with game development in a hot tub by Ken Williams at Sierra. In between, they define the hacker's amorphous motto, *"Do The Right Thing."*

Read this book on stories about humans who have the pulse on the future. But they did it their way, regardless of what others thought about them. You'll learn what it was like *before* technology was a primary cultural driver. These hackers made computers *do what they shouldn't, which no one asked for*—ages before the Internet became a pinnacle of humanity (but will be our undoing).

Masters of Doom by David Kushner (2003)

Masters of Doom[10] could be the missing fourth section of *Hackers*. Take two Gen Xers, John Carmack and John Romero, with their untapped software engineering passions. Mix in the late 1980s when computer games were prepackaged and cookie-cutter. As they cut their teeth in the industry, Carmack and Romero pushed the boundaries farther than they imagined.

This book dives deep into the eventual development of Doom,[11] its shareware release, and how these passionate engineers built a radical empire of new violence in gaming. *Masters of Doom* highlights the anti-corporate working conditions of making something new. They changed the literal game underneath the industry where it stood and inadvertently coerced politicians to birth the ESRB rating system.[12]

If you like a story of people working toward solving problems, you want to read this book. Their results are in the work they released. They had the hacker motto, *"Do The Right Thing,"* quoted by Steve Levy. It will resonate if you have had any time with id Software games in the past three decades. Between John Carmack's extension of breaking technical boundaries of 3D graphics, John Romero's killer design aesthetic, and the impact of the team's forceful creative leader, Tom Hall, who questioned tools like virtual reality, this book does not disappoint.

Honorable Mentions

The Cathedral and the Bazaar by Eric S. Raymond (1999)

The Cathedral and the Bazaar[13] contain essays from leaders in the development trenches who believe *all bugs are shallow, given enough eyeballs*. They discuss the desire for free software, which led to the accidental revolution. Eric's book highlights the passion prominent within the Linux kernel development process that overspilled, becoming what we know as "Open Source."[14] This book will change your mind on how software is developed by people who hold radical opinions about free software creation. Read this one!

Hackers and Painters by Paul Graham (2010)

In Hackers and Painters,[15] Paul Graham's eloquent writing style crystallizes a series of essays about being a nerd, working in technology, startups, and what it means to be a "hacker." Paul famously said *"it's hard to do a good job on anything you don't think about in the shower."* Read this book to understand the origins of being a problem solver. And he is one. Paul founded the machine to fund big ideas that changed an industry into present-day tech. That apparatus is an accelerator called Y Combinator, which birthed unicorns like Airbnb and cemented idea exchange with Reddit and Hacker News.

Peopleware: Productive Projects and Teams by Tom DeMarco and Timothy Lister (Third Edition, 2013)

Peopleware: Productive Projects and Teams[16] contains inspiring essays about setting up and orchestrating a well-oiled software engineering shop. It includes articles tackling what team formation should look like within an organization and recommends office space setup!

While this book does not directly highlight human feats, it consists of the seeds to evolve into the results of all the other books written above, hence why I include it. I recommend this book to anyone in software who wants to influence getting stuff done in a great environment.

Conclusion

These five well-written books (and honorable mentions above) are solid reads of the human workings within technology. My only wish is that there are many more like it. They are a small slice of what has been achieved in software. Each compelling story needs telling.

Take a moment to grab at least one of these this holiday and enjoy.

9

Do Great at Working Remotely

Be Effective and Successful Outside the Office

IN THIS ESSAY, I'll share what I've learned from working remotely (and leading distributed teams) over the years.

Working at home is a mental game. These tips will keep the reader productive, effective, and balanced.

Before Arriving at Work

Here are my essential tips right before heading "into work."

➜ **Keeping a routine.** As if going to work, keep the ritual the same. Eat breakfast as planned. Shower and dress the part. Signal that we are ready to begin working. Placing "the uniform" on improves concentration and pride in the role.

➜ **Walk to work.** Without commuting, stress will be reduced, but work and personal life boundaries will be hard to discern. So in the absence of travel, go for a walk! The action will set the mood as if arriving at the office. Benefits compound health and mind,[1] like listening to focused podcasts during the trek.

While at Work

Once arriving home, here is what is essential "while at work."

➜ **Find a particular place in the home.** Having a different space in the house is vital as a dedicated place to work. Preferably a room with a door is best. However, this is a luxury for many. So carve an area that is work only.

➜ **Equipment does matter.** Having a fast computer and a reliable Internet connection is essential. And the accessories are also crucial. Having noise-canceling headphones helps to reduce distractions. For those that want to go further, buy a professional mic and boom stand to improve presence quality in audio-video conferences.

➜ **Standing up is essential.** There is a reason why standup desks are pedantic in the software industry.[2] They do matter. While many do not have one at home, it will be a good investment. Regardless, it is essential to switch between sitting down and standing up when working. Do this frequently, like at the office.

➜ **Transition into work.** While it is incredibly convenient to join the first meeting of the day "cold," it is a good practice to "burn in" before. Having this half-hour to sync on goals can make remote work highly productive.

➜ **For all meetings, video is always on.**[3] Now at home, it is imperative to cue into the human side of working. It makes sense to keep the video "on" for most meetings. Smile, and be social. We all desire this connection. Facial expressions do build trust. If you cannot, that's okay. Let them know your video will be off.

➜ **Be intentional in communicating effectively.** The prominent benefit of remote working is the periods when one can be productive. In software, we enter deep work,[4] and it's lovely. However, we must balance this with intentionality. Actively reaching out to others on the proper channels is essential. Whether it's for the team, a follow-up, or if the role demands it, do it well.

→ **Active follow-up in minutes, not hours.** The contract above goes both ways. For those that seek contact, be sure to intentionally answer incoming messages in a timely manner. If someone cannot actively engage, suggest a time to chat. Swift acknowledgment is critical for all incoming team messages.

→ **Take lunch. It is essential to step away from the desk during lunchtime.** Take the time to decompress. Go out and get fresh air, too. As a subtle side effect, lunches will be cheaper and healthier since groceries are at home.

Work With the Team Well

As the reader works, apart from the tips above, they can perform "well with the team."

→ **Intentionally build team culture.** Team building is essential, and there are plenty of ways to gather remotely. We can take the lead! Your teammates want to know about us. Set up a time for regular socializing, online happy hours,[5] and brainstorming sessions. Do it frequently by inviting everyone.

→ **Make artifacts easily discoverable.** With remote work, hallway conversations happen less frequently. Keeping a central place of knowledge (such as a wiki) is critical to organize artifacts such as decision and design docs. Importantly, be proactively transparent on progress and point out tools the team uses.

→ **Persistent video hangouts may help.** For those teams that require collaboration, having a centrally located video chat open during working hours can work well. Anyone can bring forward a topic and actively discuss it. Virtually tapping on another shoulder is possible with this setup.

→ **The ability to flex with time zones.** Distributed teams span across the world. Remotely working from home can provide flexing hours to accommodate active contribution and being present at team rituals.

→ **Regularly meeting in person is paramount.** After all, we are storytelling humans, and it is crucial for those working remotely to meet in person. Once a quarter or during times that require heavy lifting, such as launching a product, is a good suggestion. Most importantly, it builds an irrefutable human connection.

After Work is Done

Just as we arrive at work, we must leave it. Here is what is essential in "leaving work."

→ **Finish up and call it a day.** Be disciplined by saying goodbye to the team members. Do so at a particular time or logical break when it's time to leave! Finish up by letting them know and closing out the apps which connect us. For me, I'll slide into a hobby[6] that is unrelated to work.

→ **Close the door.** As discussed above, with a separate space, exit the area as if we left the office. Signal the end of the day by closing the door. No further work will be done today, physically and digitally.

→ **Build relationships outside work.** While most of our time is now at home or in a transitional space, continue strengthening relationships outside work. Being intentional about maintaining old and new bonds,[7] which is essential for wellness!

Finally

Here are my parting items on remote work.

→ **The most critical skill set is written communication.** Remote working demands a higher form of written communication.[8] Apart from actively doing work, continually improving skill sets on spelling, grammar, rhetoric, and being mindful of the impact on others. There are tools out there[9] that can assist in writing well.

→ **Go for it!** You got this! Remote work requires purpose, intention, and transparency. You will do your best job with a bit of practice and keeping these tips in mind. The benefits can be amazing.

DSR

How to Crush Your Next Team Demo

AFTER YEARS OF OBSERVING and participating in successful software engineering demos, here is practical advice I would like to share with you.

→ **You must appease the demo gods.** They will either smile down on you or wreak havoc. It all boils down to preparation. Prepare your demo by walking through it beforehand. Keep it stable, don't change it or rush it last minute. Don't overdo the prep, though.

→ **Spend a moment to introduce yourself.** Yes, many times, I had no clue who the person was even in the same organization. Introduce yourself—what you do and the team you're on. I want to know more about you and may seek you (and others) after for a chat on the impressive demo.

→ **Spend 90% on the context, 10% on the walk-through.** I have sat through demos where *"the why"* of the feature isn't discussed, and the audience has yet to grasp its value. So, discuss the goal first. Then, talk through what you are to demo. Finally, in a few short-strokes, click the buttons that make things "happen" for the customer's delight.

→ **Face the audience, speak louder than usual.** Some demos encourage those to face the same way as the audience. Attempt to break that cycle by going up to the podium. Having that courage is lovely.

→ **Focus on one central point, and stick to it.** Try not to demo many things, stick to one primary value. I have seen demos where so many concepts are presented. I appreciated their hard work. But what was important?

→ **Slides aren't necessary, but they can support you.** Slides can tell the story. Outline what you are to demo. Highlight the challenges you faced and speak about upcoming future work.

→ **Make sure the audience can see what you see.** Lean on the presentation modes in your software so that those can see the work presented. Many times I could not see what was going on. Increase font size for distant readability. I want to see the details.

→ **Always do it live!** Walk-through the demo on the device, with a live connection, the way customers see it. Have that covered? Challenge yourself by going as far as live coding.

→ **But plan a quick backup when the gods strike down.** Demos are rife with failure. Here is a secret. Create a video or screenshots of the walk-through of what *would* happen if the demo begins to fail. Talk through it. The audience will be glad, and the gods appeased.[1]

→ **Prepare a shortlist of proposed questions.** Give the audience a chance to ask questions. A recent tip I heard and experimented with, expect your audience not to have any questions. If so, present a proposed list of items to the audience. There is a good chance it will start a fantastic conversation.

➜ **Don't worry, and you're doing great.** Every demo is a chance to learn about yourself and the audience. The team is there to support you. Even with failure, there is the opportunity to improve the experience for your customers. It is also a chance to increase shared context. Do this at every opportunity!

DSR

11

Be a Rock Star at Pull Requests

I'VE REVIEWED THOUSANDS of pull requests over my career. Here are my tips for building an inclusive learning environment while delivering value.

For the Author and Reviewer

→ **Keep it small and iterative.** By focusing on the intent, small deltas allow the reviewer to provide a timely, high bandwidth review. It's hard, but the author should resist batching work.

→ **Signal intentions with labels.** Whether it's with prefixes in the subject line or if the tool supports tagging, use these liberally to signal when work is in progress. Tags can communicate context, such as the size of the review, or if the work is associated with a milestone.

→ **Provide a clear context.** Define the problem and solution of the pull request in the description.[1] It will provide exceptional value to the review, and includes historical information for onboarding others.

→ **Review your commits and provide comments in the review.** Reduce the ambiguity by immediately self-reviewing your own newly minted pull request. Provide a proactive summary to lines that need clarification so that the reviewer has a clear context.

→ **Be open to feedback, always.** The reviewer likely has good intentions. Take the feedback well by asking questions and making suggestive edits now, or deferring them in an agreed manner. Respectful reviews are useful ones.[2]

→ **Capture conversations in the tool.** Many times, discussions had occurred outside the pull request. However, that knowledge is missing for others. Follow up, and write the outcomes in the tool. This action will immensely add context for others.

→ **End with approval and summary comment to signal completion.** At the end of the review, add a summation paragraph. The feedback will give a recap, acknowledge the great work, and build trust between reviewer and author.

→ **An empathetic review is additive attribution.** Show that you care deeply for both the code and the author. Take your suggestive edits and file them on top of the pull request. The continued courtesy builds collaborative teams.

For the Team

→ **Prefer pairing over pull requests.** Pairing provides the same value as a pull request review with the benefit of real-time results. Work toward a system that, if significant pairing has occurred, the team should provide a way for those individuals to merge without a pull request.

→ **Make it easy for those to receive a timely review.** Make the ritual of code review easy for newcomers to receive a timely review. Some teams I've seen have precise time ranges for review, others have set SLA's. Either way, be inclusive and welcoming. The reviewer pulls.

The author shouldn't need to push.

→ **Always look to improve the tooling to avoid nits.** High bandwidth pull requests lean on the direction of the codebase, not the format. Keep investing in tooling so that the human review shines. Every small comment (a nit), is an opportunity to automate away.

→ **Embrace a to-do list.** The biggest gem of pull requests is potential improvement opportunities. Capture them, embrace them, LOVE them. And above all, keep track of them, and get them done at the next iteration.

→ **Iterate on a descriptive template.** Some teams have contributing philosophies to pull requests. I've seen groups work on checklists so that the pull request is comprehensively complete. Find an instrument that moves towards completeness.

→ **Make it easy to run the work locally.** Avoid surprises in failed builds. Emulate everything that happens in the pull request locally. Whether it's pre-commits, static analysis, or tests, move to make it dead simple for anyone to run the build in one command.[3]

→ **Encourage ratcheting over gatekeeping.** Keep measuring the health of the codebase and if abstractions are understandable. Do not expect perfection; expect learning and improvement on every review. Remember, there are engineers at all levels on the team. Are you growing them without frustration?

→ **Pull requests are about cross-pollination learning.** Respect other's efforts in their pull request. Context and opinion rules software engineering. Make these philosophies apparent to the author. Clear expectations make great partners. Starters could be a contribution guideline. Bug catching and code consistency are side effects of the review.

Finally

➔ **Keep it fun.** I once observed a team where they challenged themselves by writing clever haikus and prose in each summary. Doing this hundred (ah, thousands) of times developed a team of Hemingway's. Try adding to the playful habit. Engineering is all about curiosity and learning from play.

12

The Joy of Collecting Timeless Engineering Posts

HIDING ON THE INTERNET are brilliant software engineering posts. They idle behind a few strokes of a query, having a quality set apart from the endless but helpful question and answer threads.

I recently discovered another collectible gem. This one is titled *When Bad Things Happen to Good Characters.*[1] I'm not exactly sure who the author is.

What I enjoy about posts are their unassailable attributes. They unquestionably bring deep *nerd joy*. What do I mean?

→ **They are titled intelligently.** The subject is well thought out, with a play on words, but never mincing the impact. They are associatively memorable.

→ **The subject is succinct.** The story never wanders about something soft, they get right to the heart of the matter.

→ **There is playful humor.** The tale doesn't take itself too seriously. Somewhere in the post, there is a joust for a genuine laugh.

→ **Has clear examples.** Finding a phenomenon many engineers experience is hard. What's harder is capturing examples that are vivid in one go.

➔ **Brings the joy of partnership.** When a teachable moment surfaces, the content demands to be shared openly. Whether it's mentoring an engineer or someone who summons technological prowess, it's revered.

➔ **The content is timeless in nature.** A post like *When Bad Things Happen to Good Characters* is unlikely to age. It lives for years without decay. It will always make me happy, now that I have it in my possession.

• • •

I CAME ACROSS *When Bad Things Happen to Good Characters* as my teammate pursued a damned character encoding defect. For a moment, I thought, "wow, a language to describe this awful mojibake." I shared it, and we laughed nervously together about the *wild animals* eating umlauts for breakfast.

And so, the post was added to my list,[2] primed for the future.

I appreciate its pragmatic approach. It fits in a wide spectrum of engineering posts of principle or practice that invoke feelings of joy, brilliance, and supreme craft. Oh, how such an author distills experience into so little writing and then makes it timelessly shareable.

If by chance you were wondering, we solved the encoding issue by setting the *right* code page,[3] keeping the wildebeests at bay.

13

Ten Self-Care Tips for a Great Vacation

AS I SAT ON A BENCH on my vacation, watching my better halves[1] browsing in the *Olde Shoppes*, I identified my *vacation behaviors* to maximize decompression and minimize exhaustion. With the goal of self-care and peaceful continuity, I wrote a list of practical actions to promote a healthy relationship with my employer.

Starting with My Manager

A great vacation starts with a good relationship with my manager.[2] In time, I'll discuss supportive vacation needs, who can manage the team in my absence, and uphold ongoing work so I can enjoy the time away.

Occasionally, stepping away from what I own is a challenge. By checking in periodically, my pattern had caused stressful vacations, a regular occurrence—until I burned out.[3] After breaking down, I said no to my illicit behaviors.

Self-Care Tips for a Better Vacation

Assuming relations with the manager are great, and project management[4] applies resource adjustments to meet goals, practicing self-constraint begins with a list of reasonable guidelines. What are my patterns of self-care?

1. **Pressing pause on meetings.** Committing to meetings during a break, especially in the middle, is a recipe for a ruined holiday. The worst is to acquire a time-sensitive action item during the meeting. It's best to leave the sessions until I return.

2. **Setting away messages.** To signal clear intentions, I set an away message, decline meetings in the vacation path, and place an out-of-office block on the calendar. If an appointment is necessary, I'd know by the owner's response to my declined invite. We will reschedule when I return.

3. **Emails and Slack can wait.** Responding to a message[5] can interrupt my vacation. Checking for who sent a message has an exacting mechanism, as I may be called to action, which inflicts stress.

4. **Reassign stories and tasks.** My assigned duties may be incomplete as I step away for vacation. Before leaving, I'll communicate expectations to those who await results, asking for a team reassignment or alternative closing strategy. To uphold my reputation, I'd like to leave with questions answered about unfinished work.

5. **Leave the notebook behind.** During vacations, I avoid taking my work notebook with me. Keeping a distance from the accessibility is essential, and communicating my intention of space is a courtesy to the team. And if I am scheduled for on-call support, I partner with a teammate to create an override.

6. **Limit screen time.** Since computers and phones are accessible around me, I'd sometimes drift into working on passion projects during vacation.[6] Balancing this time is a conscious effort, and it's

sometimes essential to say no, stepping away from the screen.

7. **Balancing domain knowledge.** While being an expert in a particular product area[7] has its benefits, it has a way of coming back to me while taking a vacation. So if I suspect I am the primary contact, I proactively share knowledge, promoting a convo of support. I'll work towards providing the team with a delegate in my absence.

8. **Consider contiguous days.** Achieving decompression within a few short days can be challenging for me—taking a Friday to extend the weekend for relief usually falls short. So, I try to take contiguous work days. My ideal length of time is at least one week.

9. **Asking for giveback days.** I'll speak to my manager about *giveback days* for those vacations where I am required to act unexpectedly. Few managers will proactively give these credits to those they call in, but for those who forget, ask. Importantly, I've learned I was critical, so I'll attempt to balance out the knowledge next time.

10. **Compartmentalize FOMO.** My fear of missing out is a constant reality. I must believe the team will cover.[8] The work will be there when I return, so it's best to take the vacation fully, diving into diversions and enjoying those around me.

What I Do Reflects on Others

Discovering these common-sense items took time. More so, to have the self-restraint to say, "No, don't do that!" Of course, I sometimes drifted too far, scolding myself for acquiring information I've stewed on[9] for the remaining time off.

How I behave on vacations has a reflective property within the team. Whatever I do, is what they *may* do. I'll remember to take a better break, returning well-rested and at my best for the team. More so, my family will appreciate my efforts to be present.

DSR

14

The Not So Small Things of Developing Software

REFLECTING ON MY software experiences,[1] I've formed a catalog of deep curiosities. Here is my list of all the *not-so-small* things I learned about creating software.

Defaults rule the perceived experience. What comes shipped in software is what sticks to its adopters. I've learned what is preset in software, such as settings and default preferences, shapes a first impression. That impression predicts an excellent experience from a flawed one. Adopters of my software rarely see past the defaults. Those who do are my power users.

→ **Rubber ducking clarifies intent.** When I speak to a rubber duck about issues, it solves my problems. When it doesn't, I'll take another step, talking to a human about what I am to do. Performing these two actions has a consistent effect. Speaking increases the odds of achieving what I've said, solving the problem in a shorter time.

→ **Communicate using video often.** Context is needed when a problem is discussed in conversation. Today, sharing motion capture has become effortless. Why not cut a gif or movie[2] of the observation? Since I've used gif creation, it has helped me cast a broader net to solve my problems faster.

→ **The most straightforward answer is the right one.** Debugging is a process of deep information gathering and logical deduction. If my approach goes "off the ranch," I'll tie back the fantastical thinking[3] (or blame the framework) for such woes. Instead, the solution to my problem is a straightforward answer.

→ **The answer comes the following day.** While rubbering ducking is half the strategy to unstick my problem, the other half is to step away and let my mind stew.[4] The solution to a problem will come the next day. Whether showering, exercising, or chewing breakfast, an explanation from yesterday's woes will bubble up.

→ **Deprioritizing quality for delivery.** When revenue is on the line, humans will set an immovable date. Next, consistency and quality will forgo priority in delivering software. So when delivery is declared, its scope, but precisely, quality, is at stake. Said plainly, not everything worth doing is worth doing well,[5] which is a difficult lesson for me as a former perfectionist.

→ **Instability at the edges.** When I develop software,[6] the middle parts of the system are stable. Instability lies at the edges, the seams, and the software setup. Therefore, I test software presets to ensure edge cases are tested thoroughly.

→ **Scripting things remain essential for automation.** Writing manual instructions is a step toward automation. I've achieved this by do-nothing scripting,[7] a great way to capture actions performed in an environment. Taking the scripts I wrote, I'll hammer them into a future pipeline that builds software continuously.

→ **A route to innovation is through tooling.** Creating tools for software engineers is a perfect environment to develop novel solutions to common problems. Tooling demands invention since it's hermetic to a difficulty that needs solving. Interestingly, since the tool's focus is on the immediate resolution of someone's pain, there is a chance of discovering an untried solution.

→ **Naming and grouping things remain complicated.** Aliasing software components requires a choice of cute[8] versus descriptive. I've participated in teams of senior engineers where services are tagged "creatively."[9] While labeling does not have an answer, organizing those names is clear. Grouping by concern,[10] not by type, is an excellent strategy to keep my sanity in check.

→ **Grains of salt in applying quality acronyms.** My engagement in pursuing quality software contained acronyms over the years. DRY, YAGNI, AHA, TDD,[11] and PAGNI,[12] to name a few. While all these are reasonable guidelines, easing their application in construction is a route for sanity. Over-application of such methods leads to developing into a corner. It's a matter of judgment and moderation. If I had to haul them all away, the one I would keep is KISS. Over-complexity destroys clarity.

→ **Interviewing requires specific practice.** Interviewing is a core part of maintaining my career.[13] My interviewing experiences have been challenging. I've succeeded, but in others, I have failed, sometimes humiliated. While every interview I've participated in was fair, some felt like intellectual hazing. I say this because the complex challenges raised in discussions do not appear on the job. So practicing is a skill set in itself.

→ **Distance between teams breeds contest.** Having experience working with collaborative teams over the years, I've witnessed that distance equates to competition. As isolation increases, so does the perception. It takes filling the gaps between people to avoid disharmony. But I learned sometimes I could not smooth out the edges, a reality of participating in a group of software engineers.[14] I had to let go.

→ **Remote work is a mental game.** I support remote work and its flexibility for engineers to do their job well.[15] Just like interviews are a skill set, so is working remotely. Lately, the impact of a world-shifting pandemic has caught up to me. My journey has been a long adventure[16] of becoming productive in the new environment.

→ **Support systems become collateral to burnout.** It was uncomfortable when I was engaged in a time-consuming project for months. Wrapping software engineering into a career is a recipe for experiencing burnout.[17] I found it crucial to find a support system to lean on. Software engineering requires deep thought. With its intensity, my support system had become collateral. To put the brakes on solving issues, I purposefully said no.

→ **The urge to become an expert gardener.** While plenty of my contemporaries swear by the craft, few quit to become expert farmers—due to exhaustion. At a point in my career, I see a precise repetition of events. Planning, developing, testing, and shipping software. Specifically, dealing with the politics in-between with a growing list of shelved projects. It may be time for me to take up gardening.

Conclusion

While this list is a living document, it captures my *not-so-small* things about software creation. While developing software, these essential concepts are front of mind while creating solutions. In time, embracing them will lead to further discoveries. I am sure I missed a few other core concepts, which I will add later.

DSR

15

Do You Have a Forever Project?

MY INTERESTS TEND to have a long tail—re-blooming decades later. Their revival is shaped by a life-altering catalyst, sparking a renewed interest in good feelings.

Lately, I've dug deeper into these curiosities, nurturing a set of passions. Retro-gaming[1] is one of them, and short-form writing[2] is another, but most important is reviving my exhaustion in software development.

So when the global pandemic unrolled with my family sheltered away, I inventoried my life for meaning, taking stock in what I had. That time of unease reminded me of my early years behind the monitor, locked away, tinkering with a project with others on the Internet. Uncovering these feelings opened a long-standing desire to continue something I started so long ago.[3] Some call it a passion project, but I'd like to call it a *forever project*.

Deeper than a Passion Project

My *forever project* involves developing video game modifications. "Modding" is an enveloping environment, exercising skills of artistry and software engineering.[4] Important in this writing is to label what I am experiencing. Do others resonate with a similar stimulus in their immersive projects?[5]

Labeling an effort like a *forever project* gets me thinking deeply in meta. In my own experience, a forever project is a unique designation. Its revival is a miracle, and its timescale lasts decades. I found my forever project by pursuing a hobby, which had become my software career. But then I burned out,[6] and when world events affected daily life, I rediscovered where it started.

What Makes a Forever Project?

My *forever project* is a continuous stream of effort in the background. Deeper than a side project, side quest, or a passion project, my forever project has challenged me, and its feedback comes in waves of interest. This project is a sidecar making life enjoyable. I describe it as a pedantic feeling of excitement, a rush of good emotions while creating something meaningfully valuable.

So, what defines the attributes of a *forever project*?

→ **Surrounded by others, old and new.** A *forever project* will have a support community. Different groups of people, over time, tend to come and go within the project. It may even become increasingly popular.

→ **It goes on for decades.** As in its name, a *forever project* tends to go on indefinitely. The project will depend on a community supporting its revival. It will go through periods of contributions and, other times, enter dormancy. However, it will come back with roaring nostalgia into something modern.

→ **A feedback loop that never gets old.** The *forever project* resists staleness, continuously demanding solutions to problems. During the day, the answers to issues will naturally come. There is a tendency to a cycle, but it's not formal; the rules are casual.

→ **Not attached to a company or job.** *Forever projects* aren't connected to an entity that optimizes revenue or pursues an industry. However, it will attract those who see the concept as profitable. For the creator, an introduction to a new career. In my case, a rejuvenation of creativity.

→ **Bubbles with excitement, challenging at all levels.** A *forever project* provides a feedback loop touching different skill sets of interest. A forever project delivers to a community, adding value to it.

→ **At most, a handful in a lifetime.** Since the timescale is exceptionally long, its efforts compound, altering the path of one's life, *forever projects* occur only a handful of times.

→ **Without a concrete plan but has a form.** A *forever project* will tap into skill sets by growing them, for example, shipping things over perfecting them.[7] Participating will exercise the skills picked up over the years, with control and finesse, without all the rules. Its actualization is learning with an impactful result.

→ **Promotes progeny and resists fading away.** *Forever projects* continue even after their original authors stepped away. Or if the contributors are forcibly removed from their creative chairs.[8] The project is open for anyone to contribute, preferring to share its passion now over the risk of losing enthusiasm soon. No matter how *personal* a forever project may feel, it attracts contributors because of its inevitable community impact.

Creating Without Many Constraints

After rediscovering my *forever project*, I've been engaging with the effort for over a year. Its attributes are *invisible*, and why I write this to memorialize my experience in pursuit of the medium.

Perhaps having numerous interests increases the chance of discovering the next *forever project*. But more so, having one has made me happy. I'm creating again without all the rules, formalities, or politics.

Do you have a *forever project*?

16

Video Gaming Concepts for the Uninitiated

WATCHING MY CHILDREN play provides exciting observations. Their behaviors are organized into distinct concepts. I'll tinker, associating their manners with unrelated ideas. Then, it came to me. I crave comparable actions while playing *video games*. In this essay, my goal is to label them.

As an uninitiated developer[1] who could not hold a candle to gaming theorists, I believe the following behaviors make gameplay fun. At the same time, the results trigger my children's laughter at loftier decibels while at play. My fascination is this question: *Do these behaviors transcend to video game mechanics, delivering higher fidelity?*

The List of Uninitiated Attributes

So, I created a list to answer the question.

→ **Physical possession of objects.** Holding on to things is an essential ability. While video games have inventories of collecting possessions, few have allowed players to hold onto objects in space. Grabbing onto two items is better. How about even more?

➜ **Picking up objects and throwing them.** While holding things is excellent; picking them up and manipulating them in space is perfect. Why not throw them at something? Better strength means adequate velocity. Start laughing because there is plenty to throw.

➜ **Damage and destruction of objects.** Objects are damaged if enough force is applied. Things can be destroyed too. Of course, laughter increases with the amount of destruction, to a point before it becomes out of hand. Specific items can be destroyed in video games, with lots to explore.

➜ **Hiding without others knowing.** Also known as *stealth*, this concept has the stimulating effect of protection. Cloaking oneself leads to laughter. Being hidden provides a feeling of opportunity. Games have analyzed this concept over the years, but there is much to explore.

➜ **The permanence of objects.** Objects which remain strewn across an area is an expression of disorder, especially if these objects are revisited later. Going back to what was placed earlier is of interest. Things are rarely accumulated in video games, as resources are reclaimed.

➜ **Repeat and retry.** Reprising one of the items above or below, doing it repeatedly. The same goes for these concepts in video games. A solid rewind/repeat mechanism is yet to be developed,[2] but systems have been tried.

➜ **Full brights and environment.** Nothing gets the kids laughing if there is play at night, in the snow, or an environmental change. Environmental space is the same as in video games. There are copious amounts of effects. Recently, glowing objects, or full brights, are often used for improved visual style.

➜ **The fluidity of movement.** Kids like to climb to inaccessible areas. They jump around and laugh when their perspectives are altered, looking upside down! The same goes for virtual reality; lately, games have opened up into fantastic "acrobatics," "parkour," vertical play, moving fast, and flying upside down.[3] There are mechanics left undiscovered.

→ **Chaos in quantity.** Increasing the number of objects makes kids go nuts. Think of a ball pit where there are thousands of similar items. So in video games, in a gray box or sandbox, with lots of abilities to spawn them. Chaos mode, where objects are at insane levels, makes for an exciting, time-consuming experience.

→ **Pretend building.** Nothing gets my kids' minds flowing with ideas when they pretend to build. Either sandcastles or pillow forts, it's a lot of laughter with creative imagination like *substitution* and world-building in the small. The same sentiment stirs within video games. Making things virtual is a captivating topic worth investigating its value.

→ **Mutator configurations.** Kids have a way of inventing the play in which they engage. They make things up, configure their toys in a particular way, or change the environment with unique rules such as copious amounts of pretend lava. So too, are nice to have with video games. Changing up its composition is a must-have. Unfortunately, games limit their options.

→ **Playing with invented rules.** Governance and policy are unmistakable qualities enabled in video game communities— involving others increases the fun factor. By keeping score,[4] kids create play rules in which inspirit the experience, bringing out their disagreements!

Is it Fun?

From here on out, adults invent intricate rule sets, ending my list. Those were my observations about video games, my kids, and what I crave while playing. But how do you quantify fun? Having these qualities alone does not equate to joy. A combination of them will provide incentives.

I'm sure I missed other attributes which are a part of gaming elements. Of course, numerous mechanics are well-known within the community. My goal here was to list out these observations. How they connect will be a topic I'll explore as I find other patterns.[5]

Sandboxed Limit Seeking

Limit seeking is a pattern, where a player pushes the rules of the system (or of a leader).

Regardless of age, players tend to test boundaries of the system they are in. How fast a car can go, how much one can hold, how sharp a turn can be made in a vehicle. The fun ends when the boundary is exceeded, and a consequence is tolled.

In 2004, Garry's Mod was released. It is a sandbox game which provides a world of manipulative objects which broke the mold of first-person games.

Garry's mod is one of the many sandbox proving grounds of all of the above attributes in this write-up. And user generated content provides endless rules, objectives, assets, and plenty of creative limit seeking.

Section Three

Practices and Insight in Software

prac·tice (/ˈpraktəs/) *n.* the actual application or use of an idea, belief, or method, as opposed to theories relating to it.

in·sight (/ˈinˌsīt/) *n.* the capacity to gain an accurate and deep intuitive understanding of a person or thing.

DSR

17

Touch Typing Feels Good but Is It for Me?

A Brief Analysis of Learning to Touch-Type

MY RECENT OBSERVATIONS of "humans with keyboards" motivated me to write this essay. It seemed, people around me type in a belabored "hunt and peck" style. Even a friend proclaimed he "typed proficiently with two fingers, not ten." And so we fell into a debate. Strong opinions arose from our conversation, without an agreement if touch typing was worth the practice.

I prefer the "hunt and peck style" too.

Of course, typing style is a personal choice. No one will ever force you to do it differently. Those who are curious discover their choice. And my curiosity set me off on a diversion of improving my typing. The question to myself was "With all these years behind the keyboard, how does my style measure up? Can I do better?"

This exercise analyzes learning touch typing with speed and error measurements. I'll conclude on what touch typing feels like and if I'll switch from my self-taught typing strategy.

Motivation

With twenty years behind the keyboard, my typing style is embarrassingly inefficient and clumsy. I can measure these traits on numerous factors.

- → I do not use all of the available fingers
- → My hands move to find keys
- → I look at the keyboard to realign my position

From these points of my self taught typing strategy, I'll label it as it looks: *float typing*. I have a sense that my speed is decent but do not have precise measurements. So, let's find out.

My Typing Baseline

To measure, we need a tool. I chose the website `keybr.com` to perform typing measurements on speed and error rate. What I liked about `keybr` is its no-nonsense learning. No typing games. It has algorithms that detect weakness in learning keys. Samples of commonly strung letters in the English language are recorded. The user interface is clear, straightforward, and the statistics are excellent.

```
the from the and amnes the their the ders gold the alson ords that
and act oned the
```

Figure 17.1: One sample capture from `keybr.com`.

I start with my style of typing. My float typing predominantly uses both index fingers and sometimes middle fingers. Thumbs are on the spacebar. I utilize six fingers where needed. My fingers do not feel the keys, but land on the right keys. The hands fly across the keyboard as I type. I look at the keyboard when I cannot detect the next key's position.

First, let's look at my relative typing speed.

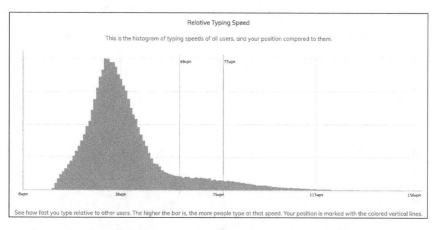

Figure 17.2: Speed of float typing, from keybr.com.

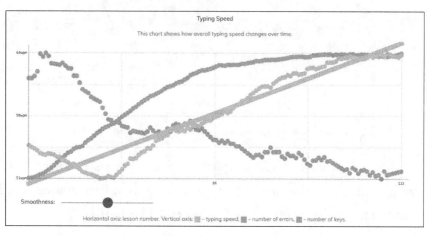

Figure 17.3: Graph of float typing baseline, from keybr.com.

In Figure 17.2, the lines marked vertically are my average and top typing speeds. Here, my average typing speed is 60 wpm (words per minute). Figure 17.3 is based on all other users that are sampled at `keybr`. From their perspective, my average speed is in the 89th percentile and my top speed is at 95%.

We can see the tool registered 132 samples, taken over the course of 35 minutes. I am comfortable with the length of testing since we see a steady line past 100 samples. Error rate and typing speed are generally consistent.

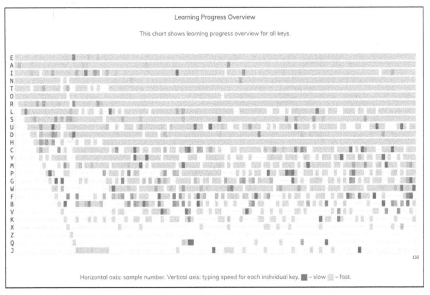

Figure 17.4: Fast/slow histogram on float typing, from `keybr.com`.

Over the course of 132 samples my typing speed is generally "fast," with some keys that are "slow." I chalk this up to unique word combinations that made me look down at the keyboard.

Touch Typing

My motivation during this exercise is to gain speed and reduce error rate. More fingers, less hand movement, and focus on the screen. After brief research, the style that addresses all three concerns is touch typing.

Touch typing is an efficient way to utilize all fingers at the keyboard. It helps minimize hand movement and decrease error rate. Touch typing's main purpose is to have eyes on the screen without looking at the keyboard to focus on typing content.

Okay, let's take a look at my metrics around touch typing.

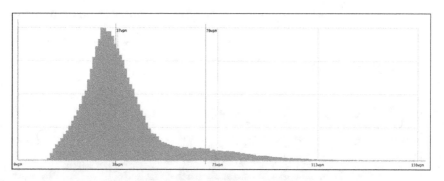

Figure 17.5: Average speed of touch typing, from keybr.com.

As we can see above, my average is much lower at 37 wpm. What is interesting is my top speed is similar to the float typing baseline. As a stretch, we can say that my "top potential" is 70 wpm. This will require significant dedicated practice. At about this point, I max out in speed and wobble in error rate.

On the following page is a graph of 1,200+ samples. This is 10 hours of practice over 25 days. We can see a plateau of error and typing speed. Over time, my average improves to 50–55 wpm.

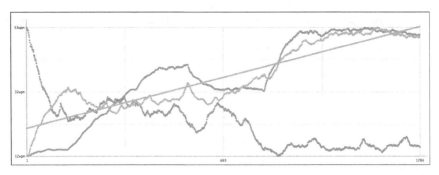

Figure 17.6: Touch typing 25 days in, from `keybr.com`.

This falls short of my self taught typing strategy at 60 wpm. From keybr's perspective, my average speed is in the 54th percentile and my top speed is at 92%.

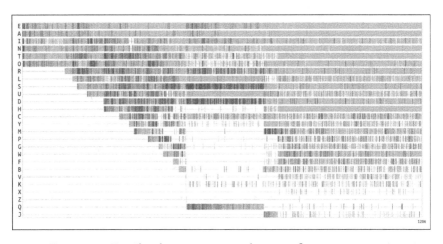

Figure 17.7: Fast/slow histogram on touch typing, from `keybr.com`.

As I become confident in touch typing, each key becomes defined and its typing speed improves. We can see above I had difficulty with R, S and D leading the tool to continually exercise my left hand. There was also a good portion of time where Q was labored upon.

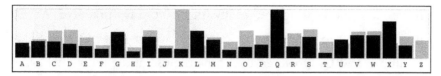

Figure 17.8: Relative miss frequency. Touch typing (light) versus float typing (dark). Lower is better, from keybr.com.

Finally, we come to errors. The review of the hit/miss ratio or relative miss frequency per key is clear. The light bars are representative of touch typing and the dark bars are float typing. The lower the bar, the better. Since I am learning, it is natural there is a higher tendency of missed keys with touch typing. Twenty of the 26 keys reported a higher error count.

Touch Typing Takeaways

The measures are clear. We can make an early conclusion. For me, there isn't a benefit in speed or error rate using touch typing. But all is not lost. If I practice, I will improve. Here are important takeaways.

It Feels Really Good

Related to muscle memory, touch typing provided a sensation of "feels good" when it came to middle, ring, and pinky articulation. For example, typing words that consist of adjacent keys produce a good feeling. Examples of words like "were," "wards," and "sad." As numerous fingers "rolled" through the keys, my dopamine peaked.

Finger Muscle Identification

Keybr identified weakness on my left fingers and right hand extremities. My middle, ring, and pinky fingers hurt as I practiced. At first, it was difficult to type sequences like "as" and keys like O versus I and finding P and Q. However, over time the use of the individual fingers became easier. I also noticed that my extremity fingers felt independent, especially the middle and ring finger.

Discipline with Home Keys

It was difficult to understand my location on the keyboard so I forced myself to "find the bumps." After every word I forcefully "reset" to the F and J home keys, felt them, then continued with the next word. This slowed me down.

Difficulty with Keys Closest to Palms

For me, touch typing minimized the movement of hands in a horizontal fashion and maximized my fingers movement on the vertical axis. I noticed that keys M and X commanded my hands to move somewhat downward, unnaturally. This could be due to the length of my middle fingers and the natural inclination of my fingers pointing upward as I rested my palms.

Looking at the Keys Inflates Numbers

I had a tendency to look at the keyboard when my hands strayed from the home keys. Words that began with B and G made me look as I typed. As noted above, I had to either stop in motion to find the bumps then go for the key or look quick and readjust. Sometimes the latter felt faster. Let's prove this.

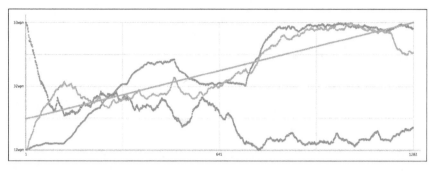

Figure 17.9: Planting my hands had a significant effect starting at sample 1,206, from keybr.com.

At sample 1,206 I forced myself to keep my palms planted, never looking at the keyboard. The result setback is seen above, as my speed dropped by 10 wpm and my error rate jumped.

The exercise was difficult as I resisted the urge to look at the keyboard. During the exercise I discovered resistance from my middle, ring, and pinky fingers from samples 1 through 650.

Conclusion

What we focus on, grows. Should this skill expand?

As I continue to practice I have found two modes of typing. If I want to type faster and with less errors, I choose float typing. When I want to feel good, both socially and from dopamine, I choose touch typing.

I will continue to practice touch typing but, looking over the data, it will take time to master. Dedicated practice will be required to throw away my self typing strategy... float typing. Will my articulation grow enough to hit high speeds if I practice?[1] Touch typing could be the answer.[2] *What is your typing style like?*

DSR

18

Deception: Degenerate A/B Testing

Questionable A/B Tests Using Dark Patterns

PICTURE A NORMAL TRIANGLE in your head. Now picture a triangle without its area. Can you? In mathematics, a **degenerate triangle** is defined as follows:

> *A degenerate triangle is formed by three collinear points. It doesn't look like a triangle, it looks like a line segment.*

It's as if the three angles of the triangle are flattened. In theory, the triangle exists, but all that remains are overlapping linear lines.

While this essay is not about mathematics, it will attempt to classify certain A/B testing methodology as *degenerate* using patterns that approach a line of user deception, also known as *dark patterns*. Then, we will review questionable large scale tests in the tech industry. Finally, we will conclude by giving recommendations on avoiding this deception by making clear statements to our users.

Before we begin, let's discuss what A/B testing is.

What Is A/B Testing?

A/B testing is based on statistical mathematics and theoretical *psychological* experimentation. There is a control "A" and a variation "B." An author of a test sends these two types to a controlled percentage of users for a variation of time in the product under test. The percentage and groups of users can be controlled by *targeting*.

Once the A/B test is completed, the data is analyzed. The analysis allows the team to steer the product in a direction[1] based on the results. These data points are inferred by the team, driving performance indicators such as *click-through rate, revenue conversion, customer retention,* or to find new indicators.

Traditional A/B testing alters the user experience, visual design, or the customer journey of the targeted system to reduce user *friction* and maximize *engagement.* Most tests are on the *surface,* where the colors, layouts, or navigation flow/behavior are altered.

A/B testing[2] has gained a particular *perception*. Consultancies have formed businesses around the discipline, just how they formed around search engine optimization (SEO). SEO gained popularity in the 2000s. A/B testing followed soon after. While SEO was beholden to secret algorithms that can change from direct control of companies like Google, A/B test logic is owned by the authors who execute them to meet goals for their stakeholders.

Data collection and tooling has increased dramatically over the past few years. The authors of A/B tests have the power to walk a fine line on a code of ethics. Let's explore these practices by defining high-level dark patterns, with the first classification under platform tools.

Pattern 1: Act on Urgency

Those who have used Android or iOS applications know what a notification badge is. Notification badges are visual indicators on the app icon that cue the user to important events. The badge is a brightly colored circle indicating the number of notifications waiting.

Example

Imagine if we push a badge with a deceptive count to represent subjective notification activity. Even when the user is logged out, they'll receive badges without significant user activity. The badge is engagement bait.

For those who are targeted, users will engage with the application to understand what was urgent. They'll engage many times, increasing chances of an outcome, because of the badge's presence.

Motto: "Urgent Notification"

On mobile platforms, that notification badge is one of many routes to execute interesting A/B tests. The platform tools will vary, but each platform engages users through high-level indicators they are familiar with. The users are wired to respond and engage, without knowing that the urgency is subjective.

Next, we will fake things.

Pattern 2: Fake It Until We Build It

Of course, there are many parts of a digital product that haven't been built completely yet. However, we want to increase engagement in some way.

Example

Recently, a group of users navigated a streaming app, looking to watch a particular movie genre. As the users typed in the search result, they were steered to partial matches.

The users engaged with the content.

Motto: "Canned Search Results"

Developing the final polished product is something we can fake, including search results. Instead of investing heavily in the perfect feature, we assemble the results into simple categories based on previous research.

Now, let's test with scarcity.

Pattern 3: Make Things Scarce

Manipulating critical numbers such as item stock, content number, and ratings are well known to consumer marketing. While these tricks work temporarily, they will backfire.

We have the power to adjust numbers to increase the outcome of engagement—to a point.

Example

Recently, a group of users shopped on a website—and the customers were experienced with commerce sites.

Let's say that one of those items that the customer absolutely needed was in stock, but only "one left." Of course, scarcity will motivate the user to act, purchasing in a timely manner.

The next day the user returned to the site to research another similar purchase—sixteen items were available. Their trust quickly eroded.

Motto: "Everything is the Last Item"

This idea can be extended to whatever the team desires and is an infringement of consumer protections. Low space, stock, rating, and a lot of things are adjustable. If your team owns a video platform, "expiring" content is another angle. Finally, anything as a number can be rounded.

Next, let's test by giving away.

Pattern 4: Give Platform Expectedly or Unexpectedly

Sometimes if we give or take away major items of the platform, it may manipulate the engagement.

Example

A group of customers on an application that offered paid content behind a paywall. This app was freemium in nature.

Access became "unlocked," and a group of users could view content for free without the paid subscription. Then time passed, and it was gone.

Some users liked the content and so they purchased the product.

Motto: "Curious Engagement Through Shock"

Opening the gates in an A/B test could be a potential opportunity to engage users. The process is to select identities to engage with them.

Additionally, moving or closing things unexpectedly will stimulate engagement and increase returns. If services that are relied on are missing, the users will visit frequently until the content returns.

Finally, we can hide things.

Pattern 5: Platform Information Hiding

One final example is the creative use of information. Here, we conduct an A/B test that manipulates information relevant to the users at the proper time and context. We either shift the information upstream or dilute it. We reduce the *friction* of information to obtain a result. Sometimes lack of information is that friction.

Example

An example is a service that relies on the live location of the available liveries in the area—maybe those parked or on break, increasing information will deliver engagement.

Group: "Shift, Adjust, and Filter Information"

We will try to alter information or direct the user to a desired action by either giving or removing information at measured points. Taking it a step further, information manipulation can be targeted to identified groups of users.

This wraps up the pattern examples. **Urgency, faking, scarcity, giving, hiding** are subjectively divisive. Are they unethical?

Degenerate Tests may be Unethical Tests

In mathematics, a degenerate triangle exists in the overarching term of *degeneracy cases*:

> A **degenerate** case where an element of a class of objects is qualitatively different from the rest of the class and hence belongs to another, usually simpler, class. **Degeneracy** is the condition of being a **degenerate** case.

The degenerate triangle is deceptive, and so are the patterns defined above. All tests are doable without the user understanding it had happened nor platforms catching authors in the act. These A/B tests are a degenerate class of e-commerce tricks which prey on *urgency*, *scarcity*, and *human fallacy*. These techniques are, in most cases, harmless but act on *deception*. The question posed here is when the human is unknowingly participating, is it ethical to run these tests?

The question has been answered by large technology companies which published their results.

A/B/Code/Deception Testing

Some years ago, both Meta and OkCupid deceived their users by running controversial A/B tests surrounding content engagement by companion matching. Then, they posted the results to the public. Opponents suggested that manipulating emotions and then matching incompatible companions was wrong. This started a long chain of responses from the community.[3]

One excellent research paper focused on this test fallout.[4] Raquel Benbunan-Fitch dubbed these as A/B/C/D testing, where she states:

*This is a deep form of testing, which I propose to call **Code/ Deception** or **C/D** experimentation to distinguish it from the surface level testing associated with A/B testing.*

Are the tests ethical? Well, the debate continues today.

The position of this author is to communicate to your customers. Let me suggest ways in which we can state our testing code of conduct.

Ethics May Start by Saying We Are "Ethical"

While the industry rolls out and scales A/B testing to their advantage, I'd like to define how we can avoid these types of C/D tests.

Here are a few ideas that are centered around communicating the use of live user testing.

1. Clearly specifying an A/B testing section in a Terms of Service
2. Publish an ethical statement and guiding principles of A/B testing
3. Visually indicate an A/B test is being performed with opt-out

The messaging presented is up to the stakeholders, and should be in plain language. The boundaries of testing must be clear.

For item three, test evangelists agree that this behavior would disrupt the results, and the test would not be valid. In "A" or "B" mode, the author requires the user to act as normal to measure correctly.

While that might be true, we would still want to give the option at an appropriate time, in user preferences or sign-up. We want to measure and satisfy the user's concern which is the *product's value*.

• • •

IN THE FUTURE, state and government agencies will define C/D testing limitations as public knowledge increases and problematic tests are uncovered. Without a doubt, companies will be caught performing highly degenerate tests that none of us could fathom.

What would be the *consequence* of being deceptive? At this time, there are **no examples** of crossing a line. We have the power to ask whether to *associate* with the authoring team that *knowingly* deploys these questionable tests or *opt-out* of these deceptive practices.

Time will tell how deceptive testing shakes out. Data, tooling, and their alignment will continue to increase testing. And increased public awareness will spur hard questions.

If there is one lasting advice, try not to deceive... too much.

DSR

19

The Decision Hypothesis

The Mythical Man-Month Hinted at Software
Decision Documents Decades Ago

SOME WEEKS AGO, I completed my third re-read of the *Mythical Man-Month* (MM-M)[1] by Frederick P. Brooks, Jr.

MM-M is a dramatic piece of authoring in software development. I consider it a *constitution* that contains delightful discoveries. Anyone who practices software development[2] should read MM-M. And reading once is not enough! Pleasure and wisdom will come from reading numerous times. The work highlights forty-five-year-old observations that hold true to this day.

This essay will describe findings in MM-M that describe how we document the *why* of *software development decisions*. It will analyze a technique my team practiced to document software decisions, providing graphs along the way.

Chapter 10: The Documentary Hypothesis

In MM-M, Fred postulates scholarly labor and its practical application in four short pages.

*Amid a wash of paper, a small number of documents become the
critical pivots around which every project's team revolves . . .*

Fred goes on to describe in three sections the required documents
for a *computer product, university department,* and documents of a
software project.

He concludes with the topic of why.

*First, writing the decisions down is essential . . . Second, the
documents will communicate the decisions to others . . . Finally,
documents [provide] . . . a database and checklist.*

From the quote Fred presents the practice of developer documentation. He targets documents such as schedule and requirements,
but how does this apply to software code?

DECISIONS.md

Some years ago, there was a process in my team to document the why
of team decisions. We created a document, called DECISIONS.md, to
provide rich detail to code architecture, dependencies, and style in a
way that explains their reasoning.

Our guiding principle? Documentation was code. And if we had to
document, *do it in the version control system* or as close to the software
workspace as possible.

Then we found a post; *Every Project Should Have a Decision
Making File*[3] by Aliaksandr Kazlou.[4] The post introduced the concept
of a version-controlled DECISIONS.md. It's a brilliant write up, and I
suspect the author is a fan of MM-M.

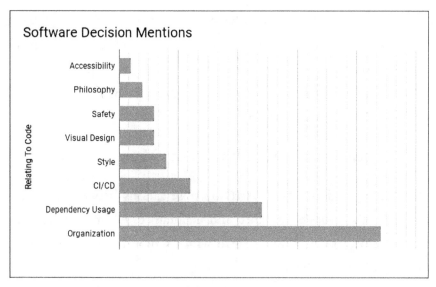

Figure 19.1: Code organization and dependency management are dominant in our DECISIONS.md.

So, we followed Aliaksandr's idea and adopted DECISONS.md in our way. I'll share a short section of ours below.

```
# DECISIONS.md

...
## Logging
As a platform team, we have decided to utilize Timber
[https://github.com/JakeWharton/timber] for all logg-
ing calls within the application. Our advantage was
the removal of an overbearing Log wrapper we had to
maintain. We wanted to get rid of its complexity.
Some other reasons for utilization of Timber are as
follows:
* Automatic tagging.
* Easy extensibility.
* Better usability in unit testing.
...
```

Once adopted, we had problems with timeliness of `DECISIONS.md` since it required constant maintenance. We also observed two truths. First, software development decisions are relentless and persistent. They can vary in intensity but are always present. Two, we have trouble keeping `DECISIONS.md` timely.

Julius Wellhausen's Work Was Lost to Many Hands

This composition was inspired by observations between the team, MM-M, the projects launched and maintained. Ultimately, I decided to write because of a lunch I had with a senior developer. The lunch brought it all together for me.

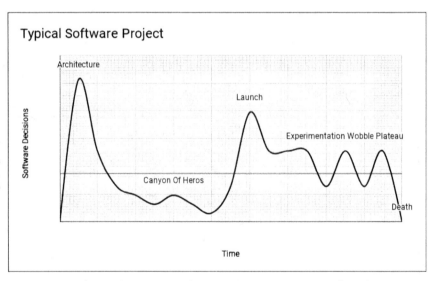

Figure 19.2: Software decisions vary during a project. Decisions prefer to be constant over time.

We debated about pull requests in our monolithic repo that went awry with inconsistent annotations and framework bloat. No team decision was made on the consistent use of nullability in preparation of our code language migration. Of course, sharing the technical details are not necessary, and these issues were the flavor of the week.

As we ate, developers were contributing to the code on an idealistic development philosophy. And no philosophy is wrong if it shares a direction. Fred's *Fragmentary Hypothesis* is in full effect when it comes to code contribution, as each contributor adds a little to its whole.

Sure enough, our lunch concluded, and we made decisions on the framework usage. When we returned, we started a discussion with the team, debated with data, and updated the DECISIONS.md document. If we hadn't, the integrity of the code will degrade over time by violating its conceptual integrity.

Fred Concluded with Self Documentation

In MM-M, Fred had difficulty grappling with separate documentation. He supported its value but pondered why developers fail to document. In the end, he stated:

> *Most documentation fails in giving too little overview. The trees are described, the bark and leaves are commented [on], but there is no map of the forest. To write a useful prose description, stand way back and come in slowly . . .*

Fred paints a contrast to spoken language. He said:

> *English, or any other human language, is not naturally a precision instrument for such definitions. Therefore the manual writer must strain [themself] and [their] language to achieve the precision needed.*

But Fred found value in explaining meaning. He said:

With English prose one can show structural principles, delineate structure in stages or levels, and give examples. One can readily mark exceptions and emphasize contrasts. Most importantly, one can explain why.

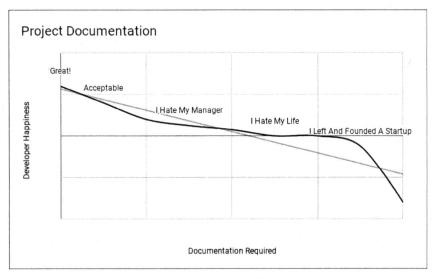

Figure 19.3: Developers do not like to document. Mundane external processes hurt developer happiness.[5]

Fred writes a chapter on marrying documentation to code. He said:

Yet our practice in programming documentation violates our own teaching. We typically attempt to maintain a machine-readable form of a program and an independent set of human-readable documentation, consisting of prose and flow charts.

The results in fact confirm our teachings about the folly of separate files. Program documentation is notoriously poor, and its maintenance is worse. Changes made in the program do not promptly, accurately, and invariably appear in the paper.

The solution, I think, is to merge the files, to incorporate the documentation in the source program. This is at once a powerful incentive toward proper maintenance, and an insurance that the documentation will always be handy to the program user. Such programs are called self-documenting.

Mr. Brooks was close to a solution, but he did not accomplish the follow through with code as documentation. Fred found that human and machine language repel each other, just as if two magnets are forced together at the same poles. Force is required to keep the connection as they move closer.

Fifty years later, *tests are the documentation on specification.* However, they, too, cannot explain why code exists as it does. Therefore, documentation has its place in the workspace. There is a high value to documenting *why* the system survives.

Code Cannot Explain the Why to Humans

Every software project has decisions which demand constant attention. The recommendation is to *document* the significant software development branches continuously, carefully, in one place. My suggestion is to try a technique like `DECISIONS.md`.

This practice serves the team by encouraging debate, focusing the resolution to a transparent file revision. The process is an imperfect electronic arbiter, serving as knowledge to onboarding engineers.

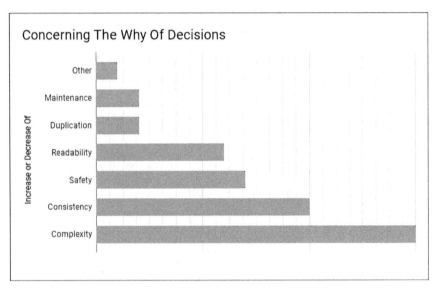

Figure 19.4: Decreasing code complexity and increasing code consistency appears to be our whys.

Code has a daft ability to communicate software decisions and their origins. Team knowledge is lost, hallway conversations are unheard, relationships end, and version control systems migrate, leading to a broken history. All that remains are the contributors that crafted pieces together over short periods. Said another way:

The decision hypothesis:

Amid constant software decisions, those of complexity and consistency become the critical pivots around which a software system survives. The decision document is a key to its revelation.[6]

Observations on the Culture of Test-Driven Development

KENT BECK, A SOFTWARE ENGINEERING leader, is the modern-day inventor of test-driven development (TDD). Kent co-wrote JUnit, a widely used testing framework, with Erich Gamma.

In his book, *XP Explained* (second edition),[1] Kent describes the axiom: at the intersection of **principles** are **values** and **practices**. When we iterate from the concept and plugin what we believe, we develop a formula.

[KISS, Quality, YAGNI, ...] + [Testing, Specs, ...] == [TDD, ...]

I respect Kent's work because of his fundamental software creations and his continued exploration of **trust, courage, feedback, simplicity,** and **vulnerability**. All attributes are paramount to the invention of Extreme Programming (XP).

TDD is a **principle** and a **discipline** that is followed by the XP community. The field has been present for decades.

In this essay, I will describe my opinion of where TDD stands in its adoption. Following, we will explore intriguing personal observations as we perform TDD. Finally, we will conclude by postulating why TDD resists standard practice.

TDD, Studies, and Professionalism

Decades since its invention, the practice of TDD remains debated in the development community.

The first question an inquisitive developer would ask is, "What percentage of software professionals use TDD today?" If you asked Robert Martin (Uncle Bob), a friend of Kent Beck, the answer would be one hundred percent. Uncle Bob believes that it is infeasible to consider being a professional if test-driven development is not practiced.[2]

Uncle Bob has been the focus of the discipline, and it is natural to discuss him as a part of this composition. Uncle Bob has defended TDD and has championed the discipline's boundaries.

To follow-up with the next question, "the definition of **practice** is the deliberate use of—but it does not specify the amount or percentage of, right?" My subjective estimation is that a majority of software engineers[3] do not practice TDD.

The reality of the situation is that we **do not know,** since the practice percentage has not been studied. The only concrete measurement we have is a collection of companies gathered at WeDoTDD.[4] WeDoTDD tracks these companies. Interviews are conducted with those who practice TDD, and that list is small. The reporting is also incomplete as other software shops are practicing TDD—but not at full capacity.

If we don't know how many are practicing, the next question is, "How effective is TDD based on measured benefits?"

Studies conducted prove TDD's effectiveness. Write-ups include well-recognized reports from Microsoft,[5] IBM,[6] North Carolina University, and the University of Helsinki.[7]

These studies report that defect density in software is reduced by 40% to 60%. In exchange, increased effort and execution time rose to 15% to 35%. These numbers are published in books and the DevOps community.

With these questions answered, the final question is, "What should I expect as I start to perform TDD?" You are in luck because I have formulated my observations of TDD. Let's review them next.

1. Develop an Approach

As we practice TDD, we begin to experience the phenomena of "calling the shot." In simple terms, the short acts of creating tests will challenge the developer. They will say aloud, "I think this will pass" and "I do not think this will pass" or "I'm not sure, let me think after I try this approach."

The developer's IDE (integrated developer environment) becomes a rubber duck of conversation. At a minimum, TDD shops should be humming with this type of conversion.

Think, then speak up about your immediate next move(s).

Verbal reinforcement is key to communication, not only to predict your next action but also to reinforce the concepts of writing **straightforward** code to make a unit test pass. Of course, if the developer becomes silent, they are wandering off the loop and must come back on the path.

2. Muscle Memory

As a developer cycles through TDD, they will experience fatigue by battling through high friction and awkward flow. The fatigue is expected as we practice. The developer will find shortcuts to improve the cycle because the goal is to reduce awkwardness and to enhance muscle memory.

Muscle memory is the key to fluidity. TDD demands it because of execution repetition.

> *Print out a shortcut cheat sheet. Learn as many shortcuts in your IDE to make your cycles efficient. Then, keep searching for more.*

The developer will become an expert of shortcuts in a matter of a few sittings, including building and running the test rig. With practice, creating new artifacts, highlighting text, and navigating the IDE will become natural. After practice, we unlock all of the refactor shortcuts such as extraction, renaming, generation, pulling up, reformatting, and pushing down code.

3. Forward Thinking

Each time a developer practices TDD, they draw a mental map on what is to be solved. In a traditional coding approach, this is not always true, as the solution can be exploratory. The developer has a goal. To get to that goal, unit tests are neglected in the process.

In TDD, the start and end of the session is ritualized. First, think, and list. Test your options. List more. Then start, do, and then think. Check off. Repeat. Finally, think, and stop.

Maintain your test list well. Check off items as you go. Never drive without one.

The list takes time to formulate and is not in the cycle. However, it should be prepared before the revolutions start. If you don't have one, getting to where you want will be difficult. Always have a map.

```
// A Test List
// "" -> does not validate
// "a" -> does not validate
// "aa" -> validates
// "racecar" -> validates
// "Racecar" -> validates
// print the validation
// have a blueberry ale
```

The practice will be smooth with a **test list**, as described by Kent Beck. The test list directs solving each cycle. Once the test list is solved, the cycle stops with a failing test.

4. Communicate with Others

As the above test list is filled out, later steps become blocked because the commitment of work is not clear. If a generated test list has guesses about the missing requirement(s), the suggestion is to stop right there.

Practicing without TDD will generate complexity. TDD performed without a list can produce the same result.

Speak up if the test list has gaps.

In TDD, understanding what to build, based on the owner's requirement(s), is the goal. If context is unclear, the test list will start to break down. That breakdown will require a conversation. And direct conversions can turn into a feedback loop of trust and respect.

5. Creates Iterative Architecture

Initially suggested in the first edition of the XP book, Kent proposed that tests drive architecture. However, there have been stories about how sprint teams crash into walls.

Tests that drive architecture decisions is unwise. Uncle Bob had agreed that architecture driven by tests is "horse sh*t."[8] A map is required, but not too far from the test lists that are being worked on in the field.

Kent identified this caveat in the book, *TDD By Example.*[9] **Concurrency** and **security** are the two significant areas where TDD is not applicable. The developer must design concurrency into the system design separately.

Create a map of organization. Have a vision that directs a few steps ahead. Make sure you are steering with the team.

TDD cannot handle **organization** of the system. Iterative architecture and TDD orchestration is challenging in practice and demands trust among all team members, pair programming, and reliable code review. Short iterative design sessions are required if we practice TDD.

6. Test Frailty and Degenerative Implementation

Unit tests have an intriguing property about them, and TDD exposes that property. They cannot prove correctness. E.W. Dijkstra had labored over this and discussed the possibility of mathematical proofs in our profession to resolve the gap.

For example, the below solves all tests around a hypothetical palindrome that the business required. It was developed with TDD.

```
// Not an imperfect palindrome.
@Test
fun `Given "", then it does not validate`() {
    "".validate().shouldBeFalse()
}
@Test
fun `Given "a", then it does not validate`() {
    "a".validate().shouldBeFalse()
}
@Test
fun `Given "aa", then it validates`() {
    "aa".validate().shouldBeTrue()
}
@Test
fun `Given "abba", then it validates`() {
    "abba".validate().shouldBeTrue()
}
@Test
fun `Given "racecar", then it validates`() {
    "racecar".validate().shouldBeTrue()
}
@Test
fun `Given "Racecar", then it validates`() {
    "Racecar".validate().shouldBeTrue()
}
```

Indeed, these tests have holes. Unit tests are frail, even for the most trivial tasks. We cannot prove correctness because if we had to, the needed inputs would be unimaginable.

```
// Too generic of a solve based on tests provided
fun String.validate() = if (isEmpty() || length == 1)
false else toLowerCase() == toLowerCase().reversed()

// Is the best implementation and solves all tests
fun String.validate() = length > 1
```

In the code above, `length > 1` is called a **degenerative implementation**. It is enough implementation to solve the problem, but it tells us nothing about the problem we are trying to solve.

When does a developer stop writing the tests? The answer is when the **business is satisfied**, not when the code author is!

TDD has benefits, and avoids us building the sandcastles we do not need. The practice is a **constraint,** allowing us to go faster, further, and with safety.

> Be aware that the unit tests are fallible. Understand their strengths and weaknesses. Property-based testing[10] and mutation testing[11] may help tie up these gaps.

No matter how frail unit tests are, they are a core necessity. They transform **fear** into **courage**. Tests allow us to refactor code mercifully. Tests guide and **document**, adding value to a project so others can contribute effectively.

7. Reveals an Assertion Completion Feedback Loop

Take a step back. For the next two points, we will visit strange reoccurrences. For the first occurrence, let's take a quick look at `FizzBuzz`. Here is our implementation.

```
// Print numbers 9 to 15. [OK]
// For numbers divisible by 3, print Fizz instead of
the number.
// ...
We are a few steps in. We now have a failing test.
@Test
fun `Given numbers, replace those divisible by 3 with
"Fizz"`() {
    val machine = FizzBuzz()
    assertEquals(machine.print(), "?")
}
class FizzBuzz {
    fun print(): String {
        var output = ""
        for (i in 9..15) {
            output += if (i % 3 == 0) {
                "Fizz "
            } else "${i} "
        }
        return output.trim()
    }
}
Expected <Fizz 10 11 Fizz 13 14 Fizz>, actual <?>.
```

Naturally, if we duplicate the expected assertion data to `assertEqualsIt`, the test passes.

As we query the test rig, failing unit tests may correctly answer their own assertions. We'll call this voodoo testing.

Sometimes failing tests will reveal a correct result.[12] Perhaps we can call these **voodoo tests**. Your mileage may vary based on test etiquette, but I have seen this happen numerous times.

8. Reveals the Transformation Priority Premise

In TDD, there are situations where we are entangled by the implementation. At some point, the testing code becomes a bottleneck to move forward—an **impasse** forms. The developer has to back out by removing a portion of the tests to advance.

Uncle Bob has experienced these impasses in his career—documenting a test order to avoid an impasse. His discovery: **as the tests become specific, the code becomes generic.**

Uncle Bob created the Transformation Priority Premise.[13] The list defines an order of refactoring to achieve passing tests. One should prefer the transformation order that will resist a dead-end.

TPP,[14] or **Uncle Bob's Test Calculus,** is an intriguing and exciting observation. Use his list as a guide to keeping the code as simple as possible (see Figure 21.1).

> *Print out the TPP list and place it at your desk. Refer to it as you drive to avoid impasses. Embrace an order of simplicity.*

Before we conclude, I'd like to answer a question, "What percentage of software professionals use TDD today?" My answer is, "I think the group is small." I'll explore this answer with reasons why.

Has TDD Taken Off?

Unfortunately, it hasn't. The percentage of developer practice is low at 8%.[15] Here are the author's observations as to why.

Reason 1: No Exposure to Real Testing Culture

A majority of software developers have not experienced a **testing culture**, such at XP.

The definition of a testing culture is a place where developers are deliberately practicing TDD. They are mentoring those who are not skilled. Each pairing and in every pull request is a feedback loop on building an individual's confidence, supported by engineering leadership. In this culture, managers believe in testing. When deadlines and times get tough, the test discipline is not dropped—it is strengthened.

Those that have lived a testing culture, are lucky. They apply the experience to future projects, educating others.

Reason 2: Unclear Educational Resources

Authors have written books on the subject, such as *xUnit Patterns*[16] and *Effective Unit Testing*,[17] but hardly convince teams to test.

When it comes to examples, open source projects are hit or miss with useful unit suites. In these unfamiliar projects, having tests is critical. But disappointment is inevitable—tests are not maintained.

Reason 3: Not Taught in Universities

My observation of candidates fresh out of university reveal little to no education in testing rigor. Every developer I know has learned testing afterward, with many enlightened through a testing culture experience.

Reason 4: A Career of High Test Passion Required

It takes passion to test well. To understand TDD and its benefits requires an extensive period of time.

Developers want things working, achieving what Kent Beck said: "First make it work, then make it right. Then, make it fast." I empathize that to get things working is a tough battle.

Testing is hard to do well, so let's conclude on that thought.

Conclusion

Kent's XP proposal included a simple formulation of **instinct**, **thought**, and **experience**. These three levels are stepping stones to execution quality measured by a **threshold**.

The threshold for clean test execution is high, in that it eclipses a baseline of developer experiences. Those that practice were trained in a supportive testing culture.

Software is challenging to build and organize. Testing takes it to a whole new level of enlightenment.

Early on, I had an **instinct** that testing is essential, but my test culture **experience** came later. It took years of **thought**, but without that experience of test culture, I would not have emerged above that threshold.

I believe that many developers cannot see the real benefit of test culture due to a lack of specific **experience**.

> *TDD discipline has struggled to take off due in part to the learning curve of testing. TDD requires a headspace that is unique as it is challenging.*

TDD demands **thought** and **experience**. The practice is not easy and is an acquired skill. The repetition commands the developer's throughput, continuously and relentlessly. We are all **vulnerable** in the process.

```
@Test
fun `Given software, when we build, then we expect
tests`() {
    build(software) shouldHave tests
}
```

However, TDD is an intriguing discipline and **is a tool to lean on**. Its **phenomena** should be studied in detail. If anything else, the discipline strengthens both the developer and the collective group.[18]

● ● ●

Transformation List

1.	{} → nil	8.	array → container
2.	nil → constant	9.	statement → tail-recursion
3.	constant → constant+	10.	if → while
4.	constant → scalar	11.	statement → non-tail-recursion
5.	statement → statements	12.	expression → function or algorithm
6.	unconditional → if	13.	variable → assignment
7.	scalar → array	14.	(case) adding another case (or else)

Figure 21.1: The author's graphic of Robert Martin's ingenious Transformation Priority Premise, published on The Clean Coder Blog, in 2013.[19]

DSR

21

No Description Provided

Explaining Context by Identifying a Code Review Template

SOME MONTHS AGO, one of my colleagues suggested a book. Out of curiosity, I read *Sapiens: A Brief History Of Human Kind.*[1]

It was a fascinating read. With themes interweaving throughout the chapters, one idea bubbled up that was thought provoking.

In his book, Yuval Noah Harari identifies humans who invent communication patterns that are valued. As described, a *mythical glue.*

I questioned, is there such a glue[2] that applies to our engineering profession? Do we, as engineering professionals, have a mythical bond we value?

Everything in a Pull Request

Without question, the pull request,[3] or code review, has become the lifeline of every development team who interact. Pull requests are where the team culture resides. In a sense, this is how the team communicates in a virtual public square.

As Yuval described free-market systems, money, and other valued constructs, we as engineering professionals believe in pull requests. We all understand what code review is and the value the practice provides.

Or do we?

With travels to other code reviews, something's not quite right. There are no descriptions that cleanly point out the *intent* of the change. For those that describe the difference, they appear messy and inconsistent.

The value, the glue, is diluted and does not bind well. What's the cost of a pull request when the problem is not described?

Figure 21.1: Perhaps the engineer was in a rush? The commit message was no better, and the commit diff was unclear, from github.com.

A crucial aspect of software engineering is to describe the intent of the change. We must explain *why*, as professionals.

Since our craft is global, earshot conversations will not do. Team knowledge will not suffice either. The description must be *textual* as a record.

So, what is the solution?

Call for a Unified Pull Request Template

The community has toiled with pull requests for some time. There have been numerous posts[4] suggesting process improvements.

Some of the best examples provide preferred templates[5] that guide the contributor to answer specific questions. Templates are an excellent way to understand a description of the change.

However, the community has yet to find a technique to craft descriptive pull requests. Many professional teams often skip descriptions, missing out on great opportunities to strengthen their glue.

An Example

At a familiar cadence, engineering teams update external dependencies. Sometimes, these updates are shrouded in mystery.

Figure 21.2: What are we trying to solve? What's the gain? From github.com.

Google "Butterknife?" This library is a view dependency injection SDK for Android. However, why the bump? What are we trying to solve?

With a descriptive summary, clarity will take hold. The team will grok the *opportunities* to improve.

The description template identifies the problem, the solution, and why. The template highlights testing, code coverage, measurement changes, and other metadata[6] to communicate change.

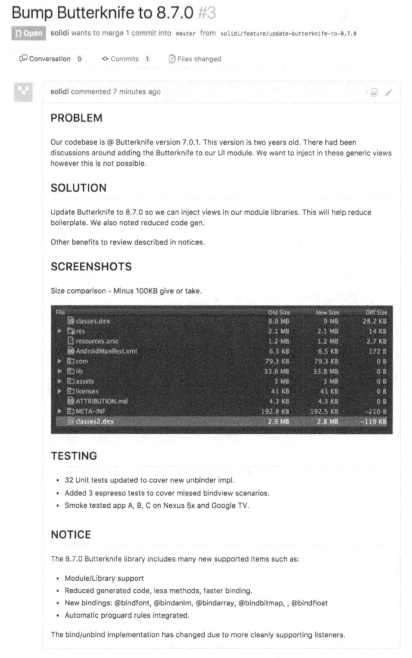

Figure 21.3: An apparent problem and solution,[7] from github.com.

The definition of a unified template starts with a *problem* and *solution*. It would behoove a team to communicate change through a template and kindly decline[8] pull requests that do not present them.

As a bonus, the template provides a descriptive commit message in a continuous integration system.

Commits May Be Overkill

Commits lack value if subject titles and descriptions are unclear.

Indeed, there have been numerous posts written about these problems over the years. A straightforward solution to non-descriptive commits is to follow the 50/72 rule.[9] This rule encourages subject and body messaging formatted in a specific way.

However, many engineers do not follow 50/72. Some engineers think it's okay to place periods at the end of subject titles. Their commits contain ticket numbers, and for seasoned engineers, these commits lie outright. Commit messages are almost too hard to get right. Writing the code was easier.

One would argue that the pull request merge commit contains the essential description, not the small iterations that came to form it. The reasoning is simple. We are not machines that can accurately remember more than seven commits at any one time, plus or minus two.[10] There are those teams that squash and rebase, so the commits were trivial.

There is no right answer to this difficulty. The only real constant is the pull request template, the opportunity described and recorded in a version control system.

Description Has Value

Pull requests take time just as much as writing code that follows consistent patterns. We value pull requests because they serve cross-pollination in engineering teams and protect user experiences valued to business.

Engineers are required to solve difficult problems. The first step is to write what the problem is, why, and how we went about solving it. Sometimes in stages throughout chained pull requests.

There are two hard things in computer science: cache invalidation, naming things, and off-by-one errors.

— Unknown[11]

Naming things is hard. However, *describing* things is harder and rife with errors. As professionals, we define the intent of change with *context* to the best of our ability.

The most correct code is that which is not written but the most correct description is one that is.

If we do not make our best attempt to describe the change, the context is lost. This lack of practice does a disservice to future contributors.

So how do we capture the value of context description, so other engineering professionals understand?

Extending Uncle Bob's Programmer's Oath

Conversations are happening in our community about our engineering profession as an organized body. We should look no further than Uncle Bob[12] sending these signals.

For some time, he has urged us as engineers, or *programmers*, to embody a set of concrete principles; otherwise, government agencies will do it for us.

Uncle Bob's argument consists of comparisons to other professional groups. One such example describes just how patients died from lack of sterilization in the medical profession; a swath of people will be at risk as software eats the world.

To correct these problems, the medical professionals organized and formed guidelines adhered to like sterilization techniques. These medical professionals handed the agencies their mottos, and hence they made their own rules. So too is what Uncle Bob is asking from us.

However, the question is, are we ready to take this on as an organized group of professionals? To answer this dilemma, Uncle Bob created nine points in the Programmer's Oath.[13]

Since programmers like to round numbers, this author will propose the ten point:

> *10. I will communicate to the best of my ability the intent of change with as much context as possible.*

Rule number ten enhances all other rules in the oath. We are writers that communicate to the best of our written abilities. And that is where the pull request fills the need.

● ● ●

THE MYSTICAL GLUE that binds us as software engineers[14] is the pull request. Let's do our part to describe the context of the *problem* and *solution* in detail so that others can contribute promptly. It starts with thinking and explaining "what" the problem is. Then we must describe the solution with the *opportunities* at hand.

Ultimately communicating the intent of change is a duty of all engineering professionals.

The Right Place?

After this chapter was written, my friend Danny Preussler replied with the following:

> *When reading Doug's article I was wondering if pull requests are the right place for documenting changes. I agree that those need to be documented but I disagree with the place.*[15]

Over time, I tend to agree. Pull requests have their place in software practice, but is it the right place for the team? That depends. Another "place" is the practice of design documents. These files capture system context through conversion.

How it's done is up to the team.

In one organization, I witnessed a simplified Python PEP process to serve conversations of large features and architecture decisions. *Also see Chapter 19 and 47 on group decision process.*

The Springboard Pattern

How to Build New Features in Isolation

A FEW YEARS AGO at an agile demo, a stakeholder made a special appearance. The team was closing in on a minimum viable product. The demonstration focused on sound effects and animations, revealing a configurable animation board. Each media experience was easy to launch in an isolated configuration. And the animation board did not depend on the extensive system. The intention was to tie-in animations of which the stakeholder agreed with.

While the team demoed, the stakeholder asked if we could evaluate the animation board for experimentation. With this feedback, the group noted the ***unrealized*** value and wrote down what to explore. Of course, this wasn't the first time the team used the technique. They made similar discoveries in future demos.[1] The team learned that feature containment provided product value in their demos.

● ● ●

FOR SOFTWARE ENGINEERS, naming things is hard. Harder still is how to communicate clearly. And in the story above, there isn't a vocabulary to describe their effort. A definition of feature containment has yet to be defined in *software engineering*.

So I propose a definition to describe the unique execution with its benefits and drawbacks. Developing and demoing in containment is an example of what I call the *springboard pattern*.

What is the Springboard Pattern?

The springboard pattern is a *visual design* pattern. Mobile operating systems that constrain viewing areas have used the pattern widely. The app launcher is an example.

Our introductory animation board fits this model. The animation board is a screen launcher and each animation is a section with its specific configuration.

When applied to software development, the springboard pattern acts as a guardrail. Features are isolated areas that are *demonstrable* on the platform. There are many benefits to engineering and product. The springboard pattern is a way to execute features incrementally.

The springboard pattern keeps dependencies in check and develops features in a cycle centered around *product demonstrations*. Here are the rules an engineer must follow while iterating.

The feature:

1. Launches from a board that includes other features
2. Can spring up with minimum setup
3. Can launch on its own and in any order
4. Defines its own state
5. Resists larger system coupling and dependencies

If we follow these rules of feature development, magic happens.

Benefits include the promotion of modularity, testability, and build-time. Additional improvements include product ideation[2] and unrealized engineering efficiency. Let's discuss these next.

Figure 21.1: Above is a screenshot of a springboard with the use of the domain language. From Android emulator SDK.

Promotes Modularity

The springboard pattern enables development of features in isolation from one another. In each design segment, the team must do their best to create a solution in ***containment***.

Dependencies will always be present, but the layers separate the feature for demonstration cleanly. The feature should be modularized and independent. As the iterations continue and demos succeed, the springboard items integrate into the extensive system. As this occurs, the team resists coupling and ensures the feature code cohesion is high. From start to finish, each item should have a weak measure of ***connascence***.

During the cycle, pattern violation can diminish the return of the modularization. Therefore, the team must make **prudent and deliberate** decisions by leaning on tools of layering, wrapping, and flow of control using dependency inversion.

Supports Testability and Build Time

The development of a demonstrable item from the springboard demands testability. The unit tests will serve as documentation of the module.

The concept of the springboard pattern promotes modularity. Its dependencies should be highly configurable. Each feature should have configurations available for its **dependency injections**. Thus the pattern supports ease of testing and mocking of the component.

By using the springboard pattern, build time is reduced, and the complexity of the codebase is normalized with each feature. Incoming features are **flagged**, conditionally built by the toolset. Features that are rejected from demos are removed.

Finally, a natural phenomenon of the springboard pattern reveals **diagnostic test tooling** of a feature. The springboard develops tools that take on a life of their own, serving to test parts of the system.

Product Ideation and Engineer Efficiency

Opportunities happen when products are deconstructed into independent pieces. In the case of the introduction example, there appeared to be an unrealized product value in the use of an animation board.

Stakeholders refer to the features of their products as cohesive constructs and use vocabulary to describe them. Wouldn't it be powerful to find a feature without friction? The springboard gives us a *learning library* and allows for *cross-pollination* between engineers and gives us a tool to locate each feature.

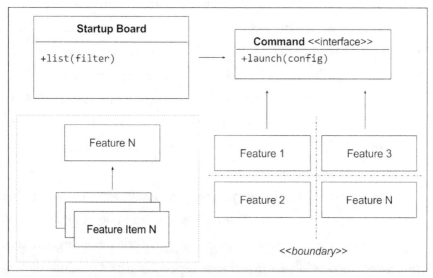

Figure 22.2: The springboard design pattern.

As an additional benefit, the engineer's work is *always available* for demonstration at a moment's notice. An isolated solution offsets the typical cost of the time to prepare for the demo.

Mileage may vary depending on the domain and the reception from stakeholders. In pragmatic terms, products must predict less and experiment more. Having the features deconstructed and isolated may indicate a different outcome or a reconfiguration of that product value.

Framework Support

The springboard pattern provides benefits that coincide with features of the framework. I'll discuss Android concerning the use of a springboard. Your framework may vary.

In the Android ecosystem, Google has launched Instant-Play Apps.[3] To support the concept, Google introduced *feature modules*. As we can see from Figure 22.2, everything that is demonstrable should be isolated. As development continues, insulate each feature from significant dependencies and optimize them for every feature. The product team will want to launch these features separately or together.

Another example of Android is the concept of isolated *activities*. Each activity launches in isolation, taking what it needs to provide an experience. If features are built-in isolated activities, reconfiguration of the pieces of an application is possible.

Finally, with the latest versions of Android, its tooling has improved. Independent modules allow for building abilities, which reduce build time. Setups that use a *flavored* code organization improves the developer's experience, especially if the product dimensions are extensive.

Before we conclude, there are drawbacks to consider.

Drawbacks

There are drawbacks to developing a springboard. The team will have to make decisions to steer clear of over-engineering.

The springboard approach may:

1. **Violate YAGNI.** "You ain't gonna need it."[4] The team should build what they need, and not a single line more.
2. **Accelerate decisions.** Deferring architectural choices is an excellent strategy to keep complexity manageable. Operating

this way will encourage code decisions.

3. **Increase complexity.** Additional logic to support layering and modularization may increase development time.

However, keep in mind that the cost paid will certainly provide a cost-benefit for code that is consistent and adaptable. *Adaptability* adds to code complexity.

Spring into Action

Developing for isolation and modularity is a practice all engineers should strive for. However, there hasn't been a pragmatic approach to these concepts and a way to describe the pattern. Now there is.

The *springboard pattern* gives us a language to our intentions in software execution. When adhering to this pattern, we manage *complexity* and increase *optionality*. Be aware of the cost of drawbacks.

The springboard pattern takes effort and drive, but the benefits are incredible to team cohesion and product impact. Implement the idea today!

DSR

23

The Next Fantastic Software Project Code Name

BORING SOFTWARE AND HARDWARE are named for what they are.

Buttoned up and formalized, application and library names like `The-App-Brand-Name`, `What-I-Do-Library`, and `Named-Service` are ordinary. Projects like `Go-to-Market`, `This-Product-Release`, `Sprint-Number`, or `Minimum-Viable-Product` are manufactured in an assembly line. And the hardware of `Domain-N-Series-Y`, `Give-Me-The-Last-Digits-On-That-VM` fades from memory faster than a trending Hacker News post.

I first experienced naming things *differently* while developing software in a team. The websites and apps we built did not have adored handles. But the blades on a server rack *did* have names. They were the *pets* hosting these projects.

Each server had a name from one of the Greek/Roman gods. `Pollux`, `Apollo`, `Castor`, all had a memorable function. `Castor` was the webserver, `Pollux` was the file server. The list went on down each metallic bay. And when we added a server, we plotted how[1] to name it well. `Hermes`, one of our later additions, was where we dropped warez payloads; it was a mess of libations.

These names and their power are *pervasive*, sticky in my mind forever. But today, naming servers this way is archaic and challenges the discussed pets/cattle metaphor.[2] If I squint hard enough, the names could be construed as fungible parts.

I still remember those machines, the projects they hosted, and the people that showed me how. I cannot remember any of the server clusters I managed since. And I haven't seen enough of this clever thinking. We need more of that geek passion while we horizontally scale to infinity.

Some Examples I've Experienced

Every label that I've encountered is a function of its culture and the people around it. It's a mix of generation, nationality, motivation, shared experiences, and values. When we play with words, a clever project handle explodes to a *code name* many can get behind.

The result is a memory hook. And those who participate are now part of the *in-group*. Calling something by a code name makes the experience inclusive and gives the group control and ownership. The name is a badge of honor, a commitment, and *undying passion* for something to succeed.

In my experience, code names rise from various contexts. And in each, there are an infinite number of ways to arrange, enumerate, and organize in an endearing, proud, or unbelievable way. They are named after science, animals, products, history, mythology, toys, animation/anime, famous adored leaders, music, and many others. The possibilities go on and on.

Let me share some examples I've experienced, which will be different from your experience.

Nostalgia

When I was involved in kid media-focused software development, handles were based on cartoon nostalgia. App names were concentrated in NickToon[3] characters Tommy, Blue, Otto, and others associated with their app function.

In that project, we created a monorepo where the streaming apps and supporting libraries were located. We called it the Aggrocrag. Named after the kids show, Nickelodeon Guts, Aggrocrag was the final challenge where contestants race up a polystyrene mountain. We got a few chuckles out of it. And then there was the common shared library that was all-knowing. We called it Olmec, named after a game co-host.[4]

I once developed a private suite of tools individually labeled as M.A.S.K. characters. Examples included Trekker and T-Bob. These libraries consisted of a developer experience toolchain, no feeling more incredible than having the complete collection of those toys and, at the same time, insight into development.

Relevant Releases

Some software projects had passion names. With the projects focused on Android app development, we went through a list of Asimov and sidekick robots. Daleks, Atlas, Yaris, and others all had a special meaning and contained changes related to robot characteristics. Obviously, Daleks was crafted to *exterminate* things,[5] removing unused features. The developers named each release in turn. The practice promoted shared ownership.

Recently, the team I managed named releases after Pokemon characters. I remember our end-of-year releases of `Haunter` and `Pidgeot`, aptly named after the American holidays. The name concept was new to these engineers. Perhaps the experience will be the motivation to name their next project.

Organization and Platforms

In one shop, two major engineering teams came together. We called the shared developing platform the `Hadron Collider`. An amalgam of different technologies in JavaScript, from render engine to UI, streamed video on many devices.

While the engineering organization was serious about its outcome, our team named existing *native* apps after non-scientific instruments. Apps were labeled after amusement park rides, like the `Gravitron`, each app's fate mixed into the organization over the course of time.

Timeline and Phases

At one point of my career, I joined a startup. We named our WebRTC communication app deploy systems after satellites launched up to space like `Telstar`, `Voyager`, and `Hubble`. Their supporting SDKs were named after *Back to the Future* paraphernalia. Both `Hoverboard` and `Delorean` powered these satellites.

Even the build servers were named in a co-tenant fashion after famous astronauts and cosmonauts like `Tereshkova` and `Armstrong`. These pipelines supported our continuous releases.

The MVP (a second iteration of the failed `Voyager`) called `Voyager 2` released. It did okay, now cruising in the ether, semi-distant, never quite achieving its mission.

Tools and Utilities

Tools and utilities typically have crafty names. Since software is focused on outcomes, the clever succinctness can be off the charts.

I've built small tools that have been discarded—naming them out of love and utility. There was `Scrapi`, a small, scrappy API scraper, `Amazement`, an iOS game where you trace out of a maze, and `Bif-Tannen`, a base index file[6] extractor tool for movie thumbnails.

And for those that authored their libraries creatively. `Import-anize`, an import organizer tool for Python,[7] was memorable.

Naming Things Make Memorable Story Telling

I've seen many series, magnitudes, and creative labels over the years. I've only shared where I actively contributed.

Code names have a rich history. The practice came from ages ago in government and the military. And further in the dawn when inventions were developed in Edison's Menlo Park. Engineers are creative. They are inventive, even with project names.[8]

I find code names are *sentimental* hooks in the playful nature of the software craft. It's about the culture of the engineers, something that we enjoy doing.

These aliases are a prescription to the ambiguous. Engineers long for a territory to raise their flock of beautiful software and hardware. Damned the boredom of names like `This-is-an-App`, or `Some-`

`Service`. Instead, let's have the `Anti-Gravity-Device` and `Newtons-Gravitational-Laws`.

The power of these labels is in telling stories—*galvanizing people*—where the hook is the code name we discuss in the hallways. Software engineers need to believe in their projects.[9] But without the naming practice, there isn't much fun. It's not memorable. There isn't much play. *Another sprint ends in the bin, semantically tagged.*

Let's create the next fantastic code name. I plan to.

IV

Section Four

Reading and Writing

read·ing (/ˈrēdiNG/) *n.* the action or skill of reading written or printed matter silently or aloud.

writ·ing (/ˈrīdiNG/) *n.* the activity or skill of marking coherent words on paper and composing text.

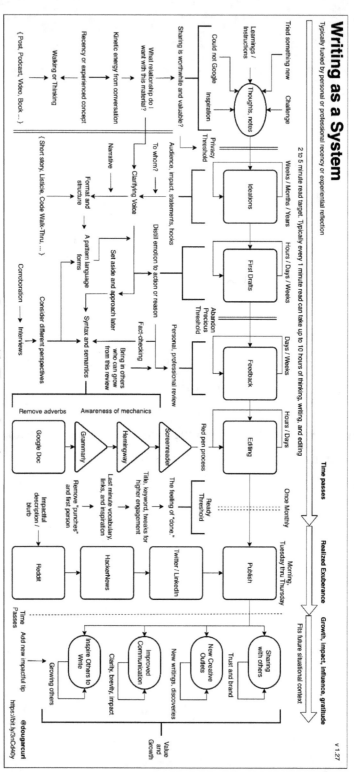

Figure 24.1: The Writing as a System diagram.

24

The One About Blogging

Mapping the Process After Years of Learning

I HAVE LEARNED ALOT about my motivations while blogging over the past years—everything from self-reflection to clarifying intentions. I've also discovered the process itself. While I could write a long-winded post about this meta, let me share what I've learned in a visual. Since the majority of the population are visual learners, the following graphic should suffice.

Figure 24.1 draws out my blogging process after a few years. It will continue to improve.

Like all creative systems, blogging contains learning feedback loops. What is most interesting is the **catharsis of publishing**. Sharing these writings with others has **growth side effects**. It is impactful, rewarding, and gratifying to share the topic contained in *one link*.

The point of blogging is to start, no matter how difficult it may seem. We all have something to share. Writing helps others and also clarifies motivations. The process reinforces the learnings, and improves the skill of communication.

So, I created a diagram of the process titled "Writing as a System," which went through twenty seven iterations. To read it, look from left to right by traveling an article's journey. Start by scanning the top row to understand the significant points, then go deep within each column to appreciate its detail.[1]

DSR

25

Deconstructing My Reading Habits

Understanding My Purposeful Discipline for Knowledge

RECENTLY I HAD A CONVERSATION about my reading habits. Speaking through it, I realized the process I follow is *purposeful*. To better understand my motivations, I drew a diagram, similar to how I blog.[1] In this essay, I will step through and highlight the essential parts. By sharing my process with others, it will memorialize my important goal—writing a book.

My Inspiration for Reading Books Comes from Others

Conversation with an individual, mentor, or leader, combined with a *motivation* factor, sparks my interest to read. This recommendation aligns with a challenge I am experiencing or a skill set I'd like to improve. For instance, when I wanted a holistic view of distributed systems in software in system design interviews,[2] *Designing Data-Intensive Applications* improved my proficiency.

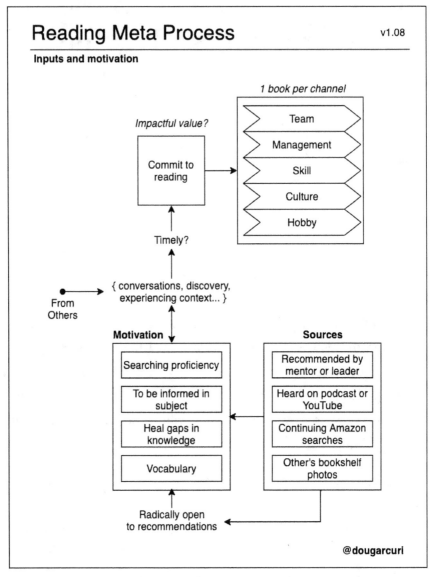

Figure 25.1: Inputs and motivation.

There are many routes to how I discover books. I am radically open to recommendations, and in some instances, I openly ask others. Book recommendations are also sourced from asynchronous mentorship—listening carefully to podcasts, YouTube, or crawling Amazon book recommendation lists. If the recommendation is *timely* and has a potential *return on discovery*, I will commit to reading the book.

My Idling Time Is Where Most Reading Occurs

My reading habits are sporadic, occurring in a gap of time where I am sitting or idling. Scheduling this time is usually not sustainable. The crucial point is I read at least a few pages a day, even if it's not chunked (such as reading one full chapter in a sitting). The books follow me, and I prefer the physical book over a digital format to keep focused.

When Reading, Note What Is Interesting

I do not entirely understand my "interesting" scale while reading books, but I know "fascinating facts" appear in the text. These artifacts are impactful quotes, an interesting idea, or applied application. Things that are **terse and succinct** positively engage me. I thought about this one for a while where interest originated from morals, values, and beliefs of my upbringing, culture, and experiences. From a skill set point of view, my "interests" are detailed information and novel application methods.

Like Robert Heaton's *How I Read*,[3] the way I track "interests" is a small system of Post-It flags and note-taking. My organization system needs improvement. Regardless, every book I've read has a handful of concepts and symbols that stick with me—creating a never-ending snowball of knowledge.

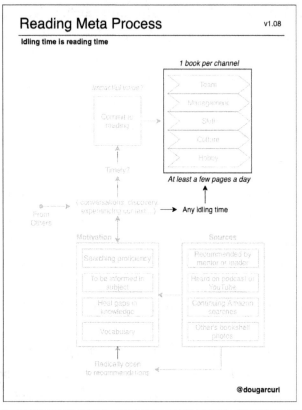

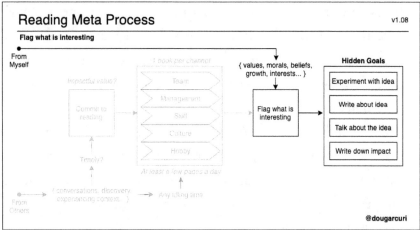

Figure 25.2, 25.3: Idling is reading time. (Grayed areas are seen in Figure 25.1.)

Completing Books Is Important to Me

When committing to a book, it is a combination of recommendations, timeliness, extracting interesting points, and understanding actions. Books I start, I finish. I believe it is essential to complete a reading because it supports my momentum to start the next book.

Books that I abandon form a new story as to why I disliked the work.

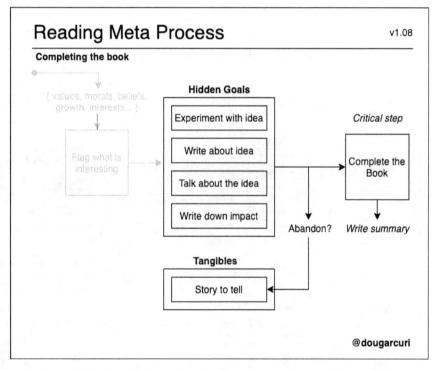

Figure 25.4: Completing the book. (The gray area is seen in Figure 25.3.)

My Outcomes and Tangibles of Reading Books

For me, reading is a process of gathering new pieces of the context.

143

Information and the experience they contain are valuable, for example, understanding *anchoring* from *Thinking Fast and Slow*, the *STARS* model from *The First 90 Days*, the *task-relevant maturity* model of *High Output Management*, and *mastering the art of letting go* from *Eleven Rings*.

Foraging **improves vocabulary.** Discovering the vocabulary builds a **mental model of the idea** expressed. The tangibles of the outcomes are clear—exercising thoughts and speaking through the topic enhances connections to others, and the process is a never-ending cycle of approximation. In some instances, books connect ideas from different viewpoints, and in the end, form new opinions for me.

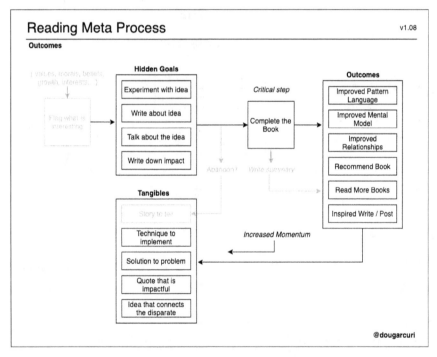

Figure 25.5: Outcomes. (The gray area is seen in the previous figure.)

My Reading Leads to Mentorship

As I read books that are purposeful in context, my goal is to **mentor others**. Telling stories of books builds trustful relationships. And the side effect is the inspiration to write openly to a community.

For example, when I read the book, *Hackers and Painters*, I connected the disparate, describing values of having a hobby[4] through "successive approximation." Reading meta books on software engineering—such as *Programming Pearls*, *Pragmatic Programmer*, and *The Philosophy of Software Design*—equipped me the vocabulary of correctness and pattern matching.[5]

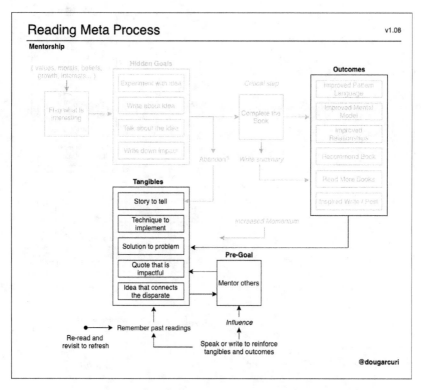

Figure 25.6: Mentorship. (The gray area is seen in the previous figure.)

Reading Leads to Writing a Book

My future goal is clear. The books I've read have **influenced me to write a book**—their content are my inspiration. My book will be a legacy of the readings and what I've learned from them.

The purpose of why I read is to write a new book for someone else—**to share what I've learned**. However, I am unsure of what *concept* to cover. I trust it will come in time.[6]

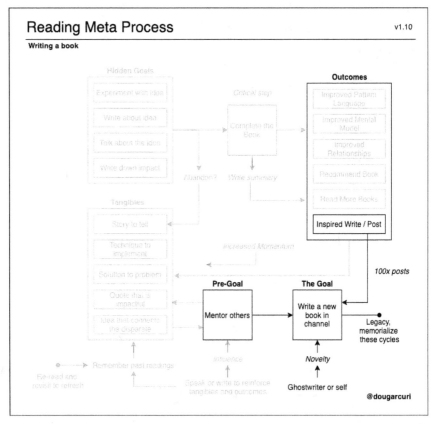

Figure 25.7: Writing a book. (The gray area is seen in Figure 25.7.)

As I noted in Figure 25.7, *100x posts* is a critical concept. By writing enough and receiving feedback guides me to achieve the goal. The format will be essay-based—exploring *concepts* to a narrative arc.

Conclusion

Reading books is a delightful process of learning. And writing is a result of reading books. The article, *How to Read Fewer Books*,[7] helped me discover my goal. My approach is not rigorous. It is **constant and continuous**. The core parts of my process are sourcing and to improve my *meta reading machine*. While I do not remember everything that I read—ideas, thoughts, and previous writings unlock new conversation. Ralph Waldo Emerson's quote describes what I feel:

> *I cannot remember the books I've read any more than the meals I have eaten; even so, they have made me.*

My reading motivation is to develop a purposeful skill set and to give back content—a creative exhaust as described by Brad Frost.[8] Your reasons may be different from mine. What works for you?

On the following page, Figure 25.7 draws the complete reading flow after eleven iterations.

The Result is Written Meta

After seven years of reading and writing, what you hold in your hand—DSR—is a result of this process. How meta is that?

Figure 25.7: The full **Reading Meta Process** experienced by this author.

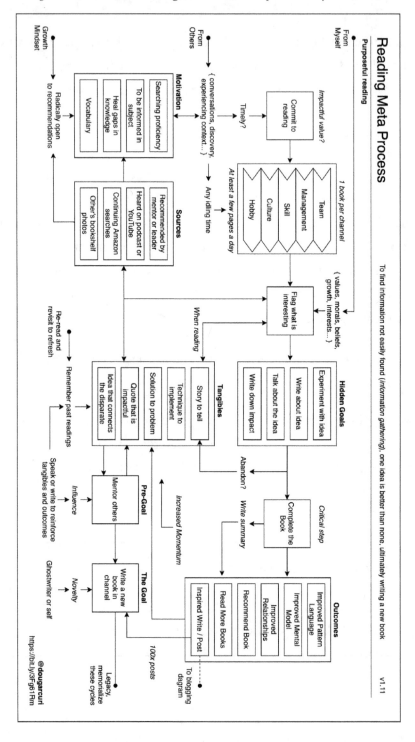

26

Rediscovering the .plan File

AT THE END OF THE YEAR, I published a long-form post[1] on discovering a computer programming career by building a game modification. In that article, I mentioned a communal practice whereby noting ideas and to-do lists originally served by the UNIX `finger` command. The command publicly exposes the content of a .plan file.

After the demise of `finger` in the late 1990s, the practice was epitomized by John Carmack[2] who had a unique approach to crafting information within. His application was romanticized in *Masters of Doom*[3] and mentioned in *Game Engine Black Book DOOM*.[4]

Since my article was published, I started a side project to rebuild that modification. My primary goal is to recapture the experience with the compatibility of the current state of the game. And in doing so, I have an interesting observation to share.

What Is LEARNINGS.md?

Out of nostalgia, I started a new .plan file[5] that captures the interesting minutiae within the small project. But with the demise of `finger`, I'm focusing every *meaningful* clarification from research,

behavior, or a [*enter your favorite search engine*] result in a file I call
LEARNINGS.md.

LEARNINGS.md is a chronological list that captures interesting
findings from the developer's perspective. With some months into the
project, it's been an investment of learning game development context,
dockerization, build pipelining, Powershell scripting, and the oddities
of cross-compilation of Linux, Windows, and macOS. Surprisingly it's
a firehose of valuable technical findings. And it's being captured.

While I have yet to see this style out in the ether, I am confident
that there are developers capturing learnings in their own way,
organizing knowledge and making it searchable. Wiki's come to mind.

And in working on so many projects, I wonder why this is such a
late discovery for me, a small gem that can be shared with others while
the sausage is made, highlighting all the things *I should know*.

Why I Like LEARNINGS.md

This LEARNINGS.md file is an unproven practice, but it encourages a
helpful feedback loop in developing software. Here are a few reasons
why I like the process:

1. LEARNINGS.md reinforces knowledge by writing down the
   findings. There is some friction to this habit; however, its
   benefit is learning concepts *spatially in time*.
2. The LEARNINGS.md file is a place to look up information when
   remembering the learning, as concepts in development come
   up more than once. I've used it as a lookup to clarify the
   technical context, e.g., resources on how to operate Docker on
   Windows within VirtualBox without Hyper-V.

3. The file is lightweight. LEARNINGS.md becomes a search index when its length becomes unwieldy.

4. LEARNINGS.md is a practice of *yak-shaving*—when there are too many tabs open in [*your favorite browser*], I'll go ahead and walk each tab, determine if there was learning from that research, write it out in LEARNINGS.md, and then close the tab.

5. Finally, the LEARNINGS.md file is useful for the next engineer as a reference of solved knowledge.

Spatial and Temporal Pedantic Reinforcement

I remember reading that .plan files were used to wax lyrical or write poems about growing old. And so I was reluctant to write about this practice because, just like a .plan file, it is a personal experience that will unlikely map to other's practices.

However, in such an environment of expert Googling,[6] I felt I had to keep track of the knowledge *somewhere*. And so I wrote.

This reminds me of an unknown quote:

> *The discovery of information is not really important. But information becomes important when it is appreciated.*

And when I'm in a jam of needing to remember a technical approach, I appreciated this file's existence. I like that it's there, a crutch, closer than [*enter your favorite search engine*]'s doormat. So I'll experiment with the LEARNINGS.md file and see where it takes me.

Realistically? The file will become a pedantic foxhole where link rot will thrive—and a life saver for the next engineer to appreciate a time-vested investigation.

DSR

27

Technically Considered Writing

WRITE[1] **TO DOCUMENT** what you're doing now, finding relief from its gripping subject. Set a publishing date as motivation. And where there isn't inspiration, tinker with the process of writing.[2] Undoubtedly the muse will return later.

What you'll write[3] will become fuzzy. Re-read your past writing[4] to remember where you were and laugh with the people you shared it with. Writing[5] transmits a once-lived perspective and style.

Writing[6] on a matter is a loop that spirals in your mind. But not after publishing it. When moving to the next, which will inevitably occur, the previous writing[7] is a compressed artifact for a future reader of your earlier thinking.

Were you clear? Did you write?[8]

DSR

28

How to Place on the Front Page of Hacker News

Exploring Content Qualities that Resonate with the Community

HACKER NEWS (HN) IS A COMMUNITY that prioritizes posts about software engineering, technology, startups, and other related meta conversations. Within HN, there is a continuous stream of topics that churn. The most engaged writings appear on the top thirty list.

Towards the end of my second decade in software engineering,[1] I began to write openly, exploring topics related to humans in software. A handful of my posts have reached its front page.

Being a genuinely curious person, I questioned why my posts rocketed to the top. So I collected the relevant information, put together a few graphs, and will share what I learned.

Introvert by Nature

My writing motivation has been an authentic outlet, a long-winded expression of myopic introversion. Making it to the front page of Hacker News is an exciting side effect of time invested.

Speaking in crowds is exhausting, but my strength is talking privately to people. In those conversations, I prioritize writing ideas.

I'll cover my essays that made it to the top of HN.

#4 Touch Typing Feels[2] Good But Isn't for Me[3] (2019) Placed 18th,[4] 24 hours

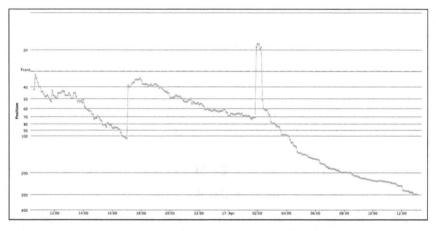

Figure 28.1: Tracking of Touch Typing Feels Good, from hnrankings.info.

Motivation: *My in-depth conversations of mechanical keyboards made me furious, questioning the effectiveness of touch typing, so I practiced.*

Learning: *My result was inconclusive. However, after I published, I tried an alternative keyboard. It improved my typing by 20 words per minute. The hardware made a difference.*

When I discovered writing, it opened up a creative outlet, transforming my overthinking into a constructive habit. But writing isn't easy to do well. The blank page is constrained to my natural writing voice. Most of all, it's easy to start but tough to continue.

#3 Observations on Test-Driven Development[5] (2018) Placed 17th,[6] 36 hours

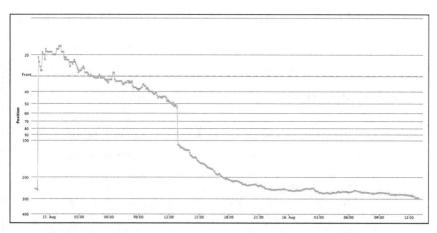

Figure 28.2: Tracking of Observations of TDD, from hnrankings.info.

Motivation: *The debate[7] about test-driven development (TDD) went long in the shop, so I had to say something—supporting it—finding helpful patterns.*

Learning: *TDD works well within small dogmatic groups but is difficult to pull off at scale. I have not found a large shop that does it, nor do I practice anymore.*

Clarity is an essential attribute in documentation. Writing requires an editing process, sometimes ongoing for weeks to achieve transparency. More so, it is when the content resonates with the reader. Connecting with an audience is the goal, so I will piece together a shortlist of what and how.

The List of What

Of my entries that went the farthest, they were intensively exhaustive in a practice of technical craft. Here are a few specific content qualities I noticed.

Content qualities that place on Hacker News:

→ To the point, best attempt at clarity in thinking to writing
→ Seeks truth through practice, data, or first-hand experience
→ Interesting graphs or media paraphernalia that surround it
→ The content is helpful and sometimes controversial
→ Builds to something important at the end of the post
→ The topic helps the reader to think or do something later

But really: Content that resonates with the audience

#2 When a Software Engineer Exits the Team[8] (2021) Placed 2nd,[9] 48 hours[10]

Motivation: *I lost numerous engineers within the continued "Great Resignation." I became a stoic for a while.*

Learning: *Most people leave their managers. However, I forgot one poignant fact. As it is for me, leaving a job was about money.*

Friends in my circle have yet to accomplish a Hacker News placement, so there isn't a peer available to compare notes. But I know people who fear speaking into the void. I was shy too, until I realized time was short, and there was so much to say. Not being able to say it in person *is the perfect reason* to write.

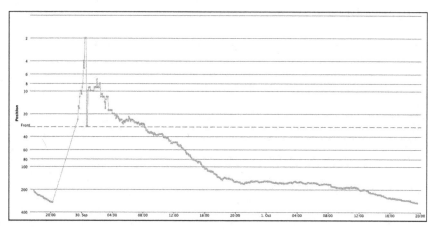

Figure 28.3: Tracking of When an Engineer Exits from hnrankings.info.

Possible shortcuts to reach the top:

→ Being popular in the community
→ An important statement concerning a product, company
→ Oversell with satire
→ Clickbait the title to spark a rolling thread
→ Post your own work when published
→ Meta post about HN or the practice of writing
→ Timely content that is the focus of the community
→ Tackle a profoundly controversial topic with impunity

Honestly: Knowing and writing to an audience

#1 Ham Radio—CQ: Personal Mastery Through Hobbies (2018)[11] Placed 1st,[12] 60 hours

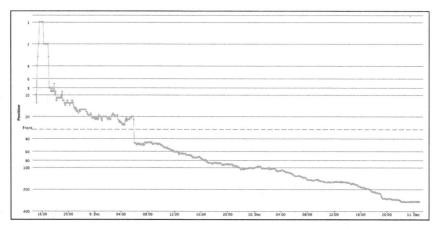

Figure 28.4: Tracking of Personal Mastery Through Hobbies from hnrankings.info.

Motivation: *When my father was battling depression for a second time, I practiced a hobby he loved—writing about it to him.*

Learning: *Constructive diversions, like a hobby, break the depressive cycle. My father recovered.*

For my entries that reached the top, I noticed a pattern in private sharing. But available tools cannot show inference. So I guess these ideas touch a nerve, for good or bad. How to place well on HN remains an educated guess.[13]

Next, let's explore comments from the HN community.

I created a "non-scientific" sentiment analysis combining the 300 comments of the four posts above. The graphs capture the HN threads at the first and second-level. The authors primarily posted on reflecting their experiences or sharing opinions with observation and practice.

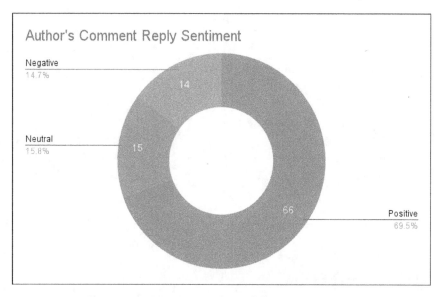

Figure 28.5: Sentiment analysis of the 300 comments.

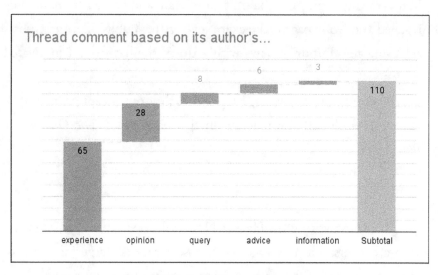

Figure 28.6: Break down of categories.

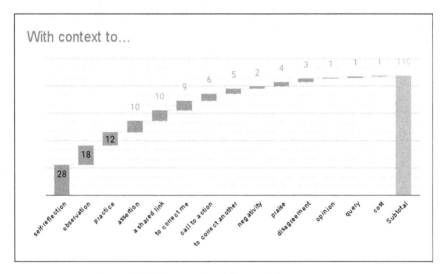

Figure 28.7: Context breakdown of the comments.

The Process of How

Many of my writings[14] haven't found an audience, nor have they reached the front page of Hacker News. After publishing, these posts achieve a few hundred views with a tip of the hat from a motivated reader.[15]

While writing for years, I tracked each idea's inception to publication. I published the diagram in this book titled *The One About Blogging, Chapter 24*.

Summary

All of my writing on Hacker News followed a process. It started with a conversation to answer what *a* reader seeks. Targeting timeless, durable content that weathers aging—scaling to *many* readers.[16] To place on HN, like anywhere else, the content must resonate with the intended audience.

Hacker News is a fascinating community to share writings. Be prepared for constructive criticism. There is no specific formula to achieve its top spot.

Other meta points that are important:

→ Experiencing something for good or bad, and sharing it
→ Privately discussing the idea with a human before publishing
→ Editing, placing it aside, cutting lots of things
→ How the writing reads aloud / red pen process[17] on a printed page
→ Timebox the goal to publish, no matter what
→ Targeting content that is relatable and timeless

Or: Be genuine with an idea and explore it to your ability, openly

---

DSR

V

Section Five

What is a ... Anyway?

role (/rōl/) *n.* the function assumed or part played by a person or thing in a particular situation.

an·y·way (/ˈenēˌwā/) *adv.* used to confirm or support a point or idea just mentioned.

DSR

What is a Software Engineer Anyway?

THE ROLE OF A SOFTWARE ENGINEER has a magnitude of dimensions. When I think of the people I've worked with over the years, here are my top appreciated attributes.

They are curious. Software engineers solve problems by pursuing truth. They prepare, weigh options, and execute optimal solutions. They communicate, write well, and are always learning.

Are collaborators at their core. Software engineers work together with others to develop and solve problems. They do not go it alone. They seek to help others and share information widely.

Teach and mentor continuously. For each problem they tackle, the process is an opportunity to show others the way. They take their time to grow these individuals in the pursuit of brilliant teamwork. When they need clarity, they create a method for teaching themselves new skills with or without training.

Partner and communicate effectively. Software engineers have supreme communication skills. They work in a complex environment where product owners, designers, architects, and teams work toward a common goal.

Dive deep into the unknown, without fear. Problems can be expansive, and they know how to break the issues down.[1] They enjoy the craft, the detail, and can orchestrate a path to its resolution when a pattern is not clear. They form a philosophy[2] and become opinionated.

Their craft has a procession to it. With toolchains and structured thinking, they embrace the concept of mise en place.[3] They invest in the discovery and improvement of their tools. The right tools are laid out to achieve the best results. They may even use insight tools[4] to improve their decisions, and are accountable for an approach.

Software is unstructured work, and they embrace it. They name and create metaphors for difficult concepts. Sometimes, they "marinate" with a problem until a solution forms. They create order[5] from entropy and automate the repetitive.

They strive for code that is human readable. They go deep into the meta of writing software: the test philosophy, the structure, and correctness.[6] Software products typically endure past the software engineer's involvement with a project. They know that well-written code that is readable and testable is essential to the success of their products.

They are a part of a community. Sometimes, in cathedrals, sometimes in bazaars, they work internally with their team or externally with open source collaborators. They participate in significant initiatives and occasionally write and demonstrate to the broader audience.[7]

They contribute ideas and are open to feedback. They have the backs of their teammates and help others when a problem needs solving. They spend their time wisely and ask for help when they have tried numerous options. They avoid silos.

Software is a creative endeavor. They love a profound technical challenge, enjoy being close to the reasons why the work needs to be solved. They appreciate being recognized while striving to be egoless.

Leaders are born from engineering teams. For those that find interest in organization engineering, or rise due to their technical prowess and empathetic strength as an inclusive collaborator, leaders emerge.[8]

The code they write is not their value. Engineers understand that formulating approaches and problem solving is their value—not the code they write. With each line of code they produce, they are learning, which has an increasing exponential impact on their current products and future society.

Knowledge Engineering

Knowledge Engineering is a profession of building decision making systems. And I think of software engineers as practitioners who harness *practical* knowledge discipline.

Software Engineering requires an immense knowledge base to construct, wire and glue data pipes together through text. And I have yet to find a phrase which describes the practice without "software."

DSR

30

What is a Software Development Engineer in Test Anyway?

DURING MY TIME IN THE INDUSTRY I have worked with talented software development engineers in test (SDETs). Also known as software automation engineers, QA engineers, and other associated titles, they practice a discipline to assert the quality and affirm the user experience.

Here are my top respected attributes.

They find issues sooner. Test engineers find proactive ways to diminish quality concerns. Whether it is reviewing requirements, participating in code review, asking engaging questions, they help identify bugs to reduce the cost of fixing latent defects. As a result, they catch defective releases well before going out the door, protecting user experiences and company reputation.

Uncover critical insights with the product team. When product requirements[1] are defined, QA engineers find ways to assert the quality of features and ensure the customer needs are met. They continuously encourage adding metric analytics for insight. In addition, they work closely to the time estimate by leading a testing plan that is concise and thorough.

Partner with software engineers. SDETs pair closely with software engineers[2] to find areas where code coverage can be placed. And apart from adding enough test coverage, they push further with code-generation, setup, and tooling that enable engineers to effectively deploy with confidence. Finally, they encourage the team to test constantly.

Actively brings in new test techniques. Whether it be mutation testing,[3] property-based testing, unit, integration, and new mocking approaches, they find ways to use these techniques and frameworks to test comprehensively. They organize and lead game days, bug bashes, and actively invest in applying methods in chaos engineering. Finally, they actively educate the team to leverage these tools.

Organizes test suites for effectiveness. When unit[4] and integration tests are developed, they promote continual improvement, organizing fixtures, stubs, and mocks efficiently. These tests support new implementations. They add end-to-end tests to assert the intentional functionality of the system. Above all, the tests are logically separated and ordered, making it easy to run the desired tests.

And promote refactoring and automation. For every test suite, test engineers improve the confidence of the product. They empower the software engineers to move forward with refactors. By doing so, their actions promote the effectiveness and investment of each codebase under test. All these suites serve as living documentation and are hermetic in nature.

They discover edge case scenarios. When requirements are challenging to automate, they quickly find the edge cases through clever exploratory testing. And with these cases, they see a way to cover these routes with record and playback, ultimately improving adopter satisfaction.

Implements advanced testing methodologies continuously. Test engineers are familiar with exotic ways to test each system. These methodologies include load,[5] stress, visual, performance, and behavioral testing. And if they are not aware, they bridge the communications with the team to those that can. This practice leads to better software acceptance outcomes.

Contributes directly to the codebase. At times, SDETs actively contribute to the software engineering side of the product. They are fearless by taking on parts of the system and then writing the tests to back up the quality of their contributions.

Are aware that flaky tests discourage testing. They actively find ways for the test suites to run smoothly. And they confirm tests either succeed or fail deterministically. They quickly stomp out test suites that are best, flaky.[6] In the end, they continue to harden the suite, so there is continued trust in the tests.

They are well educated in all the iterations of test philosophy. Testing is complex. And SDETs know all of the visual metaphors of test suites. Whether it's honeycombs, pyramids,[7] trophies,[8] hour-glasses, or ice cream cones, they build extendable test suites that find issues.

Much more than janitorial, a discipline that must happen. While slogans such as "the engineers assert the quality and QA should find nothing" encourage test ownership, and the tech companies that post insightful testing techniques in restrooms to share burdens collectively, better outcomes can be achieved with SDETs on the team. They are the humility makers, shape business reality, and execute well in this maturing craft.

DSR

31

What is a Tech Lead Anyway?

IT'S QUIET HARD TO DEFINE the tech lead role in a short post. But, here it goes.

Tech lead is a role, not a title. Any software engineer can become the tech lead. And with the part, others will look up to this leader.

The lead is the team liaison. The role shepherds change. They focus on the future state. The rapid response. The pivots from management.

Tech leads play the role of mentor and sponsor to others. They set up code reviews in a collaborative way. They handle discourse.[1] They partner with the product on feasibility, on a roadmap, priority, and estimations.

They are accountable for the developer's experience. This includes the technical debt and engineering velocity. The tooling and onboarding friction. The testing, product domain, and holding philosophies to approaches.

They write down the philosophies so that decisions are apparent. They guide others with respect—a leader who delegates as well as leads by example.

Being a tech lead can be a challenge. Managers pressure them to do the impossible. And priorities come to them in all directions. Their impact is good or bad, whether the team is pathological or generative.[2]

The lead is there to see the team succeed, to deliver. Without internal injuries, with an orchestra of collaborative engineers rising.

The brutality of being a tech lead is the demand for the individual's technical and management capability. Even though companies have split these into two ladders, the role of tech lead has intractable attributes of both. It is impossible to separate.

The team can blaze a path in the lead's absence. Whereas the real drama happens in one's head, the pure emotion of the group occurs in front of the tech lead's eyes. The lead follows through it and guides.

They lead with a myriad of soft skills jujitsu. With the technical tact unmatched. And if it all goes wrong, no worries. There are marketing opportunities.[3]

What is a Staff Engineer Anyway?

AS A SOFTWARE ENGINEER and software manager, I have worked closely with staff engineers on large strategic projects. They have responsibilities that are disparate from leading contributor roles. Here are my top recognized attributes.

The staff engineer is recognized as a leader. The staff software engineer continues to grow in their role; they become the storytellers within the teams and organizations. They market a brand, continuing to improve their craft, skill set, and lead projects. They have obtained a title that matches their designation.

Have a default bias toward action. When problems and friction forms in the systems and codebases they are associated with, they move forward not by just observing but acting and correcting the observation without asking for permission. They self-authorize to experiment and improve the systems.

Staff engineers are free electrons.[1] Staff engineers have slack time to launch experiments, finding solutions across teams. Sometimes they detail presentations about the current system's pain points. They highlight how technical actions can reduce or eliminate tension. They are held accountable for the holistic results and delivery[2] of the products they serve.

Have an impact on the systems they lead. Staff engineers are looked up to by other engineers in teams. Staff engineers guide and mentor these engineers. Their influence is not just technical contributions; they grow other developers. And these staff engineers listen and learn from others, especially novel ideas from junior engineers. With excellent soft skills, they turn good teams into great teams.

They collaborate outside with other engineers. They don't reinvent the wheel every time. When they face new challenging problems, they first look for an existing solution. If found, they utilize and expand the approach, so it is applied exponentially. They collaborate with others to form unified solutions that can scale in the organization.

Steer the business away from disastrous decisions. These engineers are held to a standard of creative solutions and delivery. When the time comes to define technical feasibility, if the business[3] is going down the path of continuous short term patching and mounting technical debt, they speak up. For those systems that may not survive long, they balance genuinely maintainable systems and delivery.

And also make the business find unrealized potential. For difficult technical feasibility projects, they recommend alternatives and find larger initiatives to improve the customer and the system's longevity. They combine technologies, find opportunities for delivery, and balance skill sets with key results while keeping it interesting for the engineers. They advocate for systemic change.

Their decisions have an impact. For the systems they design with teams, they influence the organization's critical product decisions. Understanding their impact is essential for both engineering and the business. They create the engineering brand of the organization and evangelize it to the community.

Staff engineers set the contribution track. For initiatives related to engineering brand, toolchains, and ease of contribution, they scale discipline in part with principal engineers.[4] Forming tests, decision documents, and showing the way are vital to being a reliable staff engineer.

As with principal engineers, they run initiatives. From aiming to reduce developer friction, moving to a new architecture, incident reduction, and velocity and magnitude improvement projects, they are the first engineers engaged to deliver broad impact. Involved in interview loops, they advocate for systemic change and operate inside and outside the teams to achieve results.

Align with business and leadership. With initiatives they work on and their first step toward a direction, they realize that alignment is crucial. They understand that their perspective is one of many in the organization—finding momentum towards a shared vision.

Are more than just tech leads. While "tech lead"[5] is a common designation, organizations have crafted the staff engineer title to signal to others that this is an individual contributor with extraordinary impact and influence. They balance emotive and technical excellence, and they are recognized for it.

33

What is a Principal Engineer Anyway?

I'VE HAD THE PLEASURE of working closely with talented engineers who excel in their roles. Known as principal engineers, they are leaders in their craft. Here is what I observed as I worked closely with them.

Form technical plans with the team. Principal engineers start with an idea and work toward team buy-in. They orchestrate the plan by motivating other team members and collaborating closely in achieving it. In short, they are leaders.

Lead team enablement initiatives. Typically involved in looking ahead at upcoming technical initiatives,[1] they rise above complexity to find a way to lead future missions. When that time comes, they enable developers and make teams effective.

Rapid response agents. For initiatives that require extraordinary engineering talent, they jump into a team and partner carefully to lead them to sound technical solutions. As they break the efforts down, they work closely by guiding the software engineers through gaps.

Exert external influence. The community recognizes principal engineers for their technical expertise and knowledge sharing.[2] They present practices, innovations, and inventions inside and outside of the organization.

They partner with leadership on recruiting. While principal engineers present to a broad audience, they partner with management to find new potential talent in developer communities. They recruit for expertise at developer conferences and meetups.

They mentor all engineers. Principal engineers mentor engineers to take them to the next level of their careers. They create an environment to allow them to grow. For those that are junior, they mentor. For those who are senior, they coach.

Motivate and challenge the engineering culture. These engineers help set up cross-organization engineering best practices, standards, and guidelines. They create a culture where the contribution patterns and quality are paramount. They partner closely with teams to implement them.

Are monitoring the developer experience. Principal engineers review and give recommendations on how to remove friction from the engineering toolset. They improve the delivery of software and help onboard engineers[3] effectively.

They help in design decisions. Sometimes, if there is a conflict between engineers on a design decision, principal engineers step in to help the team conclude. They discuss the pros and cons of every approach and make a decision that best scales the product.

Embody inclusive leadership. While their technical contribution is impactful to many teams, they also lead by example. They communicate well, show the way, clarify the mission, and have a can-do attitude by including others.

Are force multipliers without human directs. While they do not have reporting lines, they influence software engineers[4] throughout the organization. They help find the maximum potential of each developer.

Even without designation, they accomplish the incredible. Their attention to detail is indisputable. They achieve novel innovation to common problems. Sometimes they innovate and advance at the craft. They deliver great things by growing technology and people, even without the acknowledgment.

DSR

34

What is a Project Manager Anyway?

I'VE WORKED WITH EXCELLENT project managers (PMs) over the years. Many of them are sophisticated and technical (TPMs); here are my top recognized attributes.

Shepherds process evolution with predictability. They will find ways to keep projects on schedule by filling the gaps for the team. They are necessary meta engineers for the groups they partner with. By negotiating between engineering, product,[1] and stakeholders, they formulate the vertical slices of delivery. Evolution is achieved by iterating processes, improving the environment, and finding clear ways to prioritize.

PMs understand how to deliver. They work with management and peers to eliminate what isn't valuable from a product perspective and form plans to mitigate risks. They are the reality check, while actively listening, being able to reflect the priorities.

They are managers and understand their teams. As much as engineers and product managers partner closely with individuals, so do project managers. They conduct frequent one-on-ones and build trust with their stakeholders as much as delivering the products.

Visualize artifacts that inspire action. Clearly defining and iterating the roadmap to project completion is essential, and they envision future business opportunities. These artifacts can change behaviors into actions by clearly showing the way.

Have clarity on the technical feasibility. PMs are there to help communicate sophisticated technical feasibility or business viability to non-technical stakeholders by "Fisher-Pricing"[2]—making concepts easy to understand. They can inform, consult, or act on that information with the team.

PMs lead revelations about risks through discoveries. Just as product managers help teams reveal solutions to business opportunities, project managers unearth solutions from risks. They seek to uncover uncertainty and reduce the feeling of "hope." They resolve team blockers to meet delivery on time.

Know how to partner on the four levers of all software projects. Whether it be negotiating time with stakeholders,[3] working with management to adjust talent, improve quality, or work effectively with business to adjust the scope by dialing in priority. They are experts on these levers.

Also, they know that any project can optimize on only three attributes. Projects that are *good*, *fast*, and *cheap* are not *done*. And for those projects that are *good*, *fast*, and *done* are never *cheap*.[4] By laying tracks, they work closely with the team to optimize what matters most, depending on the team's needs.

Are aware of the meta properties of the project. That adding engineers[5] to a late project only makes it later. If the team has time to complete a project than necessary, they adequately fill it.[6] Project managers challenge and inspire those engineers with the partnership by asking for more.

Ask the right questions at the right time. Project managers form powerful questioning to inspire team ownership of feasibility, deployment, testing, and business value. They are skillful at invoking provocative operations,[7] asking thoughtful questions, so others think and act productively.

Underappreciated, they get to know what matters. Whether it's reality setting, capturing risks, time slicing, or adjusting planning bias, they go unnoticed as the project is excelling. Their role is a delicate balancing act, matching priorities from all sides. They make the sawdust edible as much as the inspirational commonplace.

● ● ●

SOME ORGANIZATIONS combine project manager with engineer manager. In this case, the following diagram may help clarify major attributes. The engineering manager's role is covered in Chapter 36.

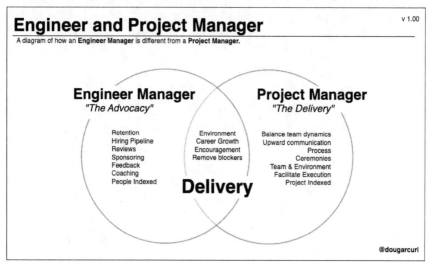

Figure 34.1: Venn diagram of engineer manager and project manager.

DSR

35

What is a Product Manager Anyway?

OVER THE YEARS, I have partnered with insightful and talented product managers (PMs). They continuously evaluate the problem set with usability, feasibility, business viability and value. Here are my top appreciated attributes.

They live with the customer problem, and ruthlessly prioritize. Product managers seek customer problems. They think deeply about the clarity of the problem and uncover its depth. As their issues are defined, they prioritize what matters to their customers.

Share data about the problem widely. Product managers investigate the issue in-depth through the market, competition, user research, and analytical tools to steer the problem to the best audience. They use A/B tests to find potential outcomes. When user feedback and data disagree, a balance is struck. These techniques are performed in an open setting with their partner's business, team, and engineering.[1]

Openly collaborates with the team and innovates. PMs work tirelessly by openly collaborating with their counterparts to engage in the problem. The collaboration includes innovating and experimenting with the problem set and using techniques like startup canvas, story mapping,[2] and personas. They incorporate opportunities to integrate with other teams in the organization. And where needed, they partner with management for resource allocation.

Know about slicing the effectiveness of the product. They instinctively know that their product suite has a general rule. A third of their products should evolve to find a top market, a third of their product is causing friction, detracting from the business value, and the final third should be abandoned as no one is using it. They help uncover these boundaries.

They are expert users of technology. While they partner closely with design and engineering, they, too, are technology experts. They know how to measure the feasibility and fundamentals of both the engineer and the customer and, at the same time, know where their limit is.

They goaltend to their customers effectively. When products roll out the door into the customer's hands, they prioritize their needs. To keep the product operational, they measure the effectiveness of the product and watch the retention curve. At the same time, they push for continuous delivery and thrive on user feedback to improve the customer experience.

Engage in innovation with engineering. Product managers explore the problem set with discovery,[3] pivoting on exploration. They bring in engineering at every point to orchestrate a direction. PMs spend the majority of their time discussing the future. Their co-location with the team is essential to keep this running smoothly.

Never backs down from the product vision, but also looks for strategic options. They trust their partners in engineering and design to increase the market, capture audience, test value, and grow their customer base. However, they never withdraw from their vision and take full accountability of the products they ship.

Holistic product management is a goal. Product managers know that half of their ideas do not work.[4] Just as products are grown, the right products are sunset, without remorse. From end to end, they manage this cycle with the vision and keep motivation high for the teams that experiment and build.

Know that the best problem has a "watch this" moment. Partnering with their team to effectively experiment and attain solutions to unanswered questions is essential. There is a moment in time with each problem, a "watch this" moment, where anyone without knowledge of the problem understands how it benefits them. With this insight, these PMs are best in their craft.

DSR

36

What is an Engineering Manager Anyway?

I'VE HAD THE HONOR of being an engineering manager (EM) for years. For EMs who are new, I want to share a handful of essential tips. Here is what I learned.

The most important action of a manager is to hire. Hiring is an intricate habit, from recruitment to onboarding. EMs are accountable for its successful orchestration. They lead team growth in the organization.

And delivery and retention are essential. Trust and continued engagement of each engineer fuel project delivery. EMs are accountable for results and retaining talent. Aligning goals and having the right engineers at the table is how they execute.

Managers and leaders are different! Managers shepherd who does what by when. Leaders show the here to there and can articulate the why. The best strive to do both.

Management is not a promotion. It's an orthogonal discipline. Managing is different from engineering. Their toolchain[1] is mentoring, coaching, feedback, and sponsorship wrapped in initiatives. These tools take a lifetime to master—an art of orchestrating people and technology.

Managers ruthlessly delegate. EMs are entrusted with "painting the picture of done." They discuss the mission, the why, and give guidance. Managers leave *the how* to the team leads,[2] so they can scale.

EMs search and source relevant context. They have an investor attitude. Managers find and point in a direction for those to learn. They share information on disciplines, trends, and what is happening in the community. EMs are meta engineers. They build and tune the talent that produces the machine.

Staying technical is essential. In software, discreteness and rational thought are paramount. The language and discipline of engineering ignite the performance of others. Managers know their limits and stay higher-ordered. Whereas the team has latitude with the craft, EMs develop a toolbox to elevate that craft further.

Like software, managers follow rituals. They follow the same feedback loop of developing software. First, make a solution work, then make it right, finally they make it fast.[3] In management, EMs build trust, place people in areas to grow, and then optimize. Developing software sometimes requires walking away for a solution— to return with options for the team.[4]

And optimization is praise. The accelerant of culture is praise. Develop a test culture by praising those that uphold quality. Develop collaboration by those that collaborate. Do some of the initial work. No matter how small, catch them doing the right things and recognize it.

But the brutality of management is the lengthy feedback loop. EMs practice patience. The satisfaction of delivery and growing those is long-tailed. Whereas the engineering feedback loop is seconds to minutes, the manager's feedback loop is weeks to months.

EMs promote a learning culture. Software is creative work. They work to build a culture that learns from the delivery of software. They encourage and capture shared learnings in the organization. EMs set time for their engineers to explore.

And they invest in their management craft. A manager invests in continuous learning. They read books, listen to podcasts, source facts, and experiment for others. There are leaders out there with the right advice. Asynchronous mentorship is all around.

EMs continuously build relationships. Managers are *organizational engineers*. To enable their teams, they focus on building alliances with everyone in the business. EMs optimize for common ground and increase optionality as projects roll on.

And they partner with product and design well. EMs collaborate on the customer journey from discovery to delivery. They barter with technology to find optimal solutions to a business outcome. EMs can demo[5] functional values in front of others.

They have to make tough decisions. Sometimes a decision is necessary. Information will be incomplete, and it will be hard. But the weight of not making the decision is worse than making one no matter how unclear the outcome.

With their decisions, fairness, and no surprises. EMs make decisions that weigh options fairly. They communicate effectively by having one-on-ones, staff meetings, and are right there with the team. There are no surprises.

And impact the lives of others. What managers say has an impact on others. If done right, they see those grow, and in turn, see themselves grow.[6] Above all, they serve the business well.

DSR

VI

Section Six

Interviewing

in·ter·view (/ˈin(t)ər,vyoo/) *v.* question (someone) to discover their opinions or experience.

DSR

37

How to Organize Your Thoughts on the Whiteboard

On Organizational Skills and the Applied Science of Gluing Lots of Things Together in the Craft of Software Engineering

SOME WEEKS AGO, a bright individual reposted on Hacker News[1] a well-thought out and succinct post about the most important skill in software development.[2] In this essay, John D. Cook reflected on the article *Organizational Skills Beat Algorithmic Wizardry*,[3] by James Hague. Both authors tackle the software engineering subject of **organization as a skill**. They contrast organizational skill to the mastery of computer science tested in interviews, taught in academia, or touted in blog posts. Their contemplation got me pondering about how interview skills are organized.

Thinking deeply about both authors' messages, I ran through my interview experiences over time and I empathize with those who experience technical interviews that are not classically trained.

My last experience was disorganized—explaining my experience in a legacy system of tangled wires.

My last completed professional project was a multi-year system that dealt with code complexity, and a never-ending rolling line of products. We fought bravely to organize the growing mess.

Both thoughts had a common thread, as they were small and large exercises in *organization.* They revolved around feelings of anxiety, vulnerability, stress, and happy moments. I (we) cared deeply about outcomes.

This motivated me to write a follow-up. Why not answer the questions posed? So I kicked the idea back and forth and stewed on one contemplation. John asked:

...how do you present a clever bit of organization?

Thinking about the question, I looked away from the screen and saw my whiteboard standing before me. My head swirled around the posts. Tough technical interviews? Organization? Managing state? Collapsing weight? Code complexity? Perhaps the technical interview whiteboard exercise could prove a salient point of software engineering all along.

So I solved typical problems at the whiteboard, confidently, all by myself.

Rarely at a whiteboard does anyone perform well. You have to hold a lot in your head, and demonstrate a didactic process. You have to communicate, but how do you convey detailed items while ignoring the voice in your head that says "hurry up!"[4] while moving around enthusiastically?

A Better Approach

At technical companies, there are whiteboard interviews. A candidate is placed in a room with a whiteboard with an individual who represents the company. They ask a question such as "build an algorithm" and we are invited to solve the problem. Then it's up to the interviewee to drive the problem to a solution.

This is where my head starts to spin out of control with anxiety and disorganization. Trumpets begin to play in my mind and my thought process becomes mangled. Time speeds up. My vision narrows and I become lightheaded.

Maybe there is a way to slow down, pace, and walk through a process with **organization**. Something I've never seen before while interviewing candidates over my years, but maybe a process can help ease the nerves and make it an enjoyable experience. To start, look at the board, and cut it up into three sections. They will be organized.

Figure 37.1: A typical 5' by 3' whiteboard cut into three sections.

Step 1: The Problem

Make sure to write down the problem in a complete sentence on top of the board. Feeling the dry-erase marker in your hand will help overcome the initial rush of "how do I solve this?"

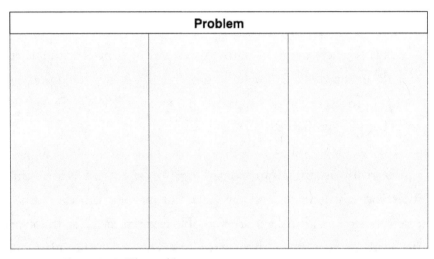

Problem

Figure 37.2: The problem statement is important to write out.

Once you have the question written down, look at it for a moment and start to think about questions. Draw the lines with ample space. Don't worry about the pause, let the interviewer know that you are thinking about questions to ask.

Step 2: Assumptions

Think about some generic questions. Like, "what programming language do you prefer?" Move to the right side of the board. No questions coming? The difficulty may contain concepts you don't know. Ask what they are. Then, start tackling the problem statement.

The first question to ask is an example of the **input** and **output.** Ask if the data is **presorted**. Write out the functional and non-functional requirements.

Clarifying assumptions can simplify the problem. As you ask every question, write each answer pair in the assumptions area. When you receive responses, get a second marker to highlight the answer. Bringing your own markers may help.

We can only hold so many items in our head, so lean on the board to capture all the knowledge. Writing the questions and answers out will slow down your approach so it is digestible.

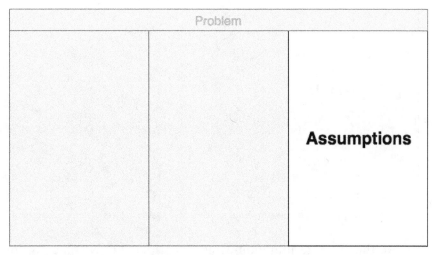

Figure 37.3: Assumptions are the questions that need answering.

Step 3: The Approach

Once you have a good number of questions on the right side of the board, physically move over to the left. This is where we will start to discuss an approach to solve the problem.

Here, very rough pseudocode, steps, and visualizations occur. Let your interviewer know that this is not your implementation, but a place where you are organizing your thoughts on the approach, with data structures and abstract data types. Draw out the solution like it's a picture.

The left box will reveal holes in our questions. As you write out your approach, stop the process if a question remains unanswered. Walk back to the right section, and write out the question and try to receive the answer.

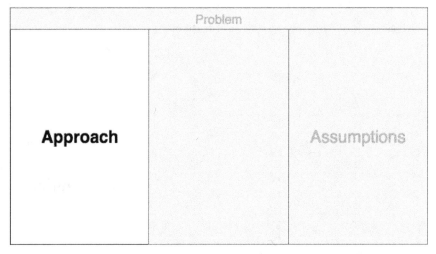

Figure 37.4: Approach is the strategy, the structure and the visualization scratch pad.

At the absolute minimum, this will happen a few times as you recognize the **average cases, best cases**, and **worst cases**. It depends on the strategy, the limits, and the constraints. Request **relaxation** on approaches such as "For this example, can I use a small set of data?" "Can I assume the input array is sorted?" Input validation is also another question generator.

Step 4: Code Implementation

Once enough "approach material" is generated, you are now ready to write through your implementation with confidence. You will be supported by both sides. Highlight and point to each step as you write the code. Carefully walk through the approach, listed to your left. As you write your implementation, go back and forth double-checking the assumptions.

Even if you struggle with the solution, you are the wizard of organization.

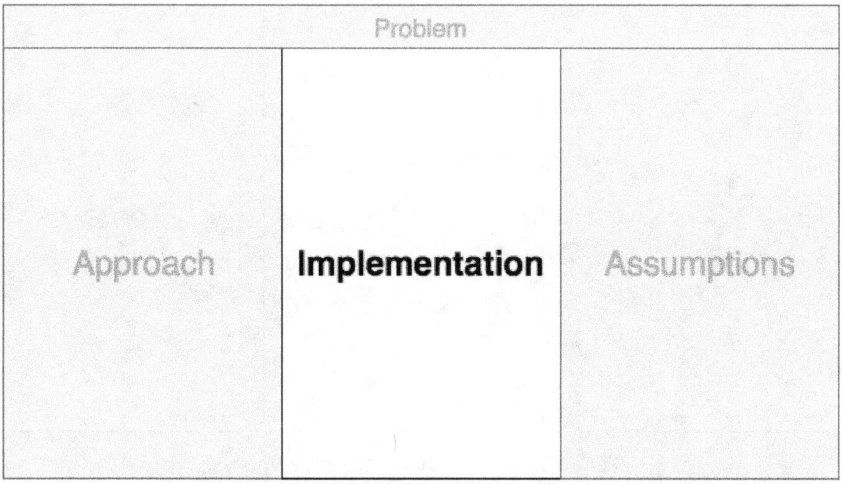

Figure 37.5: The main event is centered so it can be supported from all sides.

Of course, there is a possibility of finding improvements in the act. Walk back to the left and revive the approach, break it down, or ask for assistance. New questions pop up. Go to the right. Go back and forth from left to right to center until you succeed. You will.

Be the master of organization. If you hit a wall or find something that is just not right, remember that the sides will guide you.

Bonus Step 5: Test

If you have completed the exercise to the satisfaction of the interviewer, take the step to discuss how the solution should be tested. Use the assumptions section as a place to write test code, if you should choose to do so.

By now, it is likely safe to remove all the questions from this area. Erase the questions and write unit tests. In the end, you'll be okay because you organized with confidence.

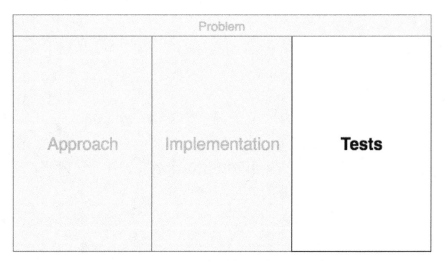

Figure 37.6: Tests should never be optional.

To Sum Up

There you go. That was a few minutes of pure organization without theory. The process leans on a few simple concepts:

1. **Sectioning:** Slicing up the problem in pieces from start to finish.

2. **Scaffolding:** The concept of temporary architecture, a supporting structure as we build around us.

3. **Gating:** We should proceed forward with the next step when we are confident about addressing the problem. Actively engage the interviewer with "Did I miss any assumptions?" or "Does my approach have holes?" before proceeding.

4. **State:** Organization is handled visually to maintain control of the problem. Avoid using an eraser.

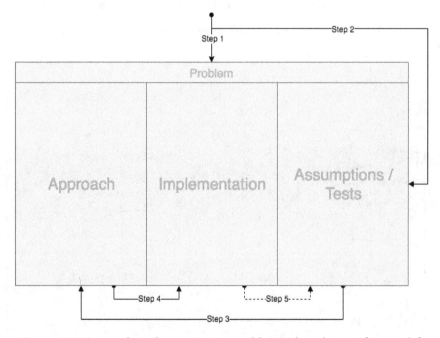

Figure 37.7: Approaching the organization problem with a solution. If you are left handed, try reversing the setup.

Conclusion

Let's finish by examining important quotes by John Cook.

You can't appreciate a feat of organization until you experience the disorganization.

I agree. This applies to projects with code, people, and those technical whiteboard experiences. But to take a step back and answer the problem with a process of organization is a feat of engineering.

John D. Cook said:

Only if the disorganized mess is your responsibility, something that means more to you than a case study, can you wrap your head around it and appreciate improvements.

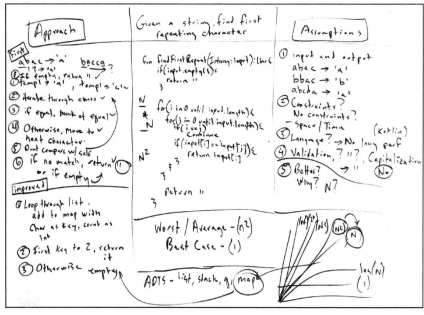

Figure 37.8: What the process looks like. Try iterating to discover new patterns.

We all have a story about the whiteboard—and we all have the stories of defeat. So, I found a way to improve my engineering mind at the same time. The result is what you have read.

Computer programming is applied science, a **pattern language**, and a **craft**. I've written a few posts[5] about linking[6] organization to system complexity. This is why I appreciated John Cook's and James Hague's thoughts on software engineering.

Walk through the steps, and you'll do great. Good luck with your next interview!

More Resources

This author does not claim to be an expert at the practice.

Since this chapter was written, many resources have appeared to assist interviewees with system design interview prep.

This author recommends ByteByteGo's *System Design Interview Volume 1* and *Volume 2* by Alex Xu and Sahn Lam. More information can be found at bytebytego.com.

Additionally, the rise of artificial intelligence will ultimately transform this human process. What will interviewing look like when machines generate correct code?

38

Find Career Freedom with a Daily Code Workout

THERE ARE TWO MAIN MODES of physical exercise, aerobic and anaerobic. Aerobics train the body to maintain output throughout distributed muscles. Its goal is to preserve oxygen levels along a strenuous distance. Anaerobic exercises target muscle groups under resistance repetitions until the muscles cannot perform further. The goal is to improve the energy output of the targeted muscle by tearing and rebuilding. Both modes have benefits associated with peak performance.

Dealing with Software

Software engineers[1] perform their craft in a similar manner. If one takes a step back, the resemblance of aerobic exercise is to solve problems, such as handling an unformed concern and unraveling it. However, engineers cannot complete the activity because they need specific "muscles" to command a solution, which requires strength to achieve endurance.

Engineers perform targeted "anaerobic" workouts to improve

problem-solving endurance to achieve aerobic results. But why perform exercises and spend time doing what seems trivial? The answer is simple, freedom to solve problems. As a benefit, career options[2] will expand when we gracefully perform various computer science skills. We choose where to spend time, motivated by solving problems.

Targets

The core engineering workout is a process of concentration and effort. It requires about one hour of practice daily. If every day is too rigorous, exercise every other day to let the mind rest. Rotate a reduced set throughout the week. Either way, working to solve known problems builds muscles in the brain, particularly the neocortex. Like code katas,[3] these exercises target building muscle memory.

1. **Temporal:** Relating to temporary space. Holding items in mind is a skill.
2. **Spatial:** Relating to visualizing how these exercises interrelate with data.
3. **Speaking:** Rubber ducking[4] through the problem challenges communication. Think: how can I teach this to someone?
4. **Recollection:** These workouts target a wide range of muscles, memorizing essential patterns. Repeating them leads to working efficiently within an integrated development environment.
5. **Abstract:** Learning something new. Discovering a new workout, we add computer science fundamentals to expand our knowledge.

The Workout

Like a physical exercise regime, these exercises require a warm-up to get the mind thinking clearly. Vigorous activities follow. After a certain amount of rotations—results include solving complex problems in less time. Craving to perform will follow, such as desiring spicy food from our TRPV1 pain receptors.[5]

Warm Up (5 minutes)

Create an array, fill it with random integers, and print it to the screen. Or execute the Fibonacci sequence[6] recursively and iteratively.

Sorts (10 minutes)

Exercise integer sorting in order of difficulty. Bubble, selection, insertion, shell, merge, quick, heap. Finalize with binary search iteratively and recursively. Describe the Big O notation[7] as well.

Maps / Hashes or Stacks / Queues (10 Minutes)

Create a naive hashing algorithm to avoid collisions. Or build stacks/queues with finding the minimum or maximum on a stack.

Trees or Double Linked Lists (10 Minutes)

Create a binary search tree by inserting nodes, printing traversals, and deleting a node. As an alternative, create a doubly linked list. Insert, delete, and print in both directions.

Graphs (15 Minutes)

Create and traverse graphs using breadth-first and depth-first search, or experiment with the Dijkstra[8] and A* algorithm.[9]

Complex (15 Minutes)

Solve a question from the *Cracking The Coding Interview*.[10] Adding these questions[11] to the workout will inspire thinking by amending the repetitive nature of the previous exercises.[12] If solving canned problems isn't attractive, build something variable.[13]

System (15 Minutes)

Rotate a complex (seen above) question and a system design question in a regular cadence. For system design questions, it starts as "Build YouTube," or "Build Google Maps." Today, free videos walk through potential solutions—some as fast at ten minutes!

The Conclusion is Core Strength

A disciplined workout is key to a healthy engineer, whether a leader[13] or an individual contributor. The goal is discipline, first to remedy the repetitions by gradually reducing the time to solve. Once achieving results, "aerobic" problem-solving exercises will come naturally because conditioned muscles are trained to execute well.

There is a certain satisfaction to these exercises. Why not strive to be a well-rounded engineer? If one hour seems lengthy, reduce the set, building toward a new goal. Importantly, push hard at the end of the exercise to finish well.

39

The One About Software Engineering Interviewing

Mapping the Process After Years of Learning

I'VE RECENTLY REFLECTED on my experiences as an interviewee in software engineering. As I trace through each interview, I have learned and improved.

I'd like to share these findings with a diagram I've built from my last search and highlight the significant bits.

Practice Role-Playing

My most impactful discovery was the value of practicing weekly with a friend. What I learned is that interviewing is a muscle. Finding a study buddy helped simulate real interview situations.[1] This practice had a tangible improvement in offers. After securing a new job, we would continue to practice, once a week for an hour, to be sharp at interviewing—recalling professional stories.

Partnering with Recruiting

I found success in partnering with recruiting as I went through the process. Being courteous, providing feedback, and asking what to expect had better outcomes. Being honest about my position in my search, expectations, and asking informed questions was an advantage.

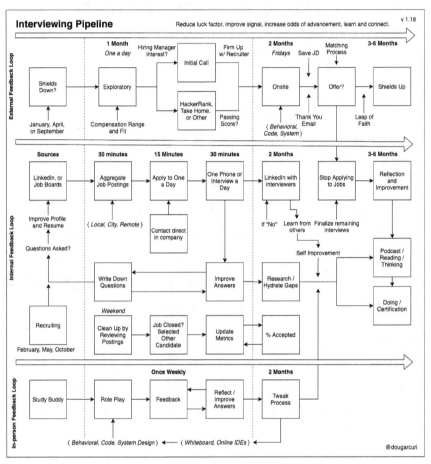

Figure 39.1: Interview process map from personal experience.

Optimal Months to Start a Search

My personal interviewing experience revealed that searching during certain months increased job opportunities and responses. It became evident that the optimal time range proceeded American holidays where high paying companies advanced their talent searches. These months were January, April, and September.

Feedback is Rare

Interview loops do not provide direct feedback on performance. Rejection was frequent, and my approach to improve was to guess what had happened. For example, if a story wasn't on the tip of my tongue, I thought about the situation and formulated an impactful answer.

Questions Improve Profile

Since feedback is rare, each question asked was an opportunity to improve my professional profile. These include the resume, social profile, and other mediums. Each item found gaps in my experience that I did not highlight as an essential experience. By fortifying these weaknesses, I appeared comprehensive over time.

Hydrating Skill Sets

Since software engineering[2] contains many skill sets, technical questions are an opportunity to learn. If a technology came up where I did not have working experience, I would build cursory knowledge by setting aside time to experiment.

Expect Technical Variations

The technical interviews required knowledge of data types and operations. Importantly, some exercises were pair based, solving a problem together. Finally, I encountered three variations of system design. The three types included building something from requirements, debugging a mal-performing system, and talking through a system established by the team and discussing tradeoffs.

Keeping Interviewing

Interviewing is tough because you are being judged for a role. There were times where I'd disagreed with the outcome. There were times I completely bombed and felt humiliated days after the interview. On occasion, organizations have requested additional interviews with me! But by thinking objectively on performance and persevering through difficulty drove me to succeed. Keep at it!

Conclusion

My approach to finding the next opportunity is to understand the system meta.[3] The result is the system diagram in Figure 39.1. By improving how I explained my experience concisely, I achieved offers.

While there is no formula to interview well, I hope that this read will prepare you for your upcoming interviews.

40

Interview Well for Your Next Incredible Engineering Role

Tips to Improve the Odds of Landing Your Next Role

INTERVIEWING CAN BE INCREDIBLY rewarding. With understanding, preparation, and reflection, you can secure your next software engineering[1] role. Here are my essential tips and walkthrough for performing a successful search.

I want to preface that these interviewing findings are based on my personal experiences and shared stories from others, so your results will vary!

Before Starting

Here are the core concepts of interviewing. By embracing these, the odds of achieving results may increase.

Interviewing is an unpredictable system. Interviewing is more than just self-preparation; it is a natural system of factors that will be beyond your control: timing, luck, relative candidates, budget changes, and the need for the position. Focus on what you can control by increasing proficiency signals. When "no" is delivered, it wasn't meant to be. Keep going! Naturally, there will be lots of rejections before the first "yes!"

Learning and reflecting reduce luck factors. For every interview, reflect on performing better. Was there a question that you did not have an answer to? Was there a problematic technical challenge[2] you couldn't build a solution to your liking? Review the questions and answers given after every conversation, then rework it by seeking better details. *The goal is to have answers at the tip of your tongue!*

It is a learning feedback loop in an unsafe environment. Interviews present challenges to candidates because values are at stake, and skills are measured. With each conversation, you are becoming a better candidate. Find someone you can lean on at this time. Receiving rejection will be hard because expectations may have been different.

Where to Begin

Now that we discussed the interviewing principles, let's talk about landing a new role.

Interviewing is a commitment. In my experience, interviews can take months of dedication before landing your first or next role. Success comes with discipline and practice. The search ends as you start the new job. *Getting there is a journey.* Work in short increments daily. Commitment is essential to achieving success!

Know about the companies you apply to. Take a look at their social media presence as well as previous employee reviews—e.g., Glassdoor. Make sure these are places you can see yourself working. Knowing the perceived company culture is essential. Look for red flags such as large amounts of employees leaving at once, frequent turnover, a weak business model, and a volatile stock price. Seek the right parts that lead to high employee satisfaction, including mentorship, learning while delivering software, and room for career growth.

Consistent procession and tracking of applications. After you commit, as each day goes by, apply to companies that align with your values and career advancement. Consistently post your resume. Track your progress with a Kanban board, or a spreadsheet, so no application goes untracked. Do not be afraid to apply to jobs you *can fail at* or if the *skill sets do not precisely match!*

Sources are everywhere. Whether it's through friends, your university campus, Internet, or your favorite tech blog, opportunities are highly available. Seek channels to post in, and spread out consistently. A variation of subscriptions can increase your chance for the next role. But don't stop there! Most importantly, lean on the power of networks of friends and colleagues to find the next opportunity. Ask those you have relationships with. They may open the door to an exciting opportunity.

Once Interviewing Starts

After starting a small conveyor belt of submissions, it may take time for someone to respond. Once they do, let's walk through what to expect.

There are different types of people you will encounter. Some are from agencies. Some are internal company recruiters. Either way, they are seeking you as a potential fit for the role. A short *exploratory call* is what to expect. *Partner with them. They are championing for you.* Let them know why you like the company and what skills you bring to the table. Finally, ask them what to expect in the interview process so preparation can be focused.

Once the recruiter advances your candidacy, expect the interview loop. If you are a fit, it's either a skills assessment or an initial conversation with the hiring manager. Be yourself and **note the questions**. If it's a skills assessment, expect a take-home assignment or a web-based one like HackerRank.

If you do well, you will advance to the final round. In many cases, a half or full day at their company's office (or remote) with a mixture of two types of interviews. The behavioral/leadership type is where you will tell stories about what and how you work. The technical interview is a coding or system design knowledge conver-sation.[3] Once complete, the process is over just as fast as it started.

The Offer and Starting the New Role

The company may take a few days before they return with an answer. If it worked, congrats on getting your first offer! You are improving by finding the role of your dreams.

When they decline an offer. Due to many candidates or liability considerations, most companies will decline feedback if you did not receive an offer. Ask! Some feedback can help you improve. Above all, be gracious and accept if you want to change.

Congrats on the offer! It's time to negotiate. When the first offer comes in, it is likely a fair starting offer for the role tailored for the experience. It will depend if it's right for you! Most companies want to secure you. If you think it's possible, there may be ways to move this needle. There may be tangibles outside of money to include in that offer. It's up to you if it makes sense. Good luck!

Clarify benefits. There are plenty of posts out there that discuss how to negotiate well. Ask questions about benefits, start date, and everything else. Make sure you understand the entire package before you commit.

Multiple offers. A purposeful search may yield more than one offer. Having these offers is an excellent position to be. Having multiple offers can give you a substantial negotiation standing point on the final package. It is up to you on how you like to proceed—take the best offer for your future.

Start with a fresh mind. Once you have signed the offer, sit back and relax. It's time to start a new role.[4] Brush up on technology and company history. Reach out and start a convo with the hiring manager on onboarding tips and thank them for taking the leap with you.

The Other Important Tips

Now that you have a holistic picture of this process and what to expect, here are my hard-won tips after going through interviews over the years.

Interviewing is a skill set. Just like programming, interviewing is muscle memory.[5] The key is to practice continuously. Keep a running list of stories you can talk through about your accomplishments. Continually update the resume. Practice the coding skill set with LeetCode or HackerRank. Do it weekly, even if it's just twenty minutes.

Career capital can help. Blogging, podcasting, and having open-source projects will help make your work shine. Crafting a professional social image is essential and will bring great conversation at an interview, securing your next role. *If you have a portfolio, highlight it!* Showcasing your work will help to "stand out" in an interview.

Find a long-term study buddy. An excellent way to practice is to role-play. Find a study buddy. Real-time feedback goes a long way. Meet weekly and rotate the interview formats from behavior/ leadership to coding/system design. An important use of time is to review the questions faced in an interview. Brainstorm together on how to formulate a better answer.

There are different channels of feedback: external, internal, and role-play. With each step in this ritual above, there are incoming learning notes. Whether you can clarify a question in your resume, update your career profile, or were asked an impossible technical problem, review with a study buddy. Take these learnings and improve!

Connect with everyone you meet in your journey with kindness. You will make connections along the way as you interview. Reach out to them, say thank you, and connect on the Internet. *Respect their process, no matter the outcome.* On occasion, new opportunities may arise, and your name may come up as being remembered as being a professional through the process.

Interviewing is a hard skill to master. Since the variables are infinite, there is no list to follow for the best outcome. The one takeaway is to be open to feedback and reflect on what you've learned. Preparation is essential, and the reflections are paramount as it's a campaign. If you keep these tips in mind, you're going to do great!

Section Seven

Being a Software Engineer

en·gi·neer (/ˌenjəˈnir/) *n.* a person who designs, builds, or maintains engines, machines, software,[‡] or public works.

DSR

Meta Skills of a Software Engineer

Learning Through Books on Correctness and Pattern Recognition

RECENTLY, A FRIEND ASKED a question about the particular skills possessed by software engineers.

What are the unique skills that software engineers practice?

Drawing from my experience led me to an opinion. I enjoy the meta of programming. The skill of learning the *meta*, or how to do what programmers do better, includes reading well-known books in context.

I took specific examples of what I read over the years, applied it to my observations practicing in the field, and I answered in a pragmatic way.

In my opinion, I would say it is the practice of **correctness** *and* **pattern recognition.**[1] *These are the skills that are unique to software engineers.*

Let's examine these skills to add context.

Correctness

Correctness is related to **how** and **why** programmers build things[2] the way they do. In organizations, it is associated with the accuracy of what the business must solve for its customers. Well written software follows this thinking.

Correctness is *how correct the "how" is*. The solution delivered should meet the customer expectations. The practice is a balance of strategy (designing) and tactics (execution).

The examination of the *how's* "how" in a vacuum appears in chapter four of *Programming Pearls*,[3] "Writing Correct Programs."

> *... keeping code simple is usually the key to correctness.*

— Jon Bentley

Pattern Recognition

Pattern recognition ties to the **organization** of **correctness** by creating the necessary abstractions and component boundaries. Pattern recognition forms modularize code. Programmers monitor duplication, find areas of reuse, and refactor complicated parts of the system. It is what software engineers[4] do well. Their attention to that detail is vigilant. Programmers recognize knowledge as it is created over and over again. Then they simplify the code.

Pattern recognition is discussed at length in the community, and there are many sources that describe their techniques. The origins where I learned about this skill reside in chapter two of *The Pragmatic*

Programmer,[5] "The Evils Of Duplication."

Make it easy to reuse. DRY—Don't Repeat Yourself.

— Andrew Hunt & Dave Thomas

A Teachable Moment

Once I answered my friend's question, they followed up with another question.

If correctness and pattern recognition are these skills, how do you teach them?

My answer was simple enough.

Locate these books, set the environment, and work through by offering examples. Set the expectation of learning and practicing these meta skills while delivering value to business. Why? Complexity. Practicing is the best investment of learning the skill of balancing complexity, resulting in engineers who are confident over time.

My mentoring focuses on these books and these particular skills. The practice made me realize there are few who invest heavily in the meta, apart from doing the work. The vocabulary of the meta is something I have an interest in. My writings on problem decomposition[6] (correctness) and organization[7] (pattern recognition) were difficult to see when in the heat of delivery.

At about the time I wrote this brief on these skills, I received a book recommendation. A professor at Stanford has been teaching a course on the meta. His study resulted in an edition of his course findings. I found out that he had the same gripe as me. I purchased the book and devoured it from chapter thirteen, *A Philosophy Of System Design.*[8]

> *Engineers tend to be very detail oriented. We love details and are good at managing lots of them; this is essential for being a good engineer. But, great software designers can also step back from the details and think about a system at a higher level.*

— John Ousterhout[9]

Conclusion

In my opinion, correctness and pattern recognition are skills[10] that software engineers do well at. The result is *higher quality software.* All other unique skills, if there are others to categorize, stem from these concepts.

I invite others to share examples of meta-skills they have practiced over time.

Fundamentally, correctness and pattern recognition have tie-ins to outcomes of complexity (also known as cognitive load). Programmers balance both so that they mitigate complexity. In essence, this is why these skills are the distillation of what they do.

Be Amazing in Your New Engineering Role

STARTING A NEW SOFTWARE ENGINEERING role can be an overwhelming experience. The first months are a dizzying mix of meetings, development, and people. But there are many ways to become successful. Here are my top tips.

Build Trust with People

My philosophy starts with people. As a software engineer,[1] good technical fundamentals support the day to day work. Software, at its core, is fundamentally about people working as a team. Focus on getting to know your teammates well.

Reach out to people and get to know them. For those that work and partner with your team, reach out, and introduce yourself and what you do. Having this small interaction starts working relationships well.

Find a partner that can pair with you. There are teammates out there that will want to see you be successful. Pair up with them and learn together.

Communication helps build partnerships. Not all communication requires purpose. Be open to team lunches. Share your interests outside of work with the team. Socializing will help forge powerful working relationships.

Show recognition. For every contribution from others, a quick thank you can go a long way. Importantly, as you start working on initiatives together, and achieve results, recognize their accomplishments.

Add Value Every Day by Learning

As you build up relationships with people, get to know the work well.

Ask questions. Whether it is about the work in flight, the product, or processes, ask questions so that you can build context. No question is off the table; in fact, asking will reveal opportunities in which you may lead.

Jump in and contribute. As you settle into your role, offer to take on a challenge by being proactive. Shadowing will help build context, build a relationship, and also move the team in the right direction. No matter how small, file your first pull request.[2]

Redraw things and learn by tracing. The systems and software you're working on are intricate. Learn by drawing out the system and collaborating with others to improve acuity. You are building value by understanding a holistic view of the system.

Meet with your manager and discuss expectations. As you learn about the people, work to understand expectations with your manager. Establish rapport by asking questions. Being on the same page is incredibly essential.

Don't know a particular technology? Learn by watching. As you start in the codebase, you will encounter technology that you may not have experience in. Build awareness by actively experiencing technology through video learning sites. A short 30-minute course will accelerate your understanding.

Spend time learning the product. Dogfooding your product is an excellent technique to understand the value you will eventually add. Having a product domain understanding will give you an extra-ordinary chance to contribute effectively. As a stretch, offer to demo[3] product work at the next showcase.

Organize Your Learning

Now that you are understanding people, and adding value by contributing, organizing what you discover can help.

Seek ways to onboard effectively. The people you work with have insight into how to onboard well at the company. Ask them. This knowledge may already be organized! A runbook or an essential checklist can give you a headstart.

Bring the outside in. There are books out there that have excellent onboarding advice. The most important book I know of is *The First 90 Days.*[4] There are also excellent podcasts and blog posts.

Start a document of all-important links. There will be disparate systems and tools. Keep a running list of all those URLs in a convenient location. Organizing bookmarks by their domain can help.

Build a glossary of acronyms. Each company has its own set of abbreviations and acronyms. As you discover them through conversation, ask what they mean, and write it down. Start a glossary, and share it with the next new employee.

Structured knowledge with a wiki. As you discover the product, it is a good idea to write out what you are learning. A personal wiki or a small library of markdown files can document your progress. The documents will reveal gaps to formulate new questions to ask. The bonus is that you can share with others.

Take on Your First Initiative

As you are onboarding well, now is an excellent opportunity to build. Take ownership of the work you will be contributing to the team.

Understand the why behind the work. As you get into taking on your first challenge for the team, it is good to ask why your work is essential. Understand the mission and shape the context so it will drive your impact.

Start small, and build up. Take on work that is achievable to build up understanding. Small accomplishments fortify your confidence.

Bring in previous learnings. As you learn from the codebase, and respect team efforts, show your way of thinking by solving the first initiative collaboratively. It's an excellent opportunity to mentor and learn even more from others.

Solve a gnarly problem. The team has many important initiatives ahead of them. Find a problem that can help the organization,[5] the product, or the environment. By taking on a gnarly issue, you will build the trust and respect of the team.

Finally

Get in there and don't be afraid! All the tips above require courage to take on. Each of these applied can be highly impactful. Be respectful and be bold! It's a journey and will take time. You will do great!

DSR

43

What's in a Career Promotion?

Deconstructing the Path of an Individual's
Advancement

RECENTLY, MY FRIEND SHARED OPINIONS on the promotion
process. I found our discussion fascinating, drawing out our thinking.
We concluded by mapping an individual's path through a career
advancement process, which I'll call the **promotion life cycle**.

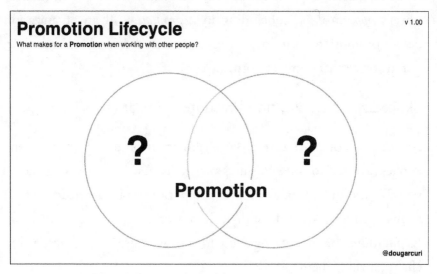

Figure 43.1: What makes for a **Promotion** when working with other people?

The life cycle defines points along the individual's journey within a business context. They are **skill sets**, **reputation**, **sponsorship**, **opportunity**, and **advancement**. These qualities are timeless but are not intended as a panacea. They depend on an individual's adaptability to a business culture, quality of relationship with the manager, and meeting personal needs.

While I cannot highlight every dimension, my goal is to draw a holistic trail for an individual's *advancement,* identifying qualities in a group of people performing work. Along the way, I'll uncover interesting bits of behaviors between people, providing hints to accelerate their relationships.

The Promotion Life Cycle

Obtaining a promotion follows a sequence of events. First, *skill sets* and *reputation* develop *sponsors* providing *sponsorship.* Next, having *sponsors* unveils *opportunities,* concluding in a *promotion.* If an organization denies promotions, a motivated individual *exits* toward *advancement.* Let me break them down to provide context.

Skill Sets and Reputation Promote Sponsors

At the start of one's career or collaboration on a new project, one applies *skill sets* to solve business problems. As time advances, people perceive the quality of their peer's application of knowledge, which forms opinions of this individual's work, creating a *reputation.* Reputations become recognized in the workgroup and leadership chains, making them *sponsors.*

Skill Sets

An individual applies *skill sets* to complete work. Skill sets are the necessary application of knowledge when performing work. Whatever the domain, the group acknowledges levels of *skill sets*. The natural course of skills development provides *eminence*, optimally tackling the job. Eminence demands an efficiency of delivery, exemplifying orchestration to their peers.

Skill Set Accelerants

→ Staying up to date with latest techniques
→ Credentials such as badges and certificates
→ Finding and participating in side projects
→ Taking on difficult work, orchestrating path finding
→ An attitude of persistence, not giving up on a solution
→ Having curiosity of how something works
→ Knowing the right time to seek help

Reputation

Reputation defines who completes the work and how. *Reputation* follows *skill sets*. Reputation aligns with how the person completes work, its recipient, and in what "bedside" matters. Reputation requires the right balance of achieving the result and doing it well with others.

One can have unique *skill sets* but lack interpersonal achievements due to poor likability, or one has an excellent reputation but lacks the required skills, requiring refinement in their craft.

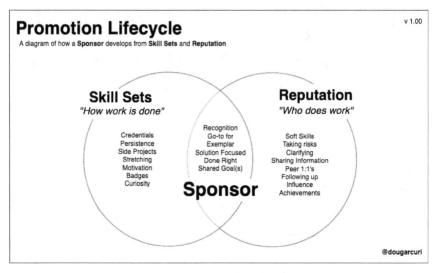

Figure 43.2: A diagram of how a **Sponsor** develops from **Skill Sets** and **Reputation**.

Reputation Accelerants

➜ Seeking what is essential in the work group

➜ Possess a high form of valency,[1] combining with others to perform

➜ Taking on risk and raising a hand when leadership needs a volunteer

➜ Securing designations that are recognized by the group

➜ Inclusive mindset for tackling business problems

➜ Bringing others in at the right times, improving soft skills[2]

Skill Sets, Reputation, and Sponsorships Promote Opportunity

Once an individual has enough *skill set* and *reputation* which is optimal for the environment, sponsors find them *opportunities*, directing the needs of new problems that require solving.

Those with potential *eminence* take on these challenges.

Figure 43.3: A diagram of how an **Opportunity** develops between **Skill Sets**, **Reputation**, and **Sponsorship**. (Previously covered areas are grayed.)

Sponsorship

Sponsors observe the work and by whom. *Sponsors* socialize with who in the group is delivering the work. People raise awareness of what is happening in the environment and often talk to one another in an initiative context. Both *skill set* and *reputation* feed into these conversations. Being visible to leadership is often a key to promotion. Sponsorship aligns with extrinsic motivators such as money and intrinsic motivators such as providing impact.

Sponsorship Accelerants

→ Foster a good relationship with the manager
→ Continue manager one-on-ones
→ Start skip level one-on-ones
→ Take on new initiatives without deferring current work
→ Mature their presentation[3] skill set and group communication
→ Increase visible achievements in execution
→ Develop brag sheet with a manager[4]
→ Being able to operate autonomously

Opportunity

Opportunity is where the new work resides. *Sponsors* discover delegation opportunities. Finding an opportunity is an excellent step toward *promotion*. Operating in the context for some time is required before recognizing the individual.

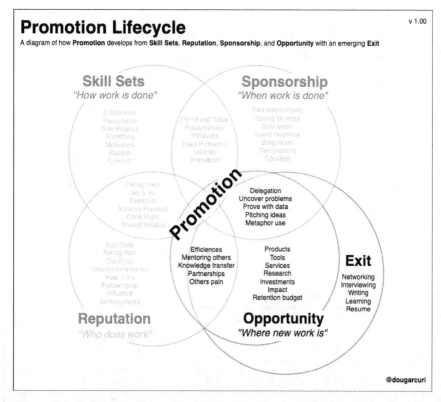

Figure 43.4: A diagram of how a **Promotion** develops from **Skill Sets**, **Reputation**, **Sponsorship**, and **Opportunity** with the emerging **Exit**.

While enough *skill sets*, *reputation*, and *sponsorship* are essential, timing and luck factor into an opportunity. One can optimize for the talent review process,[5] but not all teams have ascending options. If they do, it may require waiting in a line of succession or finding a way through the competition.

Opportunity Accelerants

➔ Finding new problems and solving them

> → Pitching to leadership new ideas
> → Asking the manager to delegate work
> → Using metaphors and having a command on domain language
> → Having motivation to advance one's career

Skill Sets, Reputation, and Opportunity Forms Promotion

An individual's journey will lead to *promotion* if opportunities exist in the environment and leadership recognizes the person doing the work.

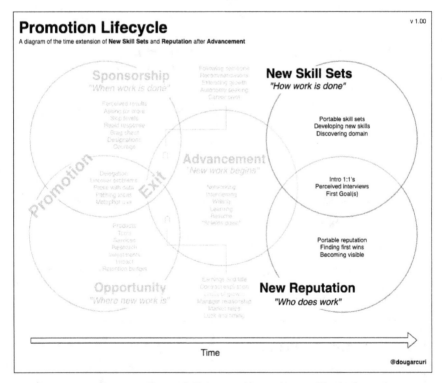

Figure 43.5: A diagram of new **Skill Sets** and **Reputation** after **Advancement**.

Opportunity and Sponsorships Promote Advancement

Suppose the individual cannot find *opportunities*. Challenges within the environment may prevent *promotion*. For example, if retention budgets do not match market rates. In that case, there is the ability to *exit*, leading to *advancement*. The individual joins a new group working on different business problems.

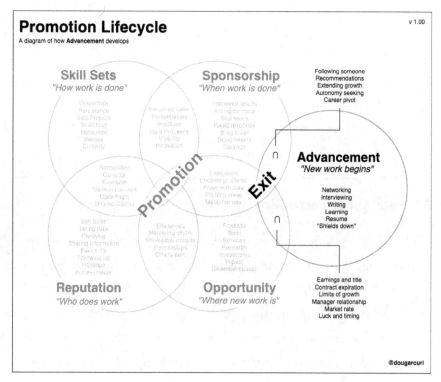

Figure 43.6: A diagram of how **Advancement** develops.

Exiting and Advancement

Adding the final piece to the framework, if an individual finds that new *opportunities* do not exist in their environment, one leaves the workgroup for an opportunity.[6] The schism is a ripcord to correct mistakes made with *reputation*, sensing their career in the organization is limited, or if *skill sets* no longer align. Leaving brings the individual a new promotion, money, or title. Hence, the *advancement* of their career.

Exiting and Advancement Accelerants

→ Following trusted individuals through prior sponsorships
→ Being informed on market rates for work performed
→ Keeping contacts and networking up to date
→ Being open to new opportunities
→ Continuous interviewing
→ Doing what's best for the individual

A Note About Portability

Following one's *promotion* or *advancement*, a life cycle repeats in timeframes. In a *promotion*, one gets to keep parts of their *reputation*. They obtain specific domain *skill sets* in a similar environment but trade-off potential accelerating *opportunities* and new *skill sets*.

In *advancement*, the person returns part of their *reputation* and *sponsorship* to the organization, discovering new *skill sets* and *opportunities* instead.

There are a myriad of reasons a schism occurs. Why someone leaves their workgroup includes seeking market rate for the work performed, limited individual or product growth, poor manager relationship, mismatch of recognition expectations, and contract expiration. Those that decide to leave may follow those who are trusted.

After following a *promotion* or *exit*, one begins seeking first goals, discovering the environment, and building a new reputation.

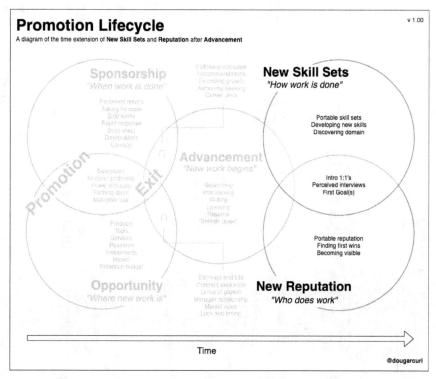

Figure 43.7: A diagram of how **New Skill Sets** and **Reputation** develops.

Conclusion

Pursuing a promotion requires *skill sets, reputation, sponsorship,* and the *opportunity* to grow. The proverbial ripcord is the emerging *exit* to *advancement* if the environment is no longer optimal. Following an individual throughout the process is called the **promotion life cycle**.

On the following page, Figure 43.8 contains the full diagram.

Figure 43.8: The full **Promotion Lifecycle** experienced by this author.

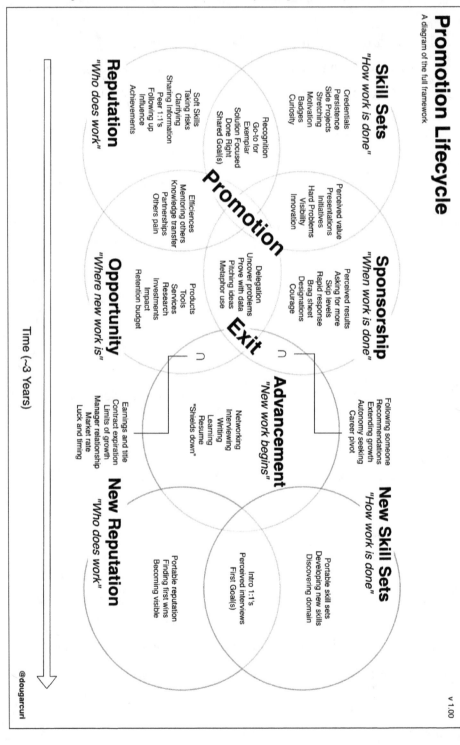

VIII

Section Eight

Being an Engineer Manager

man·ag·er (/ˈmanijər/) *n.* a person responsible for controlling or administering all or part of a company or similar organization.

DSR

Onboard Effectively in an Engineer Manager Role

Understanding My Behaviors from Starting New Roles Over the Years

ONBOARDING AT A NEW COMPANY is an immensely engaging experience, where the difference between an effective or ineffective onboarding is just an action away. As a software engineer manager,[1] I've reflected on the unique behaviors I prioritize. This essay will cover the gestalt of my successful onboarding experiences within the first 90 days.

Starting with Having Good Tact

The onboarding process is a bit of luck, timing, and keeping in mind *good tact*. Good tact is the ability to grow great relations with others— to say and do the right things at the right time, to behave in a way that promotes cooperation and reciprocity.

There is a wide range of impactful behaviors that I consider good tact. My go-to's are to make *myself available, never criticize a previous decision,* and *avoid being standoff-ish*. With these tips in mind, my initial actions include orienting within the company, shadowing, listening, building relationships, finding leaders, and succeeding at the first mission.

First, I will familiarize myself with the organizational structure.

The "I Am Here" Metaphor

In starting a new role, I orient myself within the organization. Above me, senior leaders. To the side of me, my peers, and my allies. Finally, supporting me, my directs. Building this mental model provides areas to build relations. I call this the "I Am Here" model, a radius graph of people that will help make myself and others effective.

Starting the new role, I draw a graph, labeling names, and their accountable domains. This map prioritizes people I have conversations with. The graph reveals contacts in proximity to my team.

Building Lateral Partnerships, the Skip Levels, and One-On-Ones

While building a mental model of people around me, I get to know them. For peers, having a coffee or tea with them can be effective. These connections avoid ineffective future fire drills, such as when my team needs help. This new relationship can contribute to solving an emerging problem.

I'll begin continuous rounds of one-on-ones to build trust with the team members who report to me. I start the conversation as one team—in a newly minted reoccurring staff meeting. I will announce the one-on-one meetings, the goal of the discussions, and take on questions they have. Then, I roll them out.[2]

I'll schedule skip-level meetings with other senior leaders above me. I start supporting my manager in this process. Once I have support, I'll meet with directorship and higher levels. I'll ask questions about the vision, direction, and the pain points of the organizations they lead, to calibrate where I can focus, building a horizon roadmap. These skip-levels inform me of the larger mission—the why of the work.

Listening, Seeing Inside the Team, and Setting Ground Rules

As I settle, I'll add myself to meetings *to shadow* others. I will ask questions to understand details about the processes of work and team agreements.

Remembering the "I Am Here" metaphor is essential. The initial conversations with management will inform me how to *calibrate the team goals* desired by the organization. In my opinion, an engineer manager is the *shepherd and translator* of these desired outcomes—bringing personal flair and thoughtful philosophies[3] of what needs tending.

The challenge is to balance the listening and to enact process change. Steering my behaviors is a mix of experience and intuition. I'll take a moment to review my previous experiences.

Solving the First Gnarly Problem

Some weeks in, I *pattern-match*[4] the problem in the organization. I align my team to tackle this initiative. In my years as a new manager, I realized I was hired *for something* that may have been tactical, in addition to the strategic focus of growing an organization, sponsoring others, and creating a *blast radius* going well beyond myself—the reason why managers exist. Finding my first mission and expected outcomes—*aligned to leadership goals*—is vital.

I call this "The first gnarly problem." Such problems include delivering a minimum viable product (MVP) from a team, becoming a *janitorial expert* in cleaning up the product and technical debt, being part of a reorganizing effort, or growing new teams while delivering migrations and new products. A path will appear where an approach needs directing that I'll be solely accountable! My goal is to find the essence of this mission with peers and senior management in the first weeks.

Once the task is clarified, I'll be explicit about change.

Be Explicit About Change

I have been known to repeat an expectation numerous times in front of the team. In a room of ten people, I say the "thing" ten times for one person to "get it." Being specific about change means being *explicit*. One of the lessons I've learned as an engineer manager, being implicit or nuanced is considered *cruel* to the team.

Being explicit is an easing function of reducing the *cognitive load* of the team. Providing clarity about a difference, communicating, and enacting, allows the team members to focus on what matters. The practice will reduce second-guessing motivations. Setting *expectations* is essential, such as which measures we are optimizing.

As I make the first real change to align to the gnarly problem, I identify the perceived *problematic behaviors* leaders frown upon and avoid acting that way, finding alternative routes. For example, complaining about the number of meetings but not presenting alternatives to increase their quality (such as experimenting before a pitch).

My approach to change is *to ratchet up* the team's efforts. If we as a team pivot in a new direction, I will use evidence to steer the supported decision. In addition, I remind the team of *the why* of the new work. Change builds upon other previous findings, sometimes documented.

Change Means Documenting

For decisions that have come before me, there is documentation I can discover. By seeking out these documents[5] and reviewing them with the team, everyone will understand how the previous decisions were made.

I call this *document for inversion of control*. The best way to build trust with the team is to look at documents prior (a team agreement, charter, a design doc), have a conversation, introduce a change, and bring in a new idea. And then, document it!

There will be points where my gut will tell me something needs to change where evidence cannot be presented. The best I can do is focus on the why and back it up with my experience. Then, I *write a new document*, broadcasting it to the team as a working session. The document will be a part of a decision library, ultimately scaling the team knowledge.

Sitting on the same side of the team by actively working through a plan, a decision, or some rough architecture builds trust in an *immeasurable* way. I label this as an "inversion," the document being in the middle. Including problem solvers at a higher level affirms my commitment to the team and understanding the working conditions. Team members get to know me well, uncovering the first deep problem I am held accountable for delivery.

Healing the Gaps, and Future Plans

In these first months of the gnarly problem, I attempt to *find gaps* where my specialty can shine, and I light the candle. My goal is to create a space to solve this problem. I see myself as a value add—actions like making a decision, finding others to help, applying a technical skill set, or creating the space for my team to work. I build *buffers* to solve the problem and respect the agency of the team.

As the mission is clarified, one of the challenging problems I'll solve is to remove work *burdens* and *liabilities*. The team will have work in their queue that doesn't align with the mission. It is on me to work with product[6] and project management[7] to refactor away. Creative thinking, rerouting, and renegotiating are my methods. It is always *easier to add work than to remove work*. To unburden the workstream, *to cover*, is a skill set I continue to hone for my teams.

While the team is steering to delivery, I will also get involved in OKR development,[8] KPI clarity,[9] and road mapping. These strategic exercises will become familiar, where my inputs will set the stage past the first win. Bringing in the team to estimation is vital during planning—even testing my wild guesses (also known as SWAGs). I incorporate this estimation to craft the plan, and in doing so, *own* the journey we come up with. This practice uncovers the *subsequent* gnarly problems.

In The Gnarly Problem, Hire and Find The Next Leaders

When work happens, I will see patterns of potential leaders in the team. I keep an eye on those excelling at collaboration, skill set, unblocking others, and similar behaviors *I would like to see more of*. For what I can observe directly, I set time to *recognize* their efforts and attributes.

There will be times of stress in execution. With this narrowing, the natural leaders[10] within the team rise. At the same time, I observe people doing the *glue work*, and the collaboration efforts are not visible to those who churn out the delivery. I consider glue work as daily mentorship, unblocking others, and filling gaps that aren't obvious. I call upon them and make them known to upper management.

In executing the gnarly problem, I review capacity, start the plan, and hire others. I expect hiring to begin as soon as there is a project plan. I'll reach out to recruiting, start a dialogue, and find my way to create the hiring loops. I'll make my first hire within six months.

There will be moments where I will find contributors not doing well to newly set expectations. These moments are an excellent chance to start giving *feedback* and micro-goals to each of these contributors, offering an opportunity for them to course correct. This first mission is a proving ground for adjusting the values I am bringing into the team. I will reinforce these values, being explicit and enacting change. As the manager, the team ultimately reflects what I accept, so I adjust team members according to their strengths.

Taking a Side Quest Initiative

While my main execution line is running, other problems need solving in the organization, and *no one is asking me* to lead these. Whether it is a problem my peer is having, senior management is struggling with, or an observation about the environment, this is my chance to identify and act on it.

These projects vary wildly. Some projects include improving the hiring pipelining, maturing the organization from a developer experience perspective, or running sponsorship and internships. These side quests, also called *initiatives*, may quench my thirst as an individual contributor or coordinator, and at the same time, these initiatives grow the organization.

These initiatives *grow a social network*, ultimately helping my team(s),[11] management, and peers. I find disparate initiatives exciting, potentially having a positive impact on the organization and myself. They are creative outlets.

The First Celebration at 90 Days

In the journey, the gnarly problem will come close to a resolution. My plan continues as I described above. I keep clarifying, redirecting, filling gaps, and maintaining the motivation, ensuring the team delivers the outcome. And at the correct times, I'll delegate work.

Once the outcome is achieved, I coordinate the celebration with the people and team(s) that reached the results. For me, this is the validation of a successful onboard—*to follow through with something larger than myself.*

The celebration means the onboard is complete. The process repeats, with continual refinements, improvements, the growth of others with promotions, and finding new initiatives.

Keep Going!

While onboarding as an engineer manager can be exhausting and exciting, there are points in between where there is extreme satisfaction. Seeing my team get their first win, impacting users with a superb product, promoting someone because of these accomplishments, and maturing processes is a job well done.

My onboarding goal is to apply good tact and know where I am in the organization. Then, listen, see how the team operates, be explicit when it becomes clear where I need to steer. I'll discover and solve the first gnarly problem. I'll hire, find the next leaders and give feedback to those who aren't performing. At the same time, I take on a side quest to grow my craft and the organization.

Management is a complicated arrangement of *getting people to do what they don't necessarily want to do* and becoming an umbrella to shield the team and a promoter to grow others. But in the end, I enjoy being a manager. Onboarding effectively in the first 90 days[12] is challenging as it is rewarding.

DSR

45

The Manager Stew

Management Happens Before Core Working Hours

I OVERHEARD SOMEONE SAY, "management is hard." Thank you for the courageous statement. You inspired me to write this short.

Management is extraordinarily hard. The perception of the profession is *thankless* because we play the role of business. And we get it from all sides. The company takes priority and the individual performing the role of a manager takes a back seat.

The *"how"* of management is by doing. Mentors are virtually distant.[1] I know through training and experience, working has many facets and methods. And after some years, I have invented a style of moving ideas into action. In my opinion, management's hard work is completed before core working hours.

As I began work, decisions were already made that morning.

The Stew

What is management? Perhaps it could be logically reduced to a standard set of tools. The one-on-ones, the staff meetings, the feedback, delegation, performance, coaching models, and difficult conversations. *You cannot be friends, but you can be friendly.*[2]

I would like to introduce a new multitool, primarily a compass. With some years into the profession, I have formed a pattern called ***the stew***. It is time before work that determines the day, while simultaneously holding a vision of myself, the individuals, and teams in the future.

The stew happens during a lengthy walk before work.

A Moleskine Cahier pocket[3] notebook supports my thinking time. After the walk, I jot essential items that are bouncing around in my head. A lot of these thoughts replay conversations, forming exciting threads of vision and direction.

Why?

The stew informally means a state of anxiety or agitation. As a food, a beautiful blend of savory taste simmered with time. My definition is an intense thought process marred in a cycle of logic and passion. The label was a natural fit.

The stew attempts to organize and prioritize outcomes. This thinking can include analyzing conversations, weighing fairness of actions, and identifying ownership. I replay conversations to empathize. This process is a place where positive behaviors are recognized and brought forward.

I await a new opportunity to say what was resolved in thought the same day—all thanks to *the stew*. It promotes compassionate leadership and helps steer with positive intentions.

The stew also reveals inefficiencies. And my flaws. It allows systems thinking and connecting things that would not be connected.

The stew surfaces things that need attention.

The stew is an essential strategy for leaders. For example, in the industry of software engineering where I work, leaders identify core directions. Long goalposts will emerge. "Engineers own the quality," "We never go it alone," "This is not a technology problem," "Software is about people," and "The code is the truth" are tenants that have emerged in my stew sessions over and over again.

Over a few years, I have managed *with the stew*. When exhausted, I minimize the passionate thought process by listening to podcasts (in Figure 45.1). *Listening is a way to compartmentalize the stew*. And this is where I learn about the craft of management and software engineering every single working day.

The stew is a place to continuously learn.

Conclusion

Management is about wading through the vagueness and ambiguity of interrelationships in the quest for alignment of business results. *The stew is a place to navigate.* It has revealed decision points that have eased emotional frustration. *The stew* has unveiled larger visionary goals for the teams I've led.

The result is growth in relationships and heightened performance of myself and others.

I remember numerous stews where it was painfully obvious that I tried everything to coach an individual. Through all the work, there was no other *choice—all* options were exhausted. *The stew* provided that clarity.

Do you have a similar tool?[4]

Figure 45.1: Stewing on podcasts while walking.

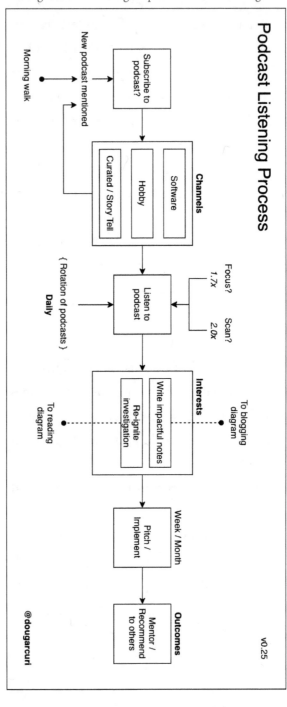

46

On Kotlin: A Reply From Management

Kotlin has Become a First-Class Language at a Tech
Conference

AS I WAS FLYING BACK from Google I/O,[1] I prepared a list of items
to present to the team. The items included "feature—
componentization,"[2] updated toolsets, life-like animation,[3] "content
first" Android TV, and new build telemetry measurement points.[4]
However, there was that—one—item I wrote down. It had two
question marks.

Kotlin? Should we adopt?

I've attended many Google I/O's. I've sat through, in person,
approximately one hundred plus sessions. While past years are fading in
my memory, this I/O conference progressed into something different.
It was memorable in a way that had real substance. Yes, Google is
moving from mobile to AI-first[5] with implications of a tectonic shift
for Android development.

● ● ●

WHEN THE UNEXPECTED announcement[6] of official support for the Kotlin programming language was revealed, engineers appeared elated. They clapped and cheered. This included many of our engineers. I smiled and took in the experience.

As managers, we must be curious. Continue to ask questions until there is understanding.

A few new sessions appeared out from the I/O scheduling veil. They focused on the Kotlin language. As a technical engineering manager, I decided to attend these newly sprouted sessions because I was curious about the endorphin rush.

Watching our engineers in the chat channels and the smiling faces, Kotlin appeared to be a big deal.

At the start of Google I/O, I knew about the existence of Kotlin, but my technical understanding was sparse. Speaking to engineers in prior meetings, my mental model of Kotlin was of a young language with potential. It was expressive. It recently made asynchronous programming easy, iterated upon by the maintainers Jetbrains. Oh yes, it also liberated code from the boilerplate.

Management should be aware of code quality. What is yours like?

Indeed, the fewer lines of code, the better for maintenance and quality.

With the Kotlin announcement being so dramatic, I thought the wave would calm during the conference duration—it wasn't to be.

• • •

AT I/O, the sessions were tweaked. Lectures included guest speakers from contributors outside of Google. This was new to everyone who attended previous years. Principal Google engineers[7] introduced the guests on the stage, and like magic,[8] they swapped speakers, taking the audience to someplace different.

Sessions were related to Kotlin. One of those sessions was *"Life is Great, and Everything Will Be Ok, Kotlin is Here."* This was one of those hosted sessions. Two staff engineers would run it from Square and Pinterest, Jake Wharton and Christina Lee.

I let the engineers know on the chat channels that this one was important and, if possible, to reserve a seat. My gut said it was going to be great.

• • •

LISTENING CAREFULLY TO our developers, there is an unspoken love for Jake and Christina. After many one-on-ones, team meetings, and discussing their work with the engineers, I've watched videos to understand that love and admiration. These are community leaders.

They, too, are now the faces of Kotlin.

As managers, actively listening is key. Acting on that listening leads to engineering happiness.

The session was split into two halves. Jake started. He explained how to convert Java code to Kotlin and built an example to where I became immersed in the details.

I was so lost to a point in which ten minutes of squinting, trying to look over others' heads, my eyes watered to focus. I had inadvertently rubbed them to regain focus—with fingers that had sunscreen on them.

My eyes began to sting, and my vision became blurry. I was fidgeting all over the place as Jake continued to smash through examples.

The Java code disappeared just like that. If only I could see it.

A few of our engineers were in the session, one right next to me. As the engineer was smiling and nodding to Jake's examples, I was having an anxiety attack. The thought of becoming permanently blinded by I/O branded sunscreen was ironic.

I was blinded by the overload of Kotlin.

But I stayed because I wanted to hear Christina and her portion of the presentation.

• • •

THE SESSION HAD a rockstar aura to it. People were waiting in line to the last minute. This was Jake and Christina, so I was determined to stay even if I could not see.

So, with Jake completing his half and my anxiety wearing off, I wondered what Christina would present. Perhaps more examples? A live demo of the conversion of an Android app to Kotlin?

No. Christina dived into a topic so fundamentally different and profound.

As managers, we should always be interested in optionality. Ask for the options from engineers.

Christina's message was one that hit hard on how to evangelize. You, management, and the team. Three points. In a sense, how to better the development life of the engineer in every organization.

The topic discussed the developer's experience. With an engineer on our team sitting to the right of me, there was a sense of unease as we sat together in the tent. I was the manager.

I kept looking center-left.

I wondered if there were other managers or stakeholders present? Was I the only one? Will they, the engineers, drag me out of the tent and beat the crap out of me?

I had sunscreen to blind them, a brilliant thought at the time. But Christina's topic was unexpected. After debating with engineers, I had come to appreciate the stance in the way that Kotlin was presented.

It took courage.

Management focuses on business value and user experience. Explain the what and why. Let engineers focus on the how.

When the session closed, I became compelled to say something as an engineering manager.[9] I was ready to march up to the microphone and ask.

How does the developer community convince Google to make Android Studio's default project language, Kotlin?

Let's remember Google is actively fixing the wrongs[10] that they have caused with Android, and now Java 8 is here. Java is the default, and Google is standing behind the language.

Christina ended at the forty-minute mark, and there was no time for Q&A.

I repeated that question to the engineer sitting next to me. He looked at me, ashamed that I was, in fact, his manager. He had no answer for me. We walked out, management beating avoided.

Management should encourage plans from engineers. Then select one. Be brave and accountable for that plan and a focal point of its execution.

• • •

MY COMPULSION OF asking the unanswered question and Christina's focus had driven me to share my experience. Outside of business dealing and internal communication, I rarely do write.

Somewhere in the middle managing engineering teams, I have never seen anything quite like it in the years of developing software. I can't remember a one-on-one or stakeholder meeting that had the same gravity. I've experienced a lot of things over the years in business. I've employed the usual management tactics of suppressing and letting it "soak."[11] Other times I'd just let it go.

I'm still learning.

It was an odd feeling as if I wronged every team that I've led. Did I "wrong" the team that asked about Kotlin?

• • •

THE QUESTION—to default to the Kotlin language—should be asked. I believe it is a question to be answered. *It could be the definitive answer for Kotlin adoption.*

Remember, Google chose Java because developers know the

language. Just think of all those Java examples that Google would need to update.

Now that Christina had equipped engineers with fundamentals, and Google had green-lit Kotlin, how does the application of those fundamentals translate?

More adoption?

If the answer is yes, the implication has more questions than answers. The fundamental problem is always the following. What is the problem you are trying to solve? Is it the right problem? Why? Yeah, boilerplate is a problem, but what else?

New staffing, upskilling, and legacy system management will be a challenge.

From what I heard, the main driver of Kotlin is developer happiness. Google even drops words like *enjoyable* and *fun* in their decision to make it official. Hell, even the method keywords in Kotlin are fun.

Management must balance happiness. Engineers do in fact build things well when they are happy.

Kotlin makes developers happy. This is not a lie. Truly every engineer I spoke to who had experienced Kotlin is happy. My latest conversation about this happiness was with an Android engineer working on medical devices. He was happy, and he wasn't looking back at Java.

Can management become happy too?

● ● ●

DURING THE PRESENTATION, Christina discussed why Kotlin is a clear choice. One slide discussed the billion-dollar mistake[12] of Java. Kotlin solves the problem by making nullability explicitly declared.

But then again, the interoperability of Kotlin is one hundred percent with Java. So is this barrier safe until Java goes away? Does NPE[13] become a decaying problem—from one million, to one billion, to a one trillion-dollar mistake?[14]

Management should encourage consistency. Make sure to communicate and promote that consistency.

As a technical engineering manager, the powerful concept ranges of *explicit-implicit* and *consistent-inconsistent* steers codebases in either a lifetime of development or a one that is abandoned. Philosophical choices[15] on these spectrums do matter.

Kotlin is here. I hope not another rewrite.

In the case of NPE's, Java makes the `null` implicitly included. Big problem. I've seen many teams make the `null` usage vague; therefore, defensive programming and NPE's are common because they do not address the extreme implicit-inconsistent delta. Some methods return `null`s, and others do not. Some parameters take `null`s, and others are annotated; others are not. Some go as far as a `null` object pattern, some not. Some mixing of optionals[16] in there, and well... you get the point. Too many code reviews discuss `null` inconsistency, but solutions are deferred.

Christina also described the concept of typed nullability and how the community uses `null`. Could this be another pitfall as an inconsistent pattern may emerge to actually using `null`? Remember, Kotlin gives us nullability because the language is tied to Java until it goes away.

Management should promote the formation of style. Own the style and improve it.

Nullability concerns will not be the case for idiomatic Kotlin, but what is idiomatic Kotlin[17] anyway? If the above is an indicator, Kotlin may be so expressive that it will introduce inconsistency among the community and in teams.

Hey, but this one last library we can't get rid of is still in... Java.

When the constraints of a previous language are lifted and the exhaustion of boilerplate removed, are there any unexpected outcomes due to expressiveness?

● ● ●

CHRISTINA RECOMMENDS using tooling on hard problems. I agree with this. Tools must do their job well. Otherwise, they are complained about until they are fixed. Google is proving this well with Gradle.

And lately, Java.

I actively encourage the engineers to focus on the interesting stuff and let the tooling do the job. It's not all about operations, features, and execution, but business requires it.

Software Engineering is about experimentation and innovation. With time in management, I have proven to myself that execution is valiant, but that engineering creativity is king, driving results through the fog of development.

Just like engineers, management should be lazy and impatient.[18]
But in the way they think.

However, since the Kotlin tooling, IDE, and language are well integrated, could we be heading in a direction where we are developing a voodoo culture?[19] If a generation of engineers grow on Kotlin, are we doing a disservice about how they grow? In which they are educated about the engineering rigors?

In my brief review of the Kotlin language, there is blazing fast support that promotes code completion. In a way that is fundamentally different from writing the standard stores and loops. The compiler does, in-fact, hide and flex the mundane.

There are magical wires that are optimized. Kotlin *vibes*.

The argument is that engineers should optimize the "hard" parts. The "efficiency-must" parts. This is a solid argument. But with the many coding exercises I've been in... Google included the ask, "What is the time/complexity of this code? Can you do better?" In Kotlin code, what is the answer? "[*shrugs,*] Depends. I don't know?" That could be an acceptable answer.

Is it acceptable? "Okay, let's switch back to Java [style] for a second to answer..."

This is a tough one. Maybe I cannot see it. Maybe I've read *Programming Pearls*[20] and *Code Complete*[21] too many times. I have been brainwashed that engineers who fail at these questions are worthy of management.

Sh*t.

• • •

CHRISTINA SAID ENGINEERS can develop apps that are stable for their users. Using Kotlin and its tooling will help avoid crashes "a lot," and the users will be happier.

In a sense, this one is a tough sell to management. Regardless of the tooling or language, it takes a village to launch stable products. It takes a consistent style, and it takes a pipeline, and that engineers own the quality.

Did I mention that engineers should own the quality?

Management should encourage a set of core engineering values, and invest time in that on-boarding.

It's tough to do quality well. To launch products consistently. To launch them quickly.

Now try it with standing up a testing culture on top, and it's close to impossible, but still plausible.

Adding new languages and tooling to the mix is up there, but maybe not as hard as a testing culture.

Do you have a testing culture?

I agree that Kotlin may help catch things sooner, but in a sense, what is the cost of that "catch sooner," and how much sooner?

Whether it's Java or Kotlin, your code reviews, pair programming, linting, unit tests, integration tests, and end-to-end tests should check items as far upstream as possible.

Kotlin may decrease risk, but again at what cost?

● ● ●

CHRISTINA'S PRESENTATION is one that challenges everyone to the maximum. I believe Kotlin deserves attention and everyone should share it broadly.

I, too, like to challenge engineers to the maximum with what we have. But in a meaningful way that is doable. This is why this session resonated.

With all this being said, I want to revisit the original question.

Kotlin? Should we adopt?

It is clear what we should do... as managers. If brave enough, work on the koans[22] to understand the developer's experience. Listen to the engineers on the benefits of Kotlin.

Listen to their wants and ask for plans.

One last thing is that we need to challenge our advocates. Adoption is not all on the community or the engineers or the teams— advocates share the burden.

Managers have partners internal and external. Push hard on them and the Google developer advocates.

Remember, the team are the doers.

To me, official Kotlin language support is now owned by Google. We must pressure them, and the developer advocates on answers as to what we should do.

Hiring managers are constrained with parameters that are difficult to avoid. Couple that with the demand for talented engineers, and it's a tough problem to solve.

It's also an unexpected problem. It's a dual-track high-level language competition.

Rare. Google never disappoints.

Advancing Kotlin adoption is a brilliant example of a live A/B test on the community.

Was that too cruel to state?

It's the truth. Both languages have their strengths, and there will be no clear victor for years to come.

● ● ●

GOOGLE WILL SET a course for Kotlin, and invest heavily in winning Java[23] legal battles, the only sure bet is that the course is unclear.

A Kotlin selection for production apps is the same as using ! !.[24] It is a risk. Perhaps calculated, knowing the costs. However, we should encourage engineers to debate and set the tone of the future.

Management usually holds the stick in the middle. Instead, encourage management to support and raise both ends.

Of course, we will use Kotlin eventually. Who doesn't want to be happy?

After this essay was published, Google followed through with Kotlin as the project default—years later. Obviously, this write-up was a hot take, highlighting timeless technological struggles.

DSR

47

In Software, Philosophy Is Delegation

How Humans in Software Transmit Direction

OVER MY SOFTWARE CAREER, I've built software apps and systems. As an engineering manager, I've noticed a pattern—a phenomenon. **Teams get their work done guided by philosophies.** This essay identifies this behavior, questions its origin, and how it's a powerful force through repetition. Let me highlight an example next.

A Short Story About a Dashboard

Recently, my team had a featured product heading to production. It was evident they needed to monitor the system before deployment. However, the goal was unclear. What are they optimizing?

Some weeks into it, I began repeating to the team that in monitoring, *we should trace the customer's pain throughout the system* (the philosophy). We would tease out the essential artifacts of the customer that made sense in an digestible format (the framework).

Of course, there wasn't a meeting stating this precisely, just informal discussions and natural consensus-building. A pattern was emerging, and it became the philosophy because of *stickiness*.

Principles Support Philosophy

As work was underway, I'd test out the dashboard. The team readjusted when we discussed the SLAP principle.[1] It was hard to reason what was on the screen because the context was mixed. Taking this feedback, the group split infrastructure health and customer pain.

What I learned is that principles (unchanging rules) help guide the philosophy and framework. Reevaluation is needed every so often. And the team continued to move it forward without the manager being there—they had agency.

In my opinion, this is a natural phenomenon of building software in teams. These types of events happened many times in my career. And the origins are difficult to pinpoint.

Philosophy Is Direction

In my experience, teams desire a single direction, *not directions*. In software engineering, defining direction is difficult because the process is intangible.[2] Software is a young profession, and there are many trade-offs. So how does one clarify an approach?

All people (the team, engineers, managers, architects, designers, and product managers[3]) develop direction. The path is summarized by multiple discussions between involved parties (engineers, leads, product people, designers, and stakeholders). Someone in the group will discover the philosophy and drive it. And that direction is an agreement between parties.

In my opinion, it is beneficial that the engineering manager[4] steers this ritual. Taking on the work may be a no-no (such as building the framework); the last thing the team wants is a manager blocking them. In exchange, they can identify and rally the philosophy.

Where Do These Philosophies Originate?

The environment in which we work and the constraints around us shape philosophies. We are optimizing for something. Knowing how to drive is where intuition is needed. The inputs are broad, but the software requires discreteness. *Philosophy is theoretical and sticky, and the framework is practical and bedrock.*

In the case above, we realized the items flowing through our pipes in a B2B system were constrained, leading to mapping customer pain on one monitor. Additional inputs came from the environment around us. One such example is heightened organizational sensitivity of observability throughout all systems—and the abundance of external support.

Philosophies crystalize delegation effectively because if a team believes in the ideology, they will work furiously in that direction. Like software delegation,[5] *a team's signature resolves by design.* This design is the commander's intent.[6] Software engineering is often opinionated, so philosophies matter. *The repeated statements are virtual commanders.*

By stating the philosophy, every engineer in the team has a unified mental model. They work through a potential framework to satisfy it. And if there is disagreement, the philosophy needs to be retooled. Ideally, anyone on the team can reshape and re-delegate.

What are the origins of philosophies? They are sourced by those that aggregate knowledge. Members who have experience can bring forward a library of available pivot points.

Philosophies Are Portable and Repeatable

In a previous role, my team would say, "let's keep our apps as dumb as possible." I realized this was a philosophy. It had an immense impact on qualitative construction through delegation.

And recently, I've had a conversation with an engineer about unit tests. What we realized is that the philosophy of testing our software had shifted. No longer was it about "every pull request[7] has unit tests," but it was "test to the design, not the implementation"—and that framework of integration tests made sense. The structure solved the problem faced by the engineers—in a monolith by the sheer exhaustion of dealing with over-engineered unit tests.

To the point, in software, *philosophies appear portable and repeatable*. I have discovered a list of these tenets in every project. Only experience will unlock these opinions in the dimensions of technical, product, design, and meta (how teams do their work).

Conclusion

Finally, I'd like to leave with a thought about how I've seen software built. Metaphorically, someone in the group muttered something resoundingly impactful about plans in a software system. Without wood, hammers, and nails[8] in the office, *philosophy is a virtual foreperson and delegates in software engineering.*

● ● ●

PHILOSOPHIES AND FRAMEWORKS are born out of problems that need solving—here is an example found on the Internet.

Another Example of the Phenomenon

In a video, Louis Castle explains[9] avoiding artificial idiocy (theory) and layering the edge cases (framework) to make an RTS (Real Time Strategy Game) pathing mechanic smart enough. As he explains subtly, "always tell[ing] people if you spend more time making sure it doesn't do something stupid, it will look smart."

Those that believe in *a way* are repeating the mantra over and over again. *This behavior is an example of the transmission of philosophical delegation.*

DSR

48

When a Software Engineer Exits the Team

My Perspective When a Team Member Gives Their Notice

BEING A SOFTWARE ENGINEERING MANAGER[1] has its difficult people bits. When a team member gives their notice to leave, it's personal *and* straightforward.

When the Notice is Given

I knew that the notice was coming. It would be rare that I was caught off-guard. The lingering *spidey sense* I've felt had been correct. I've lived with the "yeah, it's coming" weeks prior. The tip-off was the questions they ask, the doubts they have, and odd days out of office. And for those that care, a burst of contributions.

Then there is a request for a rare one-on-one before the week is out. *It's here.*

As we go through the motions, I listen, ask questions, and find levers to negotiate. But rarely do I find something to keep the person on, their mind is already made up. I respect that.

When I close the video meeting, I settle. My mind is racing. "Can I try something to bring the person back?" A list of grievances sets in, and I go through a loss cycle for days. It's a breakup. I let go.

What Happens Later

As I execute communications with the team, crafting the transition plan and the celebratory send-off, I ask myself, "What could have been different?" There are answers. I could have improved the environment, the work, the team—myself. I write the conclusions down to be taken care of, reflecting on what I've learned.

I'll leave a note. *"It was probably about money."*

There are moments during the transition where I battle an aggravated ego. But I check myself, calm down, and refocus back on this individual. I want them to succeed, and me stepping to hinder that would be incorrect. I'll send recommendations and smile. They will become a better person because of this, and so will I.

Once the person leaves, team nature dislikes a vacuum. There are opportunities for others. They step up and stretch. No one is irreplaceable, and no one is an island. But the knowledge is lost, eminence gone, and it's a pivot, for now, this new team.

Self Reflections

This notice is not the first nor the last I'll experience. Nor will the team. It is a continual procession of people, *great people doing their very best*. But this role wasn't a fit, and the timing was off. The environment was not correct. The work didn't have the impact they wanted, finding their dream job instead. Perhaps I was ineffective at communications, championing above, or slow at sponsoring elsewhere. Or the baffling outcome, their asks were all achieved as they exit.[2]

And occasionally, the software engineer[3] realized that the job was hard. They weren't performing. They knew, and so did I. And on that occasion, it's a relief.

Then I reflect on all of those managers that had experienced the same with me. I've left a few jobs this way. Now I understand a bit more. It's just business, but in no way do I sense that people can be that *frosty*. Each experience resonates.

And for those teams where I got up and left as the manager. There was a special memory leaving them where they stood. I wasn't expecting those intense feelings when walking away the first time. They don't write that in any of the books I read.

The Continual Graceful Exit

The good news is there are plenty of opportunities in software engineering.[4] It's comforting. Fluidity is what I like about the industry; it eats the world. And in some way, it grinds.[5]

In my experience, there is an interesting observation. Once an engineer, and now as a manager, many people have come and gone. In software, *people do fire themselves*, as in they leave of their own volition. It's hardly the other way around.

My goal is to treat someone well on their first as well as their last. I want the chance to cooperate later.[6] While I don't have much evidence on how other managers handle these situations, a *graceful* exit between us leads to better future outcomes. And that is how we say goodbye.

DSR

IX

Section Nine

Crossovers

cross·o·ver (/ˈkrôsˌōvər,ˈkräsˌōvər/) *n*. the process of achieving success in a different field or style, especially in popular music.

DSR

49

CQ: Personal Mastery Through Hobbies

What My Father Taught Me About Communication in Amateur Radio

SOFTWARE ENGINEERING IS MY PASSION and profession. My focus is to improve the craft and build great teams. But from time to time, I explore the skill of learning by leveraging *engineering thinking*. My goal is to find ways to improve communication, mentorship, and leadership. A way to discover new techniques is through hobbies. What follows is my personal view on *how* hobbies lead to self-improvement.

For me, it is a great moment to communicate a logical deduction since I started a new hobby of amateur radio. The "*why*" is challenging to place in words, but what I can say is my new hobby reveals a *specific and distinct* communication style. It requires *technical effort* to reach people without multi-billion dollar infrastructure. And like many hobbies, amateur radio contains a rich *vocabulary* of understanding.

Ham Radio

Amateur radio, or "ham radio," is a way to communicate without financial interest over the radio waves. The Federal Communications Commission (FCC) regulates the service in the United States, and the International Telecommunication Union (ITU) oversees the FCC worldwide. It licenses operators through an incentive examination system. Once licensed in three levels, we are free to transmit with certain restrictions. When we communicate, we identify ourselves by call signs.

We select modulations like voice, continuous wave (International Morse Code), data packets, or video. We transmit and receive for fun. Contests are run to build contacts from all over the world. But on occasion, the hobby transforms to support the resolution of an emergency or a long-running disaster. And the world has seen many natural and human-made disasters where "hams" have stepped up to help facilitate communication.

Amateur radio is rich with history, electronics, applied theory, bizarre phenomenon, and ridiculous maths when touching the edges of the hobby. Innovative technologies originate out of ham radio. From the latest on cloaking with fractal antennas to mobile phones in our pockets, they all are inventions of the hobby.

Personal Mastery and Their Axioms

Now that we know what amateur radio is, I want to pose a short formula. The key is personal mastery through a deduction of how these axioms improve ourselves and our proficiency in things.

First, we start with *personal mastery*. Personal mastery is the attempt to form a vision of yourself in the future. It has to start with *discipline* from within to see through your goal. It is a series of practices of principles applied through the journey of reaching those goals. That is personal mastery. It is a quest to seek the truth of a matter, like in a hobby.

Next, as we seek those truths, let's examine what an *axiom* is. An axiom is a shorthand for a kernel of fact, a poster sign. It is a spoken reduction of events and their goals that are self-evident. Personal mastery and their axioms feed on one another. And the axioms contain *vocabularies* that define skill and culture.

But how do personal mastery and axioms interrelate with one another? The relation is by *successive approximations*. The ability to course-correct our skill and hone in on the axioms so that we check, apply, correct, and repeat. The process is a relative comparison of what we can do better.

With personal mastery, their axioms, and successive approximation, we attempt to achieve the goal. The goal requires the examination of successive approximations saddled around *constraints*. Constraints are challenges to our axioms and limit validation on how we can achieve maximum personal mastery.

Hobbies have a wonderful ability to connect people together. Personal mastery of the hobby is ultimately a shared experience of *interdependence through mentorship*. And this is the point. My hobbies are repeating cycles of my formula.

Hobbies are explorations of personal mastery. They are the axioms divided by their constraints. They are amplified by successive approximation and accelerated by mentorship.

Example of the Application

Now that we have the formula, let's move forward with an example as we explore my thought process. Let us focus squarely on the hobby of amateur radio.

As I learn the techniques out in the world, I try to find my first axiom. And as of a few weeks ago, I concluded:

Communicate to another operator clear enough so that they understand and can respond (QSO).

Easy enough. From here, we have an axiom for our mastery. The maxim will reveal vocabulary as we go. But how does one communicate clear enough? Clarity is where personal ability comes into play. We must experiment. We must successively approximate to level up at our hobby relative to the last failure. After that exploration, here is a refined axiom of the hobby:

DX (Communicate a far distance) an operator to QSO.

As we look at this axiom, we find that there are constraints. These types of restrictions challenge us to personal mastery. These constraints pull us into ways which make us uncomfortable. **Time**, **money**, or **mental effort** are scales of being uncomfortable. Another strict examination, maybe. More time in research. More money to apply. *Vulnerability* in front of someone who knows an answer. Overcoming these challenges make us better.

With as little power as you can (QRP), DX an operator to QSO.

One way to achieve a distant connection is by using the International Morse Code. International Morse Code, also known as CW (continuous wave), is a technique of using little power to travel very long distances. It is also a challenge for most to understand and then respond in CW. It takes quite a bit of practice and discovery. And here is the final piece of the puzzle.

Hobbies are *interdependent* exercises of personal mastery and require communication with others to improve. Case in point, my father told me a story. Back in the early 1970s, he worked at the Mobil Building in New York City for Rand McNally as a trip planner.

Like most days, my father was at the desk, waiting for the next customer to draw out a road trip. An older gentleman walks in. One thing leads to another, and amateur radio is of topic. The gentleman is a high-level license holder. My father explained that he was having difficulty overcoming a crude requirement of the then license exam. The exam required a CW portion at a minimum word per minute. The gentleman gave him Coast Guard audio tapes to help him practice. Through the mentor's help, my father succeeded.

With QRP power and with 13 wpm (words per minute), DX an operator to QSO.

The man in my father's story is called an "Elmer" in the hobby. In short, a *mentor*. And hence, the cycle of personal mastery continues until a limit is reached. The axioms are tweaked until there is a collective mastery.

Of course, other axioms are *congruent* with the primary adage. In Figure 49.1, I've highlighted the primary driver of mastery. The process is drawn as a system diagram.

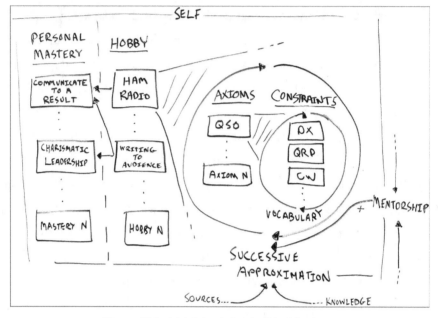

Figure 49.1: A high level visual of the ideation.

73! (Best Regards)

Hobbies are paths to personal mastery. We use axioms to form vocabulary, use a successive approximation to identify the constraints. Finally, we reach out for interdependence to become competent.

Personal mastery clarifies what is important to us. What is important to me *is how to improve the result of communication* because the practice has a desired consequence—forming a wonderful relationship with another. And the radio communication metaphor was the right fit. I could not resist but to try in this essay.

And I know I've failed beautifully at it.

Hobbies ignite a path to the truth inside one's self. When we focus our attention on learning, it is uncomfortable. We should look for the axioms, and discover their constraints. Find Elmers. They will open a world of learning, which is a beautiful thing.[1] Ponder about your hobbies and their axioms for just a moment. Are you on a path to personal mastery?

● ● ●

AND THANKS, DAD, for all this equipment to learn on. I received my first license even if it took way longer than you had hoped.

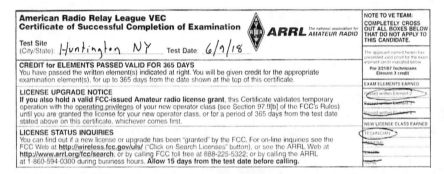

Figure 49.2: This author's successful examination card.

DSR

50

The Zen of Motorcycling and Programming

An Inquiry into Safety of Software Engineering

I'M HEADING DOWN THE PARKWAY parallel to the ocean, riding through a hot summer breeze. My engine is slowly revving by keeping a legal speed limit. I was taking it all in on my motorcycle, with thoughts of inspiration and some doubts of preservation. "Should I have checked that thing? What about this detail? Ah, whatever it is, enjoy this ride."

Unfazed, I looked over to my right, nothing but dunes, on the left, the Great South Bay. There were wispy clouds in a blue sky and a bridge in the distance. I was making my way down to OBI, a parking lot in the middle of nowhere laid up against the Atlantic ocean.

Once I parked, I removed my helmet, gloves, and jacket. The sweat from my padded kevlar jeans ran down my legs to my riding boots. I sat by my bike, on the shaded side. I wanted to think, but instead, I flipped out my phone and stared at the emails and social posts.

Some time passed. Finally, a bike pulled up, looking if it was safe to park close. An older woman jumped off her well-worn bike. I looked over and made a judgment. "Hmm, she's all geared up. My kind of rider." She slowly approached, admiring my bike and me admiring hers.

We chatted about bikes and philosophies of riding. The lady had more riding experience than I and spoke vividly about riding adventures. Then she asked about my profession.

"What do you do for work?" she asked.

I said the word.

She replied, "But what is... software programming?"

Me: "Well, in the simplest terms, we are readers. And more rarely, we are writers of code. And when we write, we likely follow checks."

Her: "What kind of checks?"

Me: "First, of course, we have *T-CLOCS* (tires/wheels/brakes, controls, lights/electrics, oil/fluids, chassis, and stands). Before we write, we read to understand. We have to *wrench* through issues first. Once we have something we can add, and this can take some time, we can jump on safely."

Me: "But before we jump on, we must wear gear. *ATGATT* (All the gear, all the time). In our writing, we wear gear to help protect us. Let's call them tests that check our writing. Tests won't protect us from everything, but it places us in a mindset that we could get hurt and are taking precautions to avoid future injury."

Me: "From there, we are worried about the visibility of that writing. We want high-vis on our code. We have others review and check it. Then code is bolted on safely."

Her: "Ah, kind of like *look twice, save a life*?"

Me: "Yes, but we take the onerous to make sure that the code will work well. We have high-vis, continuously move to be seen, and throw down the hand signals to indicate clear intentions."

Her: "Are there programmers out there that write code and avoid these checks?"

Me: "Of course. Even if it's legal, these programmers are the *lane splitters*. They go fast past others, and they win sometimes. But eventually, their odds run out, and they hurt themselves and others."

Me: "My respect for the machine is at the front of my mind, always. Just like I know that our bikes over there can hurt us. I know that the respect I have will keep me in check so *I can live to ride another day*."

Her: "You got a good head on your shoulders. But back to this software programming thing. So you are readers, and sometimes writers. Apart from these checks and tests, how do you read and write well?"

Me: "Just like we should practice our figure eights, stops, swerves, and our finesse, we need to practice our reading and writing. We should do this continuously regardless of how long we've been in the game. I didn't believe this until I recently had a very close call. I was too lazy, but I learned that if I practiced the skill continuously, the incident would have been avoided."

Her: "Yeah, it's about seat time. Safety is also about rider attitude and risk assessment."

Me: "But here is the thing. Practicing has context, and we must be deliberate on how. It must be a campaign of focus. There is quite a bit of hype all over, and you can get dragged over reading and writing things that become irrelevant. *You do need to ride your own ride.*"

Me: "Sometimes you need to follow the advice of David Hough or Ken Condon, but sometimes Maria Costello or Keith Code. Lots of time, you have to go with data, like the Hurt or MAIDS report. And sometimes you have to go with your gut. But it's the attitude in learning that matters."

Me: "We all have dropped our bikes. You learn that it is important to dust off and pick it back up."

Her: "Got it. And the computers read these writings (code)?"

Me: "Indeed, and hence how these programs work. *Just like motorcycles, software is everywhere!* But it's about people. The machines can handle all the writings just fine. They can optimize, such that they bounce over edge traps, navigate sand, and handle all sorts of different weather and traffic conditions. But humans cannot always. Sometimes ego gets in the way."

Her: "Kind of like those riders who never throw down the peace sign after you threw down first?"

Me: "Yes. There are others out there that are oblivious and need to learn what it means to throw down that peace sign. We need to mentor well and take the opportunity to show them our programming *craft*. And learning to read a lot and write a little is a challenging thing. It gets difficult since what I described is mainly performed *in teams*. And you know how difficult it is to keep group rides together."

Her: "Yeah. Every four to six riders need leads."

Me: "Right. And just like motorcycling, programming cannot be mastered."

Her: "So, you are a team of readers and rarely writers. The machines handle the optimizations, and quality is paramount to the profession. Mentoring is an important aspect, just like I have shown others how to ride safely. It sounds to me that after all this, can you *ever* enjoy the ride?"

Me: "I do. These are my opinions, but others may see it differently. Quality? The quality reminds me of that book, *Zen and the Art of Motorcycle Maintenance*."

Me: "Whether I'm classical or a romantic, I am not sure. When I read or write code or I perform an oil change or replace a stator, I keep looking at the gauges like a manic. "Did I do it right? How can I be sure? Research, apply, and *trust!*" I am stuck looking into all the details of how to do things well."

Me: "But, I..., we must do more than *look; we* all must *see* and *be seen*."

Her: "Safety Third."[1]

Me: "What do you mean?"

Her: "Just like riders are responsible for their safety, so too is every programmer."

• • •

LOOK TWICE – SAVE A LIFE
SOFTWARE
IS EVERYWHERE!!!

Figure 50.1: A future slogan of safety.

DSR

51

Driven to Optimize for Nice

Can Humans Coexist with Driverless Vehicles?

DRIVING ON MASSACHUSETTS ROUTE 28 in Cape Cod made me think. When we arrived for a family vacation,[1] numerous drivers bent the understood rules of the road. Their misbehavior made me pump the brakes, inconveniencing our last mile.

What the hell was going on?

A Driver's Primary Goal is Kindness

The driver behaviors in this area were an odd edge case. I've never experienced such "niceness" with over twenty years behind heavy machines made of steel cages and iron horses.[2] I've driven in other parts of the U.S., experiencing different regional driving attitudes, but this was different.

The misbehavior occurred on Route 28, a single-laned two-way thoroughfare with businesses on each side. Traffic was a never-ending procession of vehicles in both directions. Every two hundred feet, a car would hurry out. Those who had the right of way paused to let them in, causing those uninitiated (like me) to stop uncomfortably.

Indeed, I had the *right of way.*

I later discovered drivers gave access to the road, which otherwise would be denied entry for a significant time. As I made wild turns[3] into busy intersections, my screaming kids egged me on. But fear not, I got a blink of the headlight before I entered.

After passing through the area twice, I itched to do the same. I let go of my hardened New Yorker attitude, dropping a defensive posture. I optimized for nice,[4] no longer shaking my fist. Instead, I'd blink my lights at abandoned drivers, peer pressuring the opposing lane to yield. Laughing loudly, my family in tow thought I had gone mad. But instead, I'd become coherent with the syntax of the arranged system.

On the outside, nobody was angry. Everyone else was doing it without a care for the legal ramifications of liabilities.

Why should we care? All the drivers were kind.

Mood Generator Unavailable Within Trained Models

In my style, I like to synthesize a mix of experiences during vacation, bringing a book with me. During this trip, I read an old classic called *Artificial Intelligence (AI): The Very Idea* (1985) by John Haugeland. While the book predates newer AI thinking, it tackles a symbolic approach. The book made me question my observation about these human driving habits within context. So I formed a question:

How would a development team safely automate driverless cars in an area like this? They need to train "nicer" into their machines.

With the formal rules being bent, there was no indication of what was happening until inputs of *"Another car is crossing in front of me, but everything is nominal?* **Brake***!*" Mix in random drivers who are "uninitiated" to the process. They would wreak havoc, causing screeching brakes, while others yell out of their window, *"Yes, bend these rules, you are supposed to, dammit!"*

Indeed, automation would learn the profile in time, trading off waiting on the side of the road versus the probability of a fender-bender. Of course, AI neural networks would share data with other robots in real-time, pouring over their global positioning system. But how would it compute those who stop from speed, blink their lights, and tie up all traffic to let another pass?

Teams will train narrow models to predict routes, feeding copious amounts of data from previous reports, but no way have I ever heard they capture a mood of helping out someone who needs to get in the "right of way" when they do not qualify based on legal rules. There are *happy radicals* everywhere.

Highways and byways are easy to train, but here in the mess of "locality" is where the impossible problems cruise along.

> *To solve this problem, you'll have to train for **kind and fair**, not to be predictably safe. Yikes, is it even possible?*

The interpretation of the real-time situation's optimal path would be to cooperate immediately or risk a poor travel experience. From what I've read about artificial intelligence, developing a fleeting cooperative mood that bends the rules is crazy hard. Humans are all about uncontained self-perspectives. Machines, deterministically optimized through a metaphor of learning on a matrix map of infinite ones and zeros—not so much.

To Be Nice on the Road, Humans and Computers Must Share Critical Context

Let me be clear. I am not skeptical about the automation of driverless cars or the AI that will power them. Consumer driverless vehicles will happen, but at what timescale?[5] For instance, if humans are in the mix, these situations will make the coming driverless vehicles hard to implement safely.

In my vacation scenario, humans are making up rules for utility, feeling for others' pain of having to wait long times to enter the right of way. They want to feel good, to serve another.

> *There could be a paradox where no one wins in convenience or security. Developers will train robots to travel safely. Humans want to get there fast. Kind humans with robots wish to do both at the same time.*

If automatons are driving in these conditions, riders *within* the automatic car will be dumbfounded that their all-seeing-brain hadn't made the apparent turn. An hour would pass when it was clear opportunities existed. With each friendly human waving them on in happy anger, the AI's confidence level would never hit a proper threshold to make a move in fear of self-preservation. Empathy is not in their vocabulary.

Suppose we continue to grant human driving while autobot vehicles ramp up. When predictably safe seems paramount, how do you optimize for "friendly" within systems? It starts with mood context. People are on vacation in a land of leisure, you know? Local context is critically important to a safe ride. And context can be contrary to agreed rules.

Anyone who says engineers cannot solve the technical problem is wrong (in spite, a tenacious individual will fight through.) Finding the vector of attack by faking behavior until it becomes genuine is how they will solve it. In the process, lots of care is needed—these are mission-critical systems where life is at stake.

Do we need to remove the fallible humans, eventually?

Wheel Resistance is Less Than Futile—Tired Pressure of Political Results

In my view, there is continuing resistance to automating formal driving rules in my community. People love their driving. Their associations go deep with nostalgia, speed, and everything culturally ingrained in people spanning generations. Included are car shows, night cruises, drag racing, and everything reminding us of years past. Would anyone want to see bots driving when racing is about human drama?[6]

With driving, it's all human feeling.

For example, in the same area of Route 28, the federally mandated realignment of exit numbers proved so opinionated it has cost taxpayers money to reprint beautiful "old exit signs."[7] The advocate's passion ran deep for exiting off nostalgic single-digit numbers. Or a time when my community rejected speed cameras[8] in places where children cross streets right in front of their schools.

People dislike the peering eyes of virtual referees which surround their cars. They fight to protect their privacy and privilege. Politically? I'll brand it now, the slogan will become the "Third

Lane."[9] *Surveillance can solve our problem by knowing all the pieces on the gameboard, but humans will hinder progress.*

If behaviors indicate human resistance ahead, there is a continued price to privilege, which is tallied yearly by the National Highway Traffic Safety Administration (NHTSA). As I type, the numbers of fatalities are going in the wrong direction.[10] With automation, I like the promise of fewer deaths, lower emissions, and what it will do for us collectively, but I am not the one who needs convincing.

I savor the idea of not having to drive. But then again, I've had years of driving experience. I am content to hang up my shoes, telling stories to younger humans of how I earned my road rash battle scars. Living to tell tales of low-siding motorcycles, getting t-boned more than once, and having dreams of being covered in shattered glass as my mother screamed my full legal name seems *pedestrian* in my culture. The young ones will want to experience it too when we say "no" to their brilliant Red Barchetta[11] from a better vanished time.

Once the robots are out on the road in numbers, humans have a distinct way of learning patterns of behaviors. When incentives are understood, would it be legal for us to "game" the AI to obtain travel preference? Not everyone is lawful good.[12]

But to have robots driving and humans taking a back seat is not in the purview of the lexicon in this area of the world.

Thinly Settled Now, but Eventually a Thickly Future Problem

As our trip ended and we made our way back, I enjoyed the signs that read "Thickly Settled,"[13] a happy tour of regional flair not found elsewhere except on Route 28. The reality is these signs indicate specific changes in the rules of the road. And I wondered what happens when AI becomes intermingled with humans to its saturation.

As I write, driverless vehicles hardly exist.

My understanding of automation trials of humans *not at the wheel* has been successful in modern American cities[14] within limited optimized goals of taxiing to direct points. There are also ongoing company trials[15] with trucking AI which optimize for maximum efficiency and safety. Finally, car manufacturers offer level 2 consumer controls[16] where a human supervises the operation.

Those manufacturers who are in business should provide drivers with a "my head is burning" button. While driving, tap the button when human decision calculations are burning your head, and in this case, how I felt in Chatham, a town on the eastern tip of Cape Cod. People were blissfully shopping off Route 28—and getting in the way. The feedback could be a starting point of simulations.

While no one in the auto automation business cares about my observation of human driving attitudes at this time, once the game scales to serve many, I suspect these edge cases will flare up as potential consumer resistance. If there is a poor reception to the results of the automatons driving with mixed-in human compatriots, there will be a rejection, with favoritism of the familiar. No, I'm not talking about *safety to protect life*, but piss poor travel experiences as the humans command their preference—until they do not. Along the way, news of "death by computation"[17] will shape future reactionary perspectives.

Let's watch what control humans have on driving as we head into the mid-21st century. I suspect challenges will be raised because of the cultural significance and prestige of driving.

We need mix-controls (not currently invented) to mend technology operating within erratic human behavior. Redundant sensory controls with the red "stop button" are not enough. If capabilities fail politically, perhaps it's a side-car approach where robots fly,[18] and humans remain terrestrial in what they love.

It will be a tremendous strategy to lobby these controls *while* keeping humans happy. But for now, we will continue to ratchet the human safety features incrementally.

So, for now, enjoy the lovely human pilots in "thickly settled" areas. Let those wheels spin as drivers blink their headlights—to allow entry onto Route 28.

Figure 51.1: Will driverless AI vehicles become thickly settled?

52

Listening Alone on the Internet

My Solo Music Experience as a Xennial

A SUDDEN URGE CAME OVER ME. I craved a particular type of music. Not just any music, but the stuff that reminded me of when I was younger. I wanted to listen to Nu NRG. So I dialed them up on YouTube to share the experience—with no one else.

Who Is Nu NRG?

I'm sure you don't know Nu NRG. They were a flash-in-the-pan electronic music duo[1] that made numerous high-quality tracks during the turn of the century. Their significant self-authored hit was Dreamland.[2] Nu NRG's live sets contained high-energy melodic harmonies, such as their set from a festival called Orgasmatron. As fast as they rose in popularity, they disbanded. They left a few years of unique sounds between the golden era of trance music and the progressive style soon to come.

I cannot remember how I discovered Nu NRG. Their popularity was not expressed by family, friends, or radio media. Nu NRG didn't land at a major airport with an entourage. Their music was not recognized in my community. However, something new was happening. Groups like Nu NRG's influence rose from the earlier obscure Internet, championed by other artists.

Back then, I downloaded tracks from forums like tranceaddict.com and shared in-depth reviews with aliased cohorts. Then, I experienced them[3] live in NYC at a club called ARC. The music was too loud to speak to anyone as the duo pushed hard on their instruments. Their real-time music composition made them unique, composing high-energy music, *live on keyboards.*

Shared Experience No More

My last twenty music-listening years are these types of indulgent adventures. Nu NRG was one of many artists that have come and gone.

It all started at the beginning of the century when I primarily sourced music from the Internet. As my interest in popular music waned, I sought outlets online. My electronic music addiction was shared with a friend, the occasional clubgoer, or the millions on the Internet.

Nu NRG's music contained beats and harmonies touching on emotional tones. As with all my bedroom listening sessions, I turned off their music after receiving my high. The good memories waned, but a lingering thought remained. Glaring computer screen night sessions were undoubtedly my solo experience worth mentioning, but no one else cared.

As I grow older, sharing these listening moments remains estranged.[4] I'd have to call a friend a thousand miles away or reach out to Internet handles. But there is always the last resort. I could post a reply to a YouTube video proclaiming [*insert obscure artist here*] performed the best music of all time. Others praise their idols, famous or not—perhaps this is a normal function of aging.

The Internet Brought Me Access to Solo Experiences in Music

Of course, underground music has existed in all genres since the beginning. What I find interesting are two concepts that dominate my journey.

First, my experience has been a split duality as a Xennial.[5] When I was younger, it was shared experiences from the radio, cassettes, or CDs with those around me. This included pop, grunge, hip-hop, etc. We gossiped about music videos on MTV. But a singular cultural music stream was destined to die. Nowadays, I connect with people my age or older in an intense form of nostalgia.

When the MP3 player came, something brilliant happened. I downloaded music no one else had heard of. Access to information, especially music, was easy.[6] That's where my journey went in a different direction. I became pleasantly isolated, loading MP3s on my solid-state player. Groups like Nu NRG came to be by reaching people who once did not have access.

Secondly, since the dawn of easier access, **most** of my experiences have become an eclectic mix of music, electronica included. While I can express my love of specific genres to those around me, those people rarely connect in kind. So, my outlet is to speak into the void of the Internet. Occasionally I listen to what's playing on the radio to communicate with people. But popular music is no longer a significant stream of shared cultural consciousness. Connecting to someone in admiration of my selection of music is like discovering gold dust, a result of over-selected access.

For years, I shared my love on the Internet and discussed the latest music tracks I enjoy. I'd drag my friends to underground clubs or listen to left-field electronica, Wave,[7] and other oddities. There was even that time I took the whole team I worked with to an underground event.

No one got the vibe.

Rarely has someone in my proximity shared a similar experience.[8] Of course, on the web, my shared encounters will resonate. In-person, I seem to lack new musical connections. Thanks to the Internet, I somehow dug into comfortable solitude.

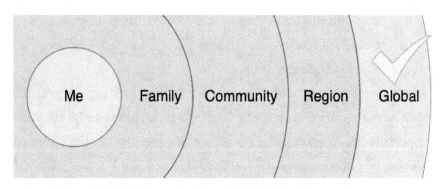

Figure 52.1: Today's music is found globally through ease of access.

• • •

IN 1969, Jim Morrison, a famous American musician of The Doors, predicted that new music "will rely heavily on electronics." He became right. But Jim failed to predict that "electronics" would *discover* music for the listener. And so, you and I listen to new music, alone.

53

A Love Letter To My YouTube Subscriptions

Cutting Cable Turned Me into a Casual Couch Farrier

WHEN I DITCHED MY CABLE BUNDLE, a transformation happened on my couch. I became a voyeur of a comforting formula, peering into the souls of once-ordinary individuals. Every day, they post content on YouTube.

And before bed, I stream their warez to my screen.

This essay is a love letter to their content after the collapse of reality TV, but before we roll it back up again.[1]

New To You (and Their Content)

Until now, my list of YouTube subscriptions was a well-held secret. The enigma was shattered after I confided with a co-worker in front of others. We got deep into the detail of unperturbed farriers shaving the hoofs of their prized heifers. From there, I realized I wasn't alone.

It's clear to me I've gone down the rabbit hole with these beautiful people. I'm in the comfort of individuals I'll never know. But are these heroes reflections of me against the LED mirror? Who are they, and what do they do? Let me share because I know you consume lovely weird sh*t, deep down too.

Nate The Hoof Guy

My co-worker and I bonded over Nate The Hoof Guy's[2] content. While I don't see Nate in his YouTube videos, I'm close up with the captivating animals getting their big nails done. I come for the exciting thumbnail descriptions of *"Blowing Bubbles"* and *"What's Stuck in this Hoof?"* I'm right there with Nate as he carves away the cow talon.

His formula is straightforward. Nate comforts the animal and gets to work. Exciting discoveries like white line defects are seen as he carves away with precision. When the abscess is cleaned up, Nate slaps on salicylic acid so no bacteria can enter. He glues on a block on the opposite hook for proper balance. The cow is released, and so am I, discharging the beautiful animal to graze.

Nate's formula repeats with at least one and a half million subscribers.

CrazyRussianHacker

It is without question there are YouTubers out there who unbox and review cool stuff. For Taras Kulakov, better known as Crazy-RussianHacker,[3] his reviews have been a staple of my YouTube diet for at least a decade. He'll take on weird man-like evaluation of tools, survival gear, and kitchen gadgets. They make me smile every time he critiques.

CrazyRussianHacker has influenced me to say, *"Let's put it to the test!"* and the joy of speaking, *"Safety is number one priority."* In real life, I'll say these quips in jest where preparation *wasn't* planned, as CrazyRussianHacker performs dangerous tests regularly. The repetitive hooks in his language have seeped into mine. And if you have been watching, I'm sure you are doing it, too.

With almost twelve million subscribers, his influence is *"No joke guys."*

Xiaomanyc

Better known as Arieh Smith, Xiaomanyc[4] delivers smiles when articulating an unsuspecting language to native speakers. He's famous because his looks do not match his impressive Mandarin and Fuzhounese skill sets. It's incredible to watch Arieh order food in an unfamiliar language while I experience anxiety about ordering a cheeseburger in my *only* language.

Xiaoma's experiences are the deepest nightmare of an introvert and the key to mastering a second language. Lately, he's been exploring additional languages, which appears uncomfortable to this polyglot. I come back because of the human reaction of others. People indeed connect on a level when their language is respected and, stunningly, when they speak their language imperfectly with passion.

Arieh is one of those people that make the human race worth preserving. Xiaoma has almost seven million subscribers as of this publishing.

Featureman

One of my latest subscriptions, Tom Williet, or Featureman,[5] was a pure joy to find. At first, I was intrigued by a wise-looking man reviewing TV dinners at their low price points. And recently, I have been watching *during* my lunch—when I eat alone. I'm drooling at his "secret dessert" reveal in every video; sometimes, they are fantastic.

But shut up and listen. He's speaking.

Featureman is a pleasant guy talking about high-processed food concerned with its economy. Until I realized he's saltier than the TV dinners. Tom has worked with Hollywood's greatest actors as a stand-in, extra, and double, spanning forty years in Hollywood. From Rock Hudson to Leslie Nielsen, he's worked with outstanding actors and actresses. And this is why I watch. Featureman's stories would make any mortal smile. God bless my vanilla pudding time with him.

Astoundingly, Tom has four hundred thousand subscribers.

11foot8plus8 (Originally 11foot8)

Vehicle accidents are scary, life-changing, and downright horrific. And in the Internet age, I've learned to swear in Russian from the glut of leaked car camera incidents. But if you look deep enough, there are misfortunes we can all laugh at, and no one gets hurt except in their wallet. 11foot8plus8[6] is a camera looking at a train bridge where unsuspecting box trucks get "can-opened" by a hungry bridge in North America. This one is a blast and my kids love it.

Jürgen Henn has been running the camera surveillance on this bridge[7] for a decade. He has a library of at least 180 truck and RV *rip-roaring* incidents that will make you cringe and then laugh at their stupidity. I mean, there is a sign flashing "*OVERHEIGHT!*"

Even after the locality raised the bridge another eight inches, videos roll in, albeit less lately! Please wait for it before the roof pops open. *Boom!* Ah, there it is.

11foot8plus8 has at least a half million subscribers.

Mr. Heang Update

Do you want to watch strong people develop a tropical paradise with hands, sticks, and pure genius? Well, you're in luck. Mr. Heang Update[8] locates you in the southeast corner of the world. Watch a few people dig into the earth; twenty minutes later, you'll find a pool, a resting area, the bbq, and even running water. How did that happen?

There is chatter on the Internet[9] that this genre is fake, and the location contains modern tools to make crafting happen. But I don't want to believe it. The editing is flawless, the video sped up, and these people are building an oasis I want to live in, even if digging machines and power tools exist behind the camera.

Mr. Heang has close to thirteen million subscribers.

Steve1989MREInfo

It is without question there is poignant interest in nostalgia. But to unbox and then eat that nostalgia is weird and *very satisfying*. Steve Thomas, or Steve1989MREInfo,[10] is making these videos of collecting, showcasing, and then eating MREs (meals ready to eat) your great grandfathers and grandmothers ate during the World Wars and your parents and friends later. And like him, I'm saying his trademarks, "*Let's get this out on a tray. Nice!*" and "*Catch you on the next one. Cool. See ya.*"

When Steve blows the finest asbestos hickory smoke from

century-old Chesterfield cigarettes, I'm relaxed like I've never been before. What's interesting is the deep knowledge I've obtained by watching the unpackaging. The engineering, craft, and intensity of developing long-distance food delivery—in combat—is an incredible science.

Steve uncans potential botulism I'll never have to experience. Since watching, I've become a savor-survivalist in modern MREs. And with Steve1989MREInfo's two million subscribers, the flavor is always good.

SB Mowing

In the land of YouTubers, watching people work is no joke. In the case of mowing lawns, that's a business with lots of money to be made. Spencer over at his channel, SB Mowing,[11] uploads videos where he donates his landscaping services to abandoned properties. I'll spend hours with Spencer with his formula of revealing what once was considered lawn and brushes.

SB Mowing is doing something extraordinary with three million subscribers watching—which is mowing lawns. I arrive for those delicious sidewalk reveals. Lifting sod off the concrete makes for a soothing experience if you are a mind-bended, neat freak like me. I come back for the straight rhythmic shots of clean edges.

Hydraulic Press Channel

In the case of Lauri from the Hydraulic Press Channel,[12] he has been at it since the 2010's. He crushes things with expensive press equipment. And I'm back, again and again, watching this fascinating man from

Finland destroying objects I've never dreamed of. And lately, he plays with fire and explosives on his frozen lake, making it all the better. Finnish people are *cool*.

Hydraulic Press Channel touches my inner soul of being a child. I liked destroying my playthings, specifically my toy cars with hammers, or at least this is what my Mom said. But with Lauri, I'm in good company without anyone yelling at me. I like him, what he does, and how hazardous the activity of crushing ball bearings produces authentic military-grade shrapnel.

With close to ten million subscribers, people enjoy this dynamic man with his classic Finnish response, "*Holy Sh*t!*" as the shards fly.

LA Beast

My final YouTuber on the list is Kevin Strahle. Better known as LA Beast,[13] a competitive eater whose videos reflect his nature of doing crazy things like eating cakes off a moving toy train while upside down on a yoga stand. LA Beast became famous for chugging a twenty-year-old Crystal Pepsi[14] and throwing it all up.

I connect with Kevin and make his videos my priority.

LA Beast lines his rooms with physical nostalgia, which connects to my deepest childhood, including Ghostbusters, WWF, Nintendo, and other oddities. He accomplishes the amazing, I drop everything to watch his next challenge. With his recent video completing a 50-mile jog, I rose off my chair, clapped, and then began crying with him on his win. Watching LA Beast is the peak of a good person trying his best at YouTube.

With three million subscribers, he's doing it well, while others are not. And as Kevin would say, *"Have a good day!"*

Link and Subscribe Below (and Click the Bell)

Of course, there are others on my list. From riding trains[15] in Scandinavia, sipping scotch in a Manx Bothy,[16] riding expensive naked motorcycles[17] in Europe, and reviewing delicious US fast food,[18] these individuals are privately celebrated and publicly embarrassing to share.

We are all watching a flavor of their creative content—captured by YouTube's awesome algorithm.

I've chosen these people because they are my new media consumption. They are doing something incredible by keeping me entertained on YouTube. And since my separation from cable, I've subscribed to these individuals, until the *next big personality arrives.*

I salute you all! And as Lauri[19] says on the Hydraulic Press Channel, *"Thank you for watching, and have a nice day."*

Seeking an Inner YouTube Personality

While we think we control the content we watch, it's clear that there are suggestive forces at work.

Waves of these individuals have risen and fallen over the decades of YouTube watching.

I don't think it was a coincidence that at least one other person got hooked on the obscure but necessary trade of farriering.

Perhaps subscriptions are a window into one's soul.

54

The Many Senses of Software Engineering

Analogs of Human Facilities to Engineering Practices

SOFTWARE ENGINEERING IS A CRAFT, intractable to describe.[1] This interest in describing *what software is* made me think about *how*. Are there facilities that constitute software engineering? So, I reflected on my past experiences. As I came up with this metaphor, I realized that individual contribution is arranged into thought processes. Our work is done in mind, writing to the machine, and speaking with others.

Based on anecdotal evidence, I settled on an everyday mapping to the human body—the *five human senses*. Seeing, hearing, tasting, smelling, and touching. We can think of each sensing facility as a separate and unique function, or as I like to think, utilizing certain parts of the mind. What follows is based on an everyday **software system**; primary groupings of what software engineers utilize.

Designing (Seeing)

With our first sense, **sight**, software engineers[2] are challenged with building systems for a need. This rarely starts as a blank slate, but in an existing structure, solving a new problem. In this application, visualization is key to its success. The system's **design** is applied through typical metaphors of gluing, plumbing, bolting on, constructing, and orchestrating.

As we see the design unfold, clarity of vision is debated. Then, we agree on the best approaches. The **abilities** are attributed to an approach we decide. For example: availability, reliability, scalability, durability. Systems and their subsystems are drawn to be seen within a line of sight.

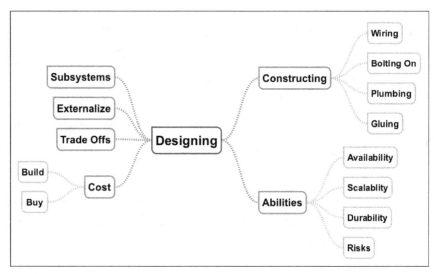

Figure 54.1: A mind map on concepts of design.

Solving (Hearing)

Once the structure begins to unfold with sight, points require an intense **hearing**. The system will require optimizations, called algorithms, in which iterating, recursing, and listening to the riddles to form a rhythmic structure that **solves** a problem. And what is of interest is listening to specific points.

In software engineering, these are the system's critical points that require a recipe to step through. And why hearing? That is because this sense is tested throughout the team by speaking through the solution. It sometimes requires a back and forth with architects,[3] analysts, and their cross-functional teams.

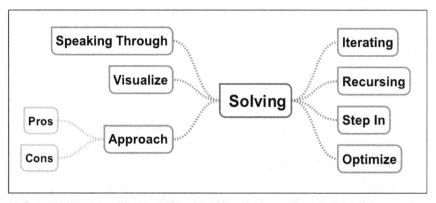

Figure 54.2: A mind map on concepts of problem-solving.

Testing (Tasting)

As the system is seen and heard, it is tested for **taste**. Taste is a subjective sense and there are many forms that people enjoy. For this system, we are **testing** by isolating, separating, and pinning dependencies. We are asserting and validating the taste of the structure. Tasting takes a few forms, whether we taste for saltiness, sweet or sour, or detect savory. We inspect at certain **levels or scales,** including unit, feature, and system testing. Tasting in the system is a continuous exercise.

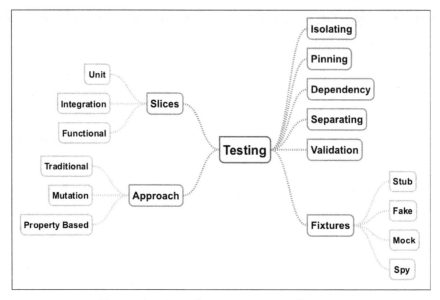

Figure 54.3: A mind map on concepts of testing.

Refactoring (Smelling)

As we continue to see, hear, and taste the system, we also smell unusual scents within our growing structure. This includes finding foul areas of the system. And once we find these accidental complexity areas, we **refactor** them using sight, hearing, and taste.

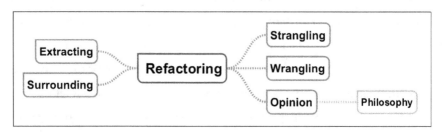

Figure 54.4: A mind map on concepts of refactoring.

We find seams by shoehorning or retrofitting items into the system by wrangling and externalizing areas that need to grow. Like taste and smell, refactoring is opinionated in nature.

Debugging (Touching)

Systems grown with the senses can operate for a time. They are new or decaying systems that require **touch**. In engineering, we call this **debugging**. We are at a loss of sight and hearing. In most structures, we are close to having a bland taste.

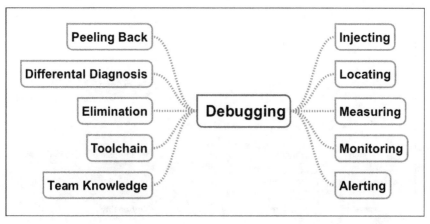

Figure 54.5: A mind map on concepts of debugging.

All that is left is the immediate feel of the subsystem. Strong smells guide us. This requires inspecting, injecting, locating, measuring, and monitoring to determine how we can further refactor and improve the system. Debugging is a highly tactile skill that requires touch. The technique is hard to describe to others because of its unique medium.

Engineering Velocity (Proprioception)

While we are operating with all senses, there is a **sixth sense**. In the human body, this sense calculates where the body is in the environment. This is called **proprioception**. Applied to engineering, this sixth sense determines how well we work with other engineers.[4] How much value we deliver.

This metaphor combines orientation, coordination, and movement of the software system. It is **engineering velocity**. We work together by empathizing and understanding others and the customer. Some *intangibles* and *tangibles* make up the concept of velocity, as seen below.

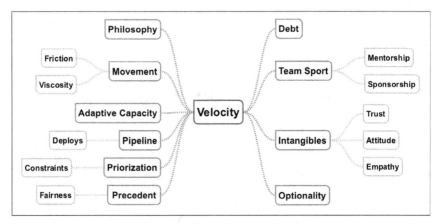

Figure 54.6: A mind map on concepts of engineering velocity.

Proprioception is tied to engineering velocity since it is a metaphor for movement awareness, with friction or ease in the system. Software is ultimately about people who develop and those who consume the value. Developing an acute sensibility of velocity requires long periods of time with experimentation throughout the organization.

Conclusion

Seeing, hearing, tasting, smelling, touching. These are human facilities.

Software engineering has similar provisions. Designing, solving, testing, refactoring, and debugging. And in all, there is a sixth sense of proprioception and its association to system movement—velocity. Engineering is applied to everyday situations through these mechanisms.

Just like senses, engineering practices can be honed and optimized. By seeking improvement in these facilities, current systems are maintained effectively, and new systems are built well. Senses are receptors that have memory. And they control a feedback loop of **continuous learning**. In each practice, invisible muscles can be trained and improved with deliberate practice by the individual and the collective.

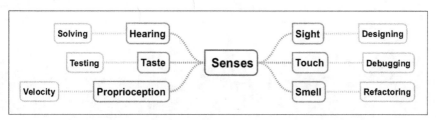

Figure 54.7: Bringing it all together.

What are other facilities typically found in software engineering?

A Missed Opportunity

Changing the respective makes for a powerful essay.

And not many essays exist on assistive technologies which programmers with impairments rely on—such as one engineer I managed who used magnification software and voice assisted technology.

There are many assistive tools but I haven't read a critical review in one place. Not much exists for those that seek assistance, and for those that are sponsors, such as managers.

Finding a comprehensive essay—a living document on the amplification of senses of each assistive technology—would be greatly appreciated. Do you know where one is?

55

Recognizing Remote Romantic Bibliophilia

ATTRACTIVE BOOK SPINES in the background of remote video calls are a source of joy to me. And on more than one occasion, I snap a quick photo, secretly loving their collection too—a pendant into the soul of this beautiful, well-read person.

I want to learn[1] with them.

For most of the pandemic, I have been happy—*grateful*—being remotely employed.[2] But my book collection sits in a small bedroom, seen in a different context. That is because my spouse is in that space, fighting COVID in projects that created vaccine formulation and mass production techniques.

And I am out here as an engineer manager[3] at my kitchen table, the team questioning my frequent house-bound geographical migrations in jest. Sometimes mimicking their virtual backgrounds of the places I've sat. I love them all.

But I wonder, do the engineers on *her* calls think that *Mythical Man-Month*[4] is an archaic titled process of medicine formulation? And for all the books I've seen, have they read through *their* titles so prominently displayed?

Regrettably, my collection has not been well-read. I'm ashamed of it. I'm trying to correct it. But I write this to end that. I am going to commit.

No book seen in my remote view will be left unread.

Regardless, my book collection[5] will continue to grow like unabated technical debt. And all these beautiful book spines leave permanent imprints in my digital shopping cart.

Oh, and that book I saw on someone else's remote bookshelf yesterday? It's on the way... borne from the brief moments of remote working and watching media interviews conducted on video-conferencing.

I recognize that every book in my collection started from a conversation. And lately, I am suffering from a one-way conversation ailment. ***Remote romantic bibliophilia disorder.***

The Books Are Piling Up

Some time after I wrote this post, I had learned the Japanese term **tsundoku**.

From a definition I found online, tsundoku is a combination of the words tsunde-oku (to pile things up and leave them) and dokusho (to read books).

The Japanese term is closely associated with "bookworm" in English, but is not derogatory in nature.

56

Short Circuiting Fantastical Debugging

DEBUGGING THINGS REQUIRES a level head. Problem-solving is an art of the *anti-freakout*. My problem is I dream of fantastical sources where the pain originates. It affects my problem-solving skills.

I'll share a story of what I mean.

Roaming Circuits

When relocating an electric circuit breaker box at a residence, there is a "certified" way to add contiguous lines. It requires a large plastic box hanging on an exterior wall containing wire splices for each circuit. These conjunctions make an exemplary engineer perpetually anxious, as splices are known to fail over time.

When we moved my home's electrical source, I became apprehensive. With an invisible electric force compounding my nerves, I was afraid that things would go wrong. Sure enough, something did go wrong, at least in my head. Fantastical visions of squirrels chewing on the lines, nefarious agents dismantling the box to disable alarms, and the elementals attacking from a well-placed lighting strike, in the night, without any sound.

Over the years, circuits have tripped for good reasons. The source of the problem *feels* a step away. These "random" flips compound my imaginary suspicions.

An Example of How to Freak Out Properly

Weeks into playing a well-loved JRPG video game[1] with my daughter, the power unexpectedly went out. My mind began to race. Was it water seeping into a specific splice, violating this circuit? Did that bluejay nest in the right place? Did the thirty-year-old 16-bit system have a malfunctioning capacitor, drawing amperage, frying the line?

Fear sank in as I considered this splice box dangerously janky.

We lost power again; I reset the breaker, squarely focusing the blame on the splice box, exposed to the elements. The device was toying with me, and sure enough, I made the mistake of the insane, flipping the breaker again, hoping for a new conclusion.

What Happened

After we lost an hour of play, I reset the circuit breaker a second time, and we played on. After some time, my daughter dispatched a boss, jumping up with excitement on her bed. At the same time, sparks flew in a specific area of the room, and the power went out again!

I freaked out. My mind immediately had a vision of terminating this splice box—I was ready to grab my soldering iron and apply twenty-year-old Radio Shack shrink-wrap in the right places. *Deus ex-circuit-breaker* robbed our gaming progress once again.

This time, I took a minute to think as my daughter's room was about to go up in flames. I applied what I've learned in software development[2] over the years. The logical deductions, inductions, and *abductions* of the electricity flooded my head. I said to myself, "keep calm and find the patterns."

Always believe in Occam's Razor. Believing in the principle of the simplest thing is not enough. But it's a good start. There was no way it could be the video game system sitting there for a time.

If the system is not well understood, it's never in the first place where you're looking. Of course, this splice box may be the source of the issue, but somehow not understanding it is a detractor to solving the problem.

If the system is stable, it's unlikely the system. Since the system has been operating on sound infrastructure,[3] there is no way it could have been anything in-between.

If the problem is new, believe it is recently introduced. It could have been the bluejay I saw that morning, but there was no evidence of a violation. I began looking at the source of the sparks immediately following the power outage.

A repeating problem is usually a misplaced configuration. Looking at a distance, all I saw was a nightlight—nothing out of the ordinary?

If the configurations are correct, it could be a newly introduced dependency. I pulled the nightlight out, realizing it was half out of the socket, with its broken metal brace perfectly wedged in-between the wall and the receptacle. My daughter sparked the chain of events by first placing the nightlight there a day before—each time we celebrated dispatching a monster, an intermittent short circuit occurred from jumping on the bed, squishing it.

Bingo. Fix applied.

Usually, It's the Simplest Solution

While the nightlight saw its end in the trash bin, I suspiciously blamed the source in error. While an established system is not often blameless, the focus should be on its added appendages. Looking into the core system is rarely necessary.

I've worked with these *splice boxes* in the past, both certified and not. In the end, the most straightforward source is to blame. It's probably a **configuration problem**, with force applied to it.

A System Problem

This real event is actually fantastical, and is a true story.

The story above demonstrates the frailty of the North American electrical outlet. Because a gap develops above the hot and neutral prongs as a plug is stressed, there is a possibility of an object wedging itself within, bridging the gap.

Where liquids and thin metal instruments are numerous, North American hospitals avoid this problem by installing outlets upside down. The gap is guarded by the grounded plug.

At the time of this publication, the National Electric Code does not specify a recommended orientation.

57

Five More Minutes

AS A PARENT, my mind is multi-threading tasks. First, enjoying my children at this playground. Second, engaging in creative engineering thinking to resolve an issue.[1] Three, observing the behaviors of other parents. One of which is the pattern of "five more minutes."

Around me, another *play project* is coming to an end. A parent over to my left loudly states to their kids, "five more minutes!"[2] Signaling playtime is about to expire, their time having fun is over.

I'm over here thinking about if I should enact the "five more minutes" decree. Should I? Probably not, I am still toying with this problem, and the scenes are nice out here in the playground. The weather is beautiful, and so is the laughter of my children.

When It's Done

I briefly teleport back to previous software engineering projects in my past. The managers would serve up the rules of play. "Five more minutes," the managers would say as the engineers blissfully play with frameworks, proof of concepts, and the art of balancing bits and bytes running around the *digital* hallways.

"Five more minutes" was met with "when it's done."[3] The managers pushed back, finding ways to get the project in scope and out the door. They enjoyed deploying tactful bribes. Those who recently crossed the chasm from engineering to management[4] knew how to reel them in by speaking their language—and those wise didn't care.

Coming back to the playground scene, I needed "five more minutes." My spouse was looking to me to make the call. I was wrestling with whether to solve the problem this way or work around it. "Daddy, I want to go higher," said one of my daughters, on the swing next to me.

My spouse looked at me with raised eyebrows.

Cutting Up the Pie

Oh fine. "Five more minutes." I let the kids know the *project* was coming to an end and we needed to ship out. "But, but!" "No, we have to go," I said to my kids. They pushed back again—for two minutes.

"Yeah, there will be a surprise when we go." Their sad eyes told the story but brightened up to the thought of something new.

In the distance was another family, also declaring "five more minutes," as if there was a recurring pattern,[5] an odd pub/sub system continued its way to each of their delegates. Another parent said the same after I committed to our departure.

We left the beautiful playground. But neither my spouse nor I checked with the stakeholders. They were the ones who wanted to play more—unfortunately, another handful of *business* problems needed solving.

I continued mentally debugging[6] as we loaded them into our car. Then it hit me; I knew what to write[7] *this* month. I just needed a way to connect the observation to the craft. Aha!

When we came back, we had their favorite surprise—pizza.

X

Section Ten

Reflections

re·flec·tion (/rə'flekSH(ə)n/) *n.* an idea about something, especially one that is written down or expressed.

DSR

58

Learning from Structures Around Us

An Observation on Software Engineering from Our Environment

TREES IN MY NEIGHBORHOOD seem to grow unnaturally. They appear as sick twisted living creatures. The reason for their ugliness is related to their proximity to electric utility lines. Their closeness is familiar in the northeast of the United States, where trees exist in the right-of-way, and extreme weather patterns are present.

Utility lines are at risk of falling tree limbs because they are vulnerable strung pole to pole. The result is the energy company must prune trees to precise distance specifications. Pruning reduces the risk of branches touching these wires and allows for repair access. When the weather is uncooperative, pruning keeps the lines protected. Yet, the result is ugly looking unbalanced trees.

The Science of Trees

In computer science, we use metaphors. The science is abstract, and construction is virtual.[1] Most development, if we even call it this, cannot be seen or touched. Regardless, we need to communicate what we see based on our world. We have to describe what is efficient. We have to talk about maxima and minima, time, and space.

Searching for data is fundamental to our science. To do so, we organize the data with structure. A tree is an abstract data type. It looks like a living tree, but upside down, as the root is at the top. We use trees to structure data so that it can be sorted and searched efficiently. Trees take on types and flavors like real trees do.

An *unbalanced tree* is a metaphor to describe an unwanted structure. The structure is not optimal for searching the data it contains. Unbalanced trees are naively grown and trimmed. They begin to slow us down due to their unchecked height. They become too high on one side.

How to Balance an Unbalanced Tree

In saving customers from service interruption, power utility authorities trim left or right. They cut where the risk is significant. The result is unhealthy trees that are unsightly. They think that the tree is performing its function, but instead, it is sick trying to survive.

There are ways to programmatically save the sick tree as it grows. Depending on the tree, we can transverse, rotate left, rotate right, or double rotate. We attempt to balance the tree so that it's healthy. Its structure becomes compact, beautiful, and elegant than its current shape.

If the unbalanced tree has enough space in front of it, there is a way to solve the blight at the root. We cut down and start over. We grow the new tree on the next pass.

Learning Cues Are Around Us Waiting for Leverage

Making way for utility lines requires mutilating trees. An abstraction of this observation would suggest that community and technology are in contention. If either is grown improperly, there is difficulty in remedying because both are supportive of one another.

The beauty of computer science[2] is *we can invent and grow structures based on our physical observations.* Ancient tree pruning techniques such as *Topping* or modern technologies such as *Drop-Crotching* may apply to computer science. Utility lines that are strung or are laid may also have their analog. How they work together may be of interest to research.

The message is to *look around outside to learn and apply what we observe, virtually.* Question if the observation could be a chance to translate a structure or system into leveraging beauty and efficiency. If we embrace the problem there is a chance for *structural invention.*

DSR

59

Software Development Is Unlike Construction

A Short on the Reasons Why

OUR FAMILY RECENTLY COMPLETED a home construction project. We took down walls and extended our kitchen into an open floor concept.

The project process and progress was clear. We initially worked with an architect by drawing up plans. We then worked with a government agency to critique and approve those plans. Finally, we partnered with the contractors in three phases—first, demolition and preparation. Second, structural, plumbing, and electrical. Finally, exterior cover and finish. At each point in time, the agency approved the work.

The project made me reflect on my profession. **While building construction metaphors are often used to describe the software development process, this is not how it works.** Here are the reasons why.

Non-Linear and Mutable in Nature

Construction can be highly linear. It follows a well-defined sequence. There are points in time where diversions are required. Sometimes alterations to the plan are made when specifics need adjustment. *Structural maladies* are discovered. Or when *safety realities* must be mitigated, such as when dangerous electrical splice boxes are found.

With software development, there is no defined sequence[1] and no silver bullet.[2] We tend to run in different directions. We shore this up with the typical "sprint zero" and include numerous inspection points. We shorten the loop of the process and respond to items in that loop.

> *Software development is a creative endeavor that is non-linear. It is fostered by discovery with no clear middle, beginning, or end. Re-work is continuous.*

Insights Are Opaque

Construction progress is straightforward and visible throughout. Software development is abstract and invisible. We use demos,[3] tools, and dashboards to make visibility available to our stakeholders and teams. At best, development is opaque and requires extraordinary effort to maintain visibility.[4] The tools lack cross-cutting dissection, relying on imperfect telemetry.[5] Inference in our tooling is nascent. Lack of observability leads to difficulty in making appropriate decisions at proper times, leading to waste, poor software cohesion, and delayed delivery.

Our mental model of software projects has misconceptions. Each contributor has a different opinion of how the process should work.

We Disagree on Common Measures

Physical construction requires building in a way that is acceptably safe and predictable. There would be no way a two-story home could stand if its main structural beam were removed. However, we are surprised at how software development projects cross the finish line with malformed structures. Software development processes, development practices,[6] and principles attempt to find common ground between engineers,[7] but there is little agreement. A continuous debate has created a void of common measures, therefore, leading to less predictability and safety.

No one can agree to a consistent scale measure. What is good enough?

Individual Personalities Prevail

Construction is physical in nature, with clear constraints. Many learnings have reinforced agreed approaches. But software development is not a mature industry, and therefore we do not follow a clear approach due to disagreement in measures. There is a high-level diversity in thought, based on assumptions. We are all exploring and learning together. There are spheres of influence that represent numerous philosophies. *Opinionated* decisions[8] are made externally and brought in internally. At best, we have *team-scrutineering* based on external community validation.

Unlike construction, software development has voices pushing and pulling the community in different approaches. The question is, who are we listening to and why?

Conclusion

Our home construction project ended on time and within budget. However, this cannot be said for a majority of software projects I worked on. What is clear are the above items. Invisible details,[9] glued together non-linearly by smart, opinionated individuals.

If construction is a poor analogy to software development, what human endeavor is its analog? Perhaps **scribing, music composition, gardening, and philosophical activity fit the process.**[10] The reasons *why* require study.

What are other differences between construction and software development not outlined here?

60

On Names: A Brief Encounter with Guido van Rossum

An Anecdote on How Names are Pronounced

LAST YEAR, WE CELEBRATED THE ARRIVAL of our child. One exciting aspect of having children is how others pronounce the new name.

Interestingly, our child's name was misconstrued unexpectedly. While normal name mangling includes mispronunciation or spelling errors, ours includes erroneous postfixes such as "Anne," and "Anna," where the root name would be sufficient and complete. I believe this resides in generational confusion where the short name was once popular, waned, and then resurged with popular conjunctive postfixes.

Frustratingly, this led to repeatedly clarifying the original name. Since our child is an infant, the disposition of the error appears higher than one that traditionally fits in the expected generational age group.

• • •

RECENCY BIAS had set in, and name wrangling was on my mind. Naming made me reflect on correctness and pattern matching,[1] which are core attributes for software engineers. So, when I traveled to Cleveland for the PyCon[2] conference as a community newbie, I picked up on a repeating pattern. Numerous presenters pronounced Guido van Rossum's name differently, the creator of the Python programming language.

Since my sense was heightened, and this inconsistency presented itself, I decided to go right to the **source of truth** on the matter. I sought detail,[3] even if trivial, with its resolution, a critical factor in uncompromising correctness.

With a penchant for seeking correctness, I submitted a clarifying question at Sunday morning's Python Software Foundation Steering Committee keynote. Unfortunately, no answer. Perhaps they weren't accepting of levity with the heaviness of his exit as BDFL (benevolent dictator for life). I left empty-handed and proceeded to the posters segment of the conference.

• • •

AN OPPORTUNITY PRESENTED when Guido came into sight as I wandered around. Then I approached. "Hey, I have a quick question..." and asked him—"How do you pronounce your name?"

Clarifying, I wanted to know what was correct. Guido proceeded with a short introduction in Dutch, respectfully turning away when pronouncing the deep-throated first syllable. He mentioned the *Jersey Shore* and its associated Italian syllables and the missteps concerning Starbucks barista scribbles. I was surprised at this third pronunciation and did not attempt to practice it.

He paused and said, "Go with Gee-Dough."

Of course, **not** the *Jersey Shore* version of *Gweedo*.

I thanked him for his breakdown of the problem and promptly left, knowing he had people calling for him. I appreciated his straightforwardness.

As we spoke, he politely declined other's queries.

• • •

OUR CONVERSATION MADE me reflect. Why did I ask this question—surely, there are more important inquiries for the inventor? Perhaps it is the affliction of my name, and everyone's who works in software since we are distributedly diverse.

I've heard my name in various ways while working and managing globally distributed teams. "Dough," "Dog," and "Duck" are common variants. In each case, I politely acknowledge a correction. And when asked my preferred name, I recommend "Doug."

I've grown to be sensitive and inclusive to other's pronunciations.

With each given correction to those I have just met, there is a sense of embarrassment, and having the chance to correct the error by causing minimal social and professional pain. It's **hard to do it gracefully**.

The root of the problem is the intense intersection of familiarity, commonality, locality, culturally, and generational. It is an intractable problem since the **measure of sweetness** is not quantifiable. Asking directly, even if the answer is clarified,[4] maybe the answer.

One time, I was at a store. When I gave my name, I saw on the screen "Doughless." I was stunned, and then shook my head in agreement. "That's accurate," I muttered.

How is your name wrangled, and what patterns have you seen?

DSR

61

When to Take a Vacation

AS THE MONTHS PASSED BY, our family's needs became routine. Rituals of lifeworks[1] seeped into everyday activities. Trepidations dulled our minds, transforming positive attitudes into resistance. Becoming irritable without knowing, we scoffed at the upcoming travel.

Apprehension set in when we prepared for leisure. Reaching our destination, we slowly uncovered devotion to family. We enjoyed the time together, creating new memories with those we love. And for a brief moment, we had become the doyen of us.

When we returned, the new routine gave way to old conventions. Our home encouraged commonplace activities. But the newly minted halcyon memories were admired, the crisp pictures we shared, and one or two newfound habits changed us forever.

There are opinions on when to take a vacation.[2] If reading this far, we are reminded it's time to take one more.

DSR

Building a Popular Half-Life Mod During the Rise of Counter-Strike

My Personal Account of Building "Cold Ice," an Underground Half-Life Mod

WHEN WE PURCHASED A HOME COMPUTER in 1998, I was consumed by PC video games. Particularly first-person shooters *Quake II*, *SiN*, and *Unreal Tournament*. Out of all of them, my favorite was *Half-Life*. The gameplay felt solid. The ambiance of the environment was immersive. The weapons felt heavy and responsive. The cast was engaging—Marc Laidlaw's plausible scenario where theoretical scientists open a portal to an alien universe was believable.

In my opinion, *Half-Life's* online multiplayer battle mode felt realistic and fast-paced. *HLDM* (*Half-Life Deathmatch*) was a place where online strangers compete to obtain "frags."

At about the same time I engaged with others in these online matches, the company that developed the game, Valve, released an SDK (software development kit) in April 1999.[1] The SDK enabled the community to modify the experience to their liking. This action made its popularity surge.

> *"My first memory of HLDM was joining a server and playing on a map called "Stalkyard."[2] The two things that sucked were the dial-up connection... and the game's awful netcode."*

Origins of Cold Ice

Before discovering *Half-Life*, I dabbled in custom configuration changes in games like *Red Alert* and *Rainbow Six*. But *Half-Life* was my gateway to real customization with computer programming—modding[3] to a community.

> *"I remember Dad buying a copy of Microsoft Visual Studio Professional from Circuit City. He looked at me, 'What is this for?' I shrugged, 'I want to mod games.'"*

My curiosity engaged. How could I modify the weapons in the game to play differently? Then, without any prior programming knowledge, I started a modification later to be called *Cold Ice*.[4]

Cold Ice[5] was fueled by changing the mechanics and "skins" (textures) of the weapons. I harnessed the digital echo-chamber of a clan—a group of people playing on the same team. The experience overtook my game consumption into a leading mod maker, an accidental producer/creator.

> *"Cold Ice was unique, immature, violent, provocative, and rather... odd. But I didn't care."*

Over time, *Cold Ice* became popular. Its concept was simple. Fast play, lots of explosions, reintroduce weapons that were cut by Valve,[6] then apply a unique winter ambiance to have a good time.

The mod's origin was discovered by accident. I found the "invert" functionality of Paint Shop Pro. After extracting the player's texture, Gordon Freeman, I recompiled it and placed it back into the pack file (a zip file the game uses to load resources).

It just so happened that the inverted texture looked cold. And hence, the mod name was born.

Curiosity on How Things Work Drives Determination

When I first picked up the SDK, I knew nothing about game concepts and how to produce results. With research, I found the instruments to make the modifications. This included a toolchain of applications and 3D modeling software. What assisted my discovery was the investigation of other's modification project structures. I would download, unpack, and review their materials.

"And in some cases, creative liberty was taken to 'borrow' others' project artifacts. In fact, I borrowed everything."

Tools like Microsoft Visual Studio Professional 6.0, Paint Shop Pro 5.0, 3D Studio Max, and Valve's Hammer[7] were learning curves for me. Still, I was determined to deliver an experience.

"That experience was a crazy good time with lots of explosive devices. And those sound effects were as hot as they were lifted from other pak0 files."

I wore many different "hats" while experimenting with modding.

One day I'd develop a web page to market the modification, the following day, I'd plug a vbsp[8] ray trace "leak" to compile a map. The next day I'd code new game mechanics. The intensity of the exploration sapped a majority of hours away from socializing in High School.

> *"I stayed up late for many nights at a time. The grit to discover was immensely awesome. Nothing else mattered."*

The tooling for *Half-Life* was a disparate toolchain. It was a grab-bag from various companies and modding teams. Since *Half-Life's* tech incremented off John Carmack's (inventor of the core technology for *Half-Life*) brilliance in design decisions and logical organization, *Quake's* tools were useful. They were implemented to explore and modify assets.

I was driven by the discovery of making things different. At that time, I was involved online with a team of players who wanted to see what we could do. This is what fueled me to keep going.

Determination Develops Skills to Glue Things Together

Understanding how to build things that were required at the time was intense. Building websites, modeling new weapons, coding game logic, 2D art, finding and creating sound effects, and building levels were unique challenges to be discovered.

> *"It was a vast playground of learning while being surrounded by invisible nerds doing the same."*

As time went by, I learned of community resources that healed my knowledge gaps. Conversations happened through forums and mailing lists. The best example was the Wavelength board. Wavelength[9] was a community watering hole, a place where we asked questions and got correct answers.

> *"There were absolutely no wikis at that time, and no Lycos or Excite search worth its salt in finding what needed to be found. Everything was bookmarked in the mind."*

Players of *Cold Ice* highly appreciated the *sound effects*. The explosive sounds, the blaring of the multiple rockets, and the new weapon effects made *Cold Ice* what it was at the time. Crafting an experience was the result of finding resources that added value to the play.

Finding knowledge and interacting with a community was a part of that toolchain. And after finding that community, my skill set could only go so far. There is a point at which specialization was needed. I had to *scale* myself. This is what happened next.

> *"What was this place? It was intoxicating with creative pleasure that nights, weekends, and summers would simply disappear."*

Impact Attracts Others

As *Cold Ice's* development went on, individuals came forward to usher the mod's development. If I had to count, it was thirty contributors over its short lifespan. People liked the mod and wanted to add new value. This included level makers, modelers, and other artists to create an experience.

This enabled me to concentrate on my expertise area. For me, it was about game mechanics and improving the gameplay, making it balanced. I really liked the programming aspect and building the libraries called *.dlls*. The libraries contained logic to make the weapons act differently. Every time I changed gaming behavior, it would have to be recompiled, and the game relaunched. This loop took at least three minutes for every change—a time before hot-swappable code.

2D art was also of interest. I enjoyed fiddling with the HUD (heads up display), the information printed on the screen. I spent hours developing a "smart HUD notification system," experimenting with mapping sprites (varying-transparency graphics). The goal was to improve real-time information and to enhance the play experience.

> *"I went through this code, compile, launch, test loop thousands of times. It was like being a magician where things kept changing to my will. It was fascinating as it was frustratingly slow."*

At the time, the people I met were centrally located on a popular chat messenger called ICQ and Internet Relay Chat, a chatroom agent. And, of course, the ubiquitous email. There wasn't anywhere near the video chat and tooling we have today.

> *"And what is odd is that the identities of the individuals remain hidden. Probably for good reason; the acne was boiling over."*

I only knew the names of one or two individuals, but we never once spoke on video in all that time. Besides, the cameras were too grainy on NetMeeting. I was on dial-up.

"The disreputable team was global. From Germany, Canada, Austria, UK, Finland, the USA, Australia, and other countries, we worked together to deliver something cool."

Contributors poured in from all channels. Whether it be voice-overs, writing documentation and READMEs, 3D modeling experts, and numerous map makers. They all taught me how to become better at each skill set. Their gifts were appreciated and leveraged.

And sharing assets also went the other way. We were invited to contribute code and artistry in the community, which we did. The mods were popular at the time. In fact, both modifications, *Trinity Command* and *Wasteland HL* (*WHL*),[10] were associated with early contributors of *Cold Ice*.

I personally loved *WHL* and *Trinity Command* because of their dedicated art direction. The feel of the gameplay was fantastic. When I had the chance to contribute to the weapons, HUD, and gameplay code, I had a lot of fun—I contributed to something larger than what we originally founded. And these founders were intensely good at the artwork, creating an atmospheric experience.

"These contributors spearheaded other mods later, a testament to growing obnoxious leaders in digital cabals.[11] And I was too obtuse to stay with them. Drama was shared between individuals and mod teams."

Mod making was collaborative at that time—in the summer of 1999, we were invited to alpha test *Counter-Strike* with the map *cs_siege*. I gave notes back to the "test party." Unfortunately, these notes are lost, but I remember that the mod was absolutely excellent. *Counter-Strike* became quite popular. So popular that Valve eventually acquired them, and the mod became a globally recognized household brand.

Software Is About Outcomes and Consequences, Not About Technology

Cold Ice rarely used version control, unit tests, and product testing that would remotely resemble a modern development shop.

However, we launched the modification versions anyway, and when things broke, we launched patches where they were needed (which happened frequently). It was a real research and development setup.

> *"Craftsmanship is a new business we buy into; which didn't exist at this time in software. Clean wasn't in the vernacular. But we all needed serious personal linting."*

Between developers and artists, the process was libertarian. We shared files through private FTP's (file transfer protocol) and sparingly used patch files. We furiously messaged each other when changes occurred. We appreciated the quickness of the releases. Nothing ever stopped the team from delivering an update due to quality concerns.

> *"We listened to the community. We recklessly launched in a way that promoted chaos."*

The outcomes of the modification were never completely validated. But in developing software, craftsmanship was never a crutch we used to validate our software existence. I didn't know at the time, nor did the community.

> *"This is not to say we didn't have discipline. That practice was harnessing the purest form of autodidactic exploration. The discipline was to ship. It was a Holy Land of craft, a geek Nirvana, a Mecca of maximum return on discovery."*

There is a lot to be said about software quality in association with predictability. To think, after writing tens of thousands of tests over my career and nudging others to do the same, we launched software without the automatic checks. We celebrated our *beta testers,* and that was refreshing, liberating, and free.

Success in the Community (1999-2000)

After several versions, *Cold Ice* made it to the *Mod of the Week*[12] located at Kevin "Fragmaster" Bowen's[13] Planet Half-Life (PHL). PHL was the central community hub located on the defunct Gamespy network.

Others in the community noticed. I remember being invited to Valve's 1999 Mod Expo[14] in San Francisco, which I declined the invite.

> *"I never pushed my parents to fly me to SF, nor was extroverted enough to go through such a frightening social event—I was acutely introverted."*

And then there was the regular PHL mailbag,[15] which the community rallied around. The replies were positive, and the trolls abrasive as ever.

"At that time, being a troll was normal fanfare. Everyone was doing it. Memes were the middle finger made in MS Paint."

Having our mod on the mail list was like being number one on an app store in a major category and receiving tens of thousands of downloads an hour. This was validation that we were doing things correctly and that the community was receptive.

Lots of people liked the play. Version 1.75, our beloved version, was the golden master build (GM)—a time when the software was burned to CDs and marked as 1.0 for manufacturing.

Cold Ice launched the beta 1 2.x update that changed how the game was played. This version visually improved the weapons and skins and experimented with an exchange system. The new version wasn't receptive, as noted in community polling.[16]

After a time, we paused the development of *Cold Ice* as I contributed to other modifications and started to branch out, learning about pure deathmatch play. *Half-Life Pro*[17] was an experiment inspired by *Oz Deathmatch*.[18] HLPro contained a mountain of configurable *cvars* (console variables) that included game modes, mutators (rules that change the way the game is played), and a redesigned heads up display.

In mid-2000, while I worked on *HLPro*, we launched a "Cold Ice SDK" of our own.[19] It appeared we "shut-down" *Cold Ice*, but that wasn't actually the case. We attempted something bigger.

Release Early and Often; Otherwise, the Value Will Be Shelved Indefinitely (2000-2002)

As we grew, we realized that the production version was highly naive.

We wanted to improve. As we were working on features, Valve broke the ecosystem by launching a non-backward compatible 1.1.0.0 update to the game. This caused labor for modders. Unless a non-trivial patch was attempted, the full crop of mods—*up to Spring 2000*—crashed on loading.

> *"Valve fixed the netcode by optimizing server messaging, which was welcomed. But in the process, the patch created an unwashed caste of mods that would forever be locked in the 1990s."*

And then we made a decision. Fix forward 1.75/2.x *Cold Ice* or attempt bigger changes? So we went with the latter and started our *rewrite*. We called it *Cold Ice Resurrection* (*CIR*). We shared the work only with our developers at the time.

The work was of higher quality than the first versions, and the maturity of the approach was light-years ahead than when we started. We grew as developers. The *evolution* was tangible.

Hundreds of hours of work were labored over the project between contributors.

The resurrection was an amalgam of many themes: *Counter-Strike, Action Half-Life,*[20] *WHL, Trinity Command,* and core elements of original *Cold Ice*. The direction was unclear, but we focused on fun gameplay and lots of mutators like *Iceman Cometh*.

We kept the rewrite to ourselves, reverting our original approach to feed the community. We informed PHL of the incoming work, and they gave us a hosting spot, but we held back from sharing. This was a mistake.

"There wasn't a feedback loop like we had with the original versions. That was the mistake that screwed us. The resurrection was directionless in its visual beauty. I was an ineffective newb for not pushing it out the door."

Over time, the project became heavy, and motivation dipped to *zero*. We stopped work and left the project unreleased. The artifacts began to decay into the digital ether. No one saw the update that we worked so hard on.

"Without a community jeering us on, we failed to grind through and ship.[21] 'When it's done' never came."

After the beta 1 source code was lost due to a hard-drive failure, we briefly started a beta 2. My last memory of *CIR* was that I wanted to modify the engine to make it snow—and then we gave up. The project was shelved in 2002, becoming our failed rewrite.

"I was pissed off. We restarted the work on a second beta with Infinity (lead contributor), but that fizzled out—and just like that, we were gibs all over the floor."

Retaining and Sharpening Skills After Failure(s)

Unfortunately, there isn't a fairytale ending like what happened to other modifications. The biggest was that of *Counter-Strike* and *Day of Defeat*,[22] which we were a part of their community.

And that of Valve, guided by Gabe Newell's vision. They grew the gaming ecosystem pie by creating the massive Steam Network.

What I can say is that for those who participated, we used *Cold Ice* to hone our skills and to grow as developers and artists. It was a great experience that I always thought shaped me as a person but left me questioning my understanding of what all had happened, quietly in my bedroom.

"The experience was like a cold night in a 'digital' football game where we won on the High School Internet. But no one was there, the bleachers were empty. Mom kept calling me for dinner."

My interesting lesson as a new software engineer[23] was *even in failure; I grew a vast skill set.* I wanted to see what may happen next, what I could learn. *I would not surrender to solving a problem*—a shower or a walk helped with unlocking a solution.

My larger observation was solid. For a project to survive, it must be surrounded by a community—betting on the team to succeed and feeding off their releases. And if the cheering is absent, *projects die.*

"There was no money in any of this. I left wondering where will I go—work somewhere and code with real people?"

The road to developing, launching, growing, and maintaining game modifications in the community had taught me lessons. As I moved forward and started my career, these experiences were not forgotten. I had a unique and valuable perspective on building things.

My *curiosity* led to a determination to achieve something interesting. And critical afterthoughts—not to plan projects as "big-bang" releases unless there is a commitment to a Valve time,[24] and to support backward compatibility where possible.

> *"And while all of the above is in the trash bin of gaming, the skill set is valid and memorialized for meatspace to come get me. I'd be stuck in a ch3wz0r[25] map, devoured like everyone else—but know better."*

Exiting the Scene

After another pause, we had the energy to craft something elegant. We soft-launched a mod called *HL Advanced (HLA)*,[26] a competitor to *Adrenaline Gamer* (*AG*),[27] which was popular at the tail end of the golden time of modding in *Half-Life*. *HLA* included all of the game modes, like one-on-one[28] arena matches. As it was a pure server-sided mod, no download was required.

The concept for *HL Advanced* included all the lessons learned on making a better mod. It even had a mini-pong game mode while waiting as a spectator.[29]

> *"I performed a solid 10,000 hours of being a troll and building things. My skill set was ready for whatever a company would throw at me. Except people skills—I had zero hours in that business."*

But *HLA* suffered the same fate as the resurrection; it was a failure. We repeated the mistake above, hiding in an unaccountable state over the brashness of launching—surrounded by trolls' feedback. But the real fear was I'd receive no feedback at all.

With all my creative energy expended, *Half-Life 2* launched in 2004. I walked away.

"In a golden era of mod making, Valve forever changed the scene. This wasn't the plain old piping data into databases, it was an exploration of a new digital art form."

Others picked up *Cold Ice's* development. A small team launched a 2.5 version.[30] But over the years, it's been inactive. Interestingly, *Cold Ice* remains a favorite on the vast Internet.[31] Some people still ask how to set up the mod, decades later.[32]

• • •

THE YEARS HAVE rolled by—I have much gratitude to those I modded with and to Valve. See my Github for those interested in contributing to the project material.[33] The code, files, and screenshots were located on an old hard-drive I found in storage. Unfortunately, artifacts are permanently missing. Maybe you have something to share?

Cold Ice Remastered

After this post was published, a mod rewrite called Cold Ice Remastered was launched.

After one hundred thousand views and thousands of downloads, the modification was back—finalizing the vision that I held in my head.

The Internet remains a fascinating place of creation. And I learned the lesson—whatever I wanted to create was possible.

Cold Ice Remastered can be found on ModDB at moddb.com /mods/cold-ice-remastered

---

DSR

∞

Final Section

Epilogue

ep·i·logue (/ˈepəˌlôg,ˈepəˌläg/) *n*. a section or speech at the end of a book or play that serves as a comment on or a conclusion to what has happened.

DSR

The World I Worked into No Longer Exists

A Personal Memoir of Remote Work During COVID-19

I PUT IN MY EARBUDS AND WALKED briskly to the train station. I hopped on a westbound express. When the train pulled up to Atlantic Terminal, I walked into Brooklyn to meet the team I'd worked remotely with for years. I've seen these people on a computer screen; now they are in meatspace at this beer garden.

I purchased a big glass of lager to relax, not knowing to handshake, hug, or stare, understanding they were real. This experience is remote work during an easing pandemic. I have an idea of what it's like, living it for almost three years.

They say working remotely is different from working remotely during a pandemic. I see what the advocates mean. My decades of working in software[1] included telecommuting—championed by proponents who advocated its full implementation. But COVID-19 had turned everything upside down personally and professionally, with an unusual type of world-ending stress. I am the lucky cardholder of a job change while the pandemic unfolded. Instead of a smooth transition into the next job, I watched the President address the nation nightly, bought cases of meals-ready-to-eat, and hastily set up my non-technical father to work digitally after forty years of mental sweat in cubicles.

Now years after the outbreak, I compare my remote experience with working with people in office spaces. Being alone is fine, but the experience has been intensely solo, surrounded by a beautiful family I've built.

No Books I've Read Give Guidance

Things feel familiar from an old world as I socialize with the people in the beer garden. As the alcohol takes hold, I do not mind the new distance from my family and children. I know we are to share pieces about each other as we avoid talking about work, but it does creep in.

I'm looking for polite cues to discuss and, at the same time, deliver a little edge on jokes. In the process, I am sure I said something that offended them. But mainly, I smile and listen in groups. When it made sense, I shared advice on being a nerd or a parent to those expecting. I have three.

But in this setting, I am consciously aware of the people who have power in the organization. Of course, I want to connect, but I avoid flying too close to the sun. It's a tricky balance now we have met for the first time in person, and no books I've read give guidance in this scenario.

In remote work, I've noticed focusing on tasks is easier than in an office setting. I grasp what is happening within the team. The experience is contrary to what I would have expected. Everything is purposefully executed, whether it be the work, conversations, or ideations. I have time to do other stuff. When it comes to focusing, there was a hump for navigating extreme freedom found, but now it's a breeze. Remote working excels at muting social interaction, distilling what needs to happen, which is excellent for present work. And for future work, innovation, and career advancement, these concepts originate from motivated individuals regardless of location.

As I mingle at this beer garden, a conversation gets serious with my manager. Socializing with coworkers above in the hierarchy often elevates the context of work. I want to discuss where we have issues, what I need for the team, and what I can do to keep the business running to expectations. I take a moment to refocus our conversation on lighter things, sharing my hobbies in my off time. But a feeling rushes over me. As soon as it started, it was over. I'll have to travel back to where I had come from, a particular place with a way of living. My bedroom community has become a partial dining room table society of randos present during the day, where time moves at twice the speed.

While my spouse has returned to the office, I'm holding on tight. These afternoon walks are the best I've experienced.

The B-Movie Psychological Thriller Script

I sometimes experience flashbacks to the height of the pandemic. My experience was from a B-movie psychological thriller script that ran for weeks as the virus invaded our entire family. With my Dad on the phone, he struggled to breathe while battling a variant. My kids were all sick, and my spouse was in bed, coughing. I'm the only one who hadn't caught it yet, but I knew my time would eventually come.

And so the time came for my seven-week-old newborn. He developed a 103 fever, and the pediatrician ordered him to the emergency room.

It's midnight, and I'm driving with him to the hospital. When we arrive, we are both called to cut the line of the walking dead. He is tested for the virus by doctors in spacesuits. As they shoved the swab up his nose, his scream was like nothing I'd ever heard. They confirmed it was COVID-19. He's placed in care and given medication as I held him. Hours go by, we bond, and it's over. His fever breaks, and we exit the hospital as the sun rises.

As I lay sick in bed days later, the experience opened my eyes to what I'll learn through a pandemic. One, permanent change is in for all of us, and I'll tell my son what happened when he's older. Two, no matter the global origin, the inevitable sickness eventually arrives. Three, horrible news often comes during these times. I discovered my Dad's cancer diagnosis. But to keep the story in context, my loving Aunt had died in the hospital from coexisting conditions.

When I think deeply about what has transpired over these years, remote work poignantly surfaces what is happening in one's life. If there are tensions in a personal relationship, they are heightened. If one feels lonely, they will feel lonelier. Remoteness will demand a desire for socialization. The cracks in maintaining one's life are openly exposed in remote work. Everything is tested because there is no escape to an alternative world.

So, I felt all of it. I vowed to strengthen my marriage, submit myself to therapy, make new friends, and find social bonds. And as I grow older, it's not all velvet. Before the pandemic, I held on to a few friends who moved away, finding comfort in those I work with in person. I was soft to a few because I desired companionship. It just depended on the first impression. Now the office does not exist.

For me, remote work is an unforgiving forcing function of truth. In a remote setting, bonds are built into a new priority. The good news is I'd reach out, seek professional help, build better relations with coworkers, and improve my relationships.

In remote work, it's everything *and* the work. One thing is sure; this is the future. Looking out the window, I feel different folding the laundry on a remote call. I smile as I walk my children to school, building beautiful relationships with them. Dad and I often speak, guiding him through his cancer treatments. Nevertheless, I'm tortured by the dedicated work ethic to show up, instilled by my parents of yesteryear. It evaporated overnight as the next generation will consider this very practice as expected. Work is getting done well. I promise myself I am a professional, but deep down, there is unresolved guilt to unlearn. So, I write to unthink, placing my once heroic cape in a box labeled as "expired."

The World I Worked into No Longer Exists

As I leave the beer garden, I say goodbye to the team. I feel immense happiness with these people. These are the individuals I'll see tomorrow on a video call, as we've always had for the past few years. We will continue to run the business as needed. My employer made it an excellent place to work in such a difficult time. And these people are kind, but I left sad knowing remote work is a place that exists in my head. I am sure others feel the same, even those who left during the

Great Resignation.[2]

Walking back, I thought a bit further about remote work. There are positives. It is a beautiful practice allowing me to refocus on what is essential in my life—my spouse, children, parents, and the software craft. If I were in an office, the new side projects I've started would be impossible. I would not get to see my children grow or support my father in fighting his illness. So I've warmed up to "remote" in a way I hadn't suspected, being a former contrarian about the practice. My story is one of the millions who went through personal whiplash, but mine persists; I've committed. I am working in a new way, which is my way. Fewer trains, getting sick, less stress, wasted time, minimal gossip, and time focused on what makes my life whole.

Close to Atlantic Terminal, I noticed the clever slogan off Flatbush Ave. It read, "The world you were born into no longer exists."[3] I reflected on this time. "Yeah, it doesn't," I smiled. I boarded the train and went back to where I came from.

Walking home, I received a text message from an old coworker from my past. "Hey, was that you on Flatbush? I saw you! It's been years. How are you doing?" I laughed loudly and replied, "Yeah, doing alright, I guess. Remember when we worked together in our so-called office? Not a chance I'm going back."

I received another text days later. "Hey all, sorry to tell you this, but there has been an exposure to COVID-19 at our party."

As I placed another swab up my nose, a belief bubbled up, "The world I worked into no longer exists."

Eventually the world self-corrected to a hybrid model of being beautifully human. And from then on, I made remote time my working paradise—as Dad defeated his cancer.

My Goal Is to Ship

My Anthem to Decades of Software Development

IN APPROACHING TWENTY-FIVE YEARS of software engineering, I live within a growing loop of memorable projects,[1] recently delivering again. In the haze of its accomplishment, I asked myself the question, "What motivates me to develop?" I've learned the answer—to embrace the never-ending chase of shipping the next thing.

Smoothing These Rough Edges

Shipping has been my goal all along. My measured reactions to people's behaviors help me see things through. When I began, this exercise was uncomfortable, but now I'll adjust to find common ground, with humor, prioritizing what is to be solved.[2]

Smoothing my rough social edges has come over time. I've learned crafting software contains invisible friction points.[3] Attributes like conflicting motivations, priorities, shiny objects, lack of testing, and over-hyped clean code can slow development. I'm sure I missed so much more, but what is clear is how lethal these could be.

For what I can control, I've overcome these challenges by mellowing combative opinions for partnership. The give and take[4] is tough to do well, and I don't always get it right.

Once disagreements settle and we see eye to eye, I find pure joy when a project aligns and exceeds escape velocity. There is a familiar feeling of being "on." The result is I'll ship with a team,[5] sharing it with the world.

In Shipping, I Cannot Switch Off

Even with years of newfound tact, what frustrates me profoundly are projects that sit on shelves. I've learned to push them to a conclusion, negotiating their way out the door. If I sensed a project was permanently stuck, I'd leave it behind, despite others who chip away at it.

In shipping, I cannot switch it off. Being "on" means my mind keeps working no matter what mental hacks I deploy. My subconscious pops the stack and bubbles up, solving problems as I breathe.

In these years, I've learned how to handle these inconsistencies gracefully. For me, there isn't a 10 to 6. Thinking happens at odd times.[6] This unmanaged cycle causes strain on my relationships that matter, fatigued by continual moodiness.

In pursuing the solutions where my motivation peaks, nothing around me seems beautiful until this burden is taken care of. When it's "on," I push others away. When it's defeated, I'm happy for a moment, hugging my loved ones. Then I come crashing back down again, discovering danger at these peaks.

When I Burned Out

Sometimes in these long-tailed moments, mistakes happen. I sacrificed my family time. The decision depended on what it meant to ship. Failing to keep balance had consequences.

With years in software and a passion for completing things, my probability of burning out was certain. In the middle of my journey, I did. I endured physical pain for months, unable to take care of myself. Amid this broken mind, my love looked after me as I recovered—and to my parents,[7] who supported me through the trial.

It isn't a wonder that this pursuit is my addiction. I know that if I open the book *Hackers*,[8] in exactly the middle, it reads, "[Software] will consume all of your spare time, and even your vacation if you let it." For me, it had. As I exited the suffering, I learned a toolset, a support network, to mitigate future mental illness.

Being "on" is a thrilling rush, but I no longer prescribe heroics. I understand there are times I must push myself to ship. Triangulating this sacred trigger has happened a handful of times in my career, and lately, my acceptance has a higher bar.

Seeing it Through Is What I Value Most

For products I've participated in, a familiar observation has formed.[9] Projects break apart after they are delivered. A new process begins, measured by the magnitude of its intended impact. Finishing a new project will require months or years of searching for the next, then when I find it, there is time invested until it's released.

It's a Regular Wash Cycle

Preparing to deliver the next requires recharged personal momentum. I learned there is limited time, so when I ship, I must be diligent by setting a date, prioritizing its list, and cutting scope.[10] This process repeats with variable excitement in a never-ending cycle. My wisdom, as in naming familiar phenomena I'd discovered along this journey, makes it easier.

There is a growing list of products I've contributed to in these twenty-five years. Many have shut down, and a rare few engaged by millions. What is certain is that after I left, a new team rewrote these popular products.

Perhaps it's a regular wash cycle. I understand these releases inherently create a perpetual maintenance burden to serve a lack of engagement. For products that kept going, iterations of teams dissolved into the ether.[11] All is not lost. I'll export the learnings to the next project. It's threading this needle and seeing the next through is what I valued most.

Here Is to Another Twenty-Five

As I age, memories have formed from my first IRC login, traveling to offices, and recently joining a Webex,[12] Discord, or whatever they choose. I desire to surround myself with dedicated people who contribute solutions to a beautiful conveyer of intractable problems. Not only because we will ship together, but because I'll learn so much from their creative thinking.

It's clear what is important to me in all these years. To finish things I begin, my individualist pursuit of dedicated execution. *My goal is to ship.* That has never changed in this beautiful dream of crafting stuff in the sand.

Here is to another twenty-five.

Acknowledgments

THANKS TO THE MANY PEOPLE who contributed and provided feedback on these essays.

In no particular order, the following people made these works possible: Danny Preussler, Mariusz Skierski, Daniel Leonardis, Scott Yelich, Emily Goetz, Jesse Conover, Chris Longo, Shawn Carrillo, Konrad Stanik, Krista Abraham, Alex Hart, James Shvarts, Arhant Jain, Len Santoro, Ross Goodman, Andrea Gordon, Matt Funk, Justin "Max" Pugliese, Mike Mathis, Evan Leach, James Burns, Pratik Dhiman, Csaba Tóth, David Shen, Tom Lawless, Timothee Bourguignon, Taji Philip, Christina Hickey, Koysul Amin, Paul Gomez, Jim Higgins, Miroslav Shubernetskiy, Sang Lee, Kamal Shaham, Manoj Sharma, Khalid Richards, Anita Anderson, Colby Stone, Ramakrishnam Sagiraju, Suhyun Kim, John Revano, Joe Dimartino, Jonathan Chu, József Pallagi, Erik Cerone, Dhimiter Bozo, SM Azizul Hoque, John Pavley, Feazan Yaseen, Annette Lin, Manoj Thopcherneni, Uta Knablein, Matt Lagueras, Amaury Rodriguez, Parthasarathy Narayanan, Andre Perkins, Nikesh (Venkata) Kommuri, Diane DiLiello, Howard Chang, Michael Virga, Ajai Purakkandiyil, Hazem Saleh, and to everyone who had contributed feedback.

I also thank my kids, who kept me honest about how many hours I spent on the laptop, and my wife, Danielle, who helped edit many of these essays. She gave feedback during the nights when we were tired. And her "thumbs up" on each published post was key—I knew at least someone had read each as we pushed through the early years of making a family.

To Steve Guyer, a former co-worker with whom I reconnected during COVID, remembering "that one project." Many people came together years ago to make it happen, and for which we share a photo I keep close. Steve gave critical feedback on some of these essays, making me think deeply.

And to the many people on the Internet, in software, who scribe well. I'll call them async mentors. We've never spoken, but your writing has influenced me, which I shared with other engineers. Paul Graham, Emma Bostian, Michael Lopp, Rachel Kroll, Will Larson, Lara Hogan, Robert Martin, and Joel Spolsky [whom I heard speak at Viacom] are among them. Of course, there are others, and I thank you all.

A special thank you to Dad for helping me debate the writing *When a Software Engineer Exits the Team* during a summer party. His reflection on his fifty years of reporting to varied management made me realize that no one knows how to do the job, and at the same time, managers create the ultimate storied legends for others to tell.

Although only a three-minute read, *When a Software Engineer Exits the Team* is the most-read piece in this varied collection. It is a short but intense, expressive essay describing what all managers go through at a nascent point in their career, which, to my knowledge, has never been written from its point of view. You'll find it in Chapter 48.

Thanks to Dad, *When a Software Engineer Exits the Team* is my most treasured piece.

Endnotes

† To the Google Docs team, here are three product requests from a book author: (1) support word breaks; (2) allow expanded document size selection (such as 9" x 6"); (3) add odd and even page margin support. [Yes, I gave up on LaTeX.] Thank you.

‡ Sectional definitions were sourced using Google English dictionary provided by Oxford Languages. In the definition "engineer," this author added the term "software." Software discipline has yet to be associated with "engineer" in dictionaries. languages.oup.com/google-dictionary-en

1. Apps Doing Sh*t

1. Arcuri, Douglas. *To SlackHQ - A Request For An Experiment*. X. x.com/dougarcuri /status/1300474757935235072

2. Cancel This App Update, Dammit!

1. Arcuri, Douglas. *Five More Minutes*. DEV Community. dev.to/solidi/five-more-minutes-5b7d
2. ————. *Apps Doing Sh*t*. Medium. medium.com/@solidi/apps-doing-sh-t-f5ffa72140db
3. ————. *What is an Engineering Manager Anyway?* DEV Community. dev.to/solidi/what-is-an-engineering-manager-anyway-4and
4. Now happens with carrier smartphone updates! I played the "delay this update" game, then lost when I needed my phone. The OS aggressively updated at an inconvenient time, delaying meeting a family member at the airport. I could not contact a loved one while my phone was updating.
5. Harding, Scharon. *Sonos workers shed light on why the app update went so horribly*. Ars Technica. arstechnica.com/gadgets/2024/09/it-was-the-wrong-decision-employe es-discuss-sonos-rushed-app-debacle

3. SemVer is Dead. Long Live SemVer!

1. Agaram, Kartik. *The cargo cult of versioning*. Freewheeling Apps. akkartik.name/pos t/versioning
2. *Semantic Versioning 2.0.0*. semver.org

3. Arcuri, Douglas. *Cancel This App Update, Dammit!* DEV Community. dev.to/solidi/cancel-this-app-update-dammit-5f6j

4. Qu, Vivian. *Outdated vs. Complete.* Simulated Annealing. vivqu.com/blog/2022/09/25/outdated-apps

5. Arcuri, Douglas. *Latest Versioning 0.1.* latestver.org

6. Yang, Edward Z. *Thoughts about Spec-ulation (Rich Hickey).* EZYang Blog. blog.ezyang.com/2016/12/thoughts-about-spec-ulation-rich-hickey

4. Reply All Considered Harmful

1. Arcuri, Douglas. *What is an Engineering Manager Anyway?* DEV Community. dev.to/solidi/what-is-an-engineering-manager-anyway-4and

2. *Getting to Yes.* Wikipedia. en.wikipedia.org/wiki/Getting_to_Yes

5. Goodbye to Saccharine Feelings of Clean Code

1. Graham, Paul. *You start out feeling you have infinite time.* X. x.com/paulg/status/1619480259556179968

2. Guzman, Alyssa. *Not sparking joy? Marie Kondo has 'kind of given up' on tidying up after having three kids.* Daily Mail. dailymail.co.uk/news/article-11687263/Marie-Kondo-says-shes-kind-given-tidying-having-three-kids.html

3. Munroe, Randall. *Code Lifespan.* XKCD. xkcd.com/2730

6. Do Laundry During System Demos

1. Arcuri, Douglas. *Do Great at Working Remotely.* Medium. medium.com/@solidi/do-great-at-working-remotely-adbfe4b7452b

2. Melore, Chris. *Shower thoughts explained! Scientists figure out why we get great ideas while washing.* Study Finds. studyfinds.org/shower-thoughts-great-ideas

3. Arcuri, Douglas. *Technically Considered Writing.* DEV Community. dev.to/solidi/technically-considered-writing-3nng

4. —————. *How to Crush Your Next Team Demo.* DEV Community. dev.to/solidi/how-to-crush-your-next-team-demo-2bb5

7. Prefer Accommodating Over Accurate App Experiences

1. Arcuri, Douglas. *Read These 5 Passionate Engineering Book*s. Medium. medium.com/@solidi/read-these-5-passionate-software-engineering-books-this-holiday-6c6ad8fbd211

2. ————. *What is a Product Manager Anyway?* DEV Community. dev.to/solidi/what-is-a-product-manager-anyway-3pc4

3. ————. *Apps Doing Sh*t.* Medium. medium.com/@solidi/apps-doing-sh-t-f5ffa72140db

4. ————. *My Goal is to Ship.* Medium. medium.com/@solidi/my-goal-is-to-ship-c772f63c278d

8. Read these Five Passionate Software Engineering Books

1. *The Soul of a New Machine.* Amazon. amazon.com/Soul-New-Machine-Tracy-Kidder/dp/0316491705

2. *Mushroom Management.* Wikipedia. en.wikipedia.org/wiki/Mushroom_management

3. *Code: The Hidden Language of Computer Hardware and Software.* Wikipedia. en.wikipedia.org/wiki/Code:_The_Hidden_Language_of_Computer_Hardware_and_Software

4. *Code: The Hidden Language of Computer Hardware and Software.* Amazon. amazon.com/Code-Language-Computer-Hardware-Software-dp-0137909101/dp/0137909101

5. *The Mythical Man Month, 25th Edition.* Amazon. amazon.com/Mythical-Man-Month-Software-Engineering-Anniversary/dp/0201835959

6. *Conceptual Integrity.* WikiWikiWeb. wiki.c2.com/?ConceptualIntegrity

7. *No Silver Bullet.* Wikipedia. en.wikipedia.org/wiki/No_Silver_Bullet

8. *Hackers: Heroes of the Computer Revolution. (Book)* Wikipedia. en.wikipedia.org/wiki/Hackers:_Heroes_of_the_Computer_Revolution

9. *Computer Lib/Dream Machines.* Wikipedia. en.wikipedia.org/wiki/Computer_Lib/Dream_Machines

10. *Masters of Doom.* Amazon. amazon.com/Masters-Doom-Created-Transformed-Culture/dp/0812972155

11. *Doom (Video Game).* Wikipedia. en.wikipedia.org/wiki/Doom_(1993_video_game)

12. *Rating Guide.* Entertainment Software Rating Board. esrb.org/ratings-guide

13. *The Cathedral and the Bazaar (Book).* Wikipedia. en.wikipedia.org/wiki/The_Cathedral_and_the_Bazaar

14. *Open Source (Practice).* Wikipedia. en.wikipedia.org/wiki/Open_source

15. *Hackers & Painters: Big Ideas from the Computer Age.* Amazon. amazon.com/Hackers-Painters-Big-Ideas-Computer/dp/1449389554

16. *Peopleware: Productive Projects and Teams (3rd Edition)*. Amazon. amazon.com/Peopleware-Productive-Projects-Teams-3rd/dp/0321934113

9. Do Great at Working Remotely

1. Arcuri, Douglas. *The Manager Stew*. HackerNoon. medium.com/hackernoon/the-manager-stew-dd59cd653728
2. —————. *Be Amazing in Your New Engineering Role*. gitconnected. medium.com/gitconnected/be-amazing-in-your-new-engineering-role-2fe005cf3e0
3. After time has passed, the idea to keep video on is contested.
4. Moore, Dan. *Cultivate the Skill of Undivided Attention, or "Deep Work."* Letters to a New Developer. letterstoanewdeveloper.com/2019/12/19/cultivate-the-skill-of-undivided-attention-or-deep-work
5. *Free online multiplayer drawing and guessing pictionary game.* skribbl.io
6. Arcuri. Douglas. *CQ: Personal Mastery Through Hobbies*. Medium. medium.com/@solidi/cq-personal-mastery-through-hobbies-f25aab2e49ad
7. —————. *The World I Worked into No Longer Exists*. Medium. medium.com/@solidi/the-world-i-worked-into-no-longer-exists-732659963058
8. —————. *Reply All Considered Harmful*. Medium. medium.com/@solidi/reply-all-considered-harmful-f895beb5eabc
9. —————. *The One About Blogging*. Medium. medium.com/@solidi/the-one-about-blogging-cd9e65a2055b

10. How to Crush Your Next Team Demo

1. McKenney, Paul E. *How to Appease the Demo Gods*. Raindrop. www2.rdrop.com/~paulmck/DemoGods/

11. Be a Rock Star at Pull Requests

1. Arcuri, Douglas. *No Description Provided*. HackerNoon. medium.com/hackernoon/no-description-provided-8d9e0f3a3abb
2. *Code Health: Respectful Reviews == Useful Reviews*. Google Testing Blog. testing.googleblog.com/2019/11/code-health-respectful-reviews-useful.html
3. Spolsky, Joel. *The Joel Test: 12 Steps to Better Code*. Joel on Software. joelonsoftware.com/2000/08/09/the-joel-test-12-steps-to-better-code

12. The Joy of Collecting Timeless Engineering Posts

1. *When Bad Things Happen to Good Characters*. HCI Bibliography: Human-Computer Interaction Resources. hcibib.org/multilingual/badchars.htm

2. Arcuri, Douglas. *Learning Notes*. Github. github.com/solidi/learning-notes/blob/main/mentoring/shared-links.md

3. *Code page*. Wikipedia. en.wikipedia.org/wiki/Code_page

13. Ten Self-Care Tips for a Great Vacation

1. Arcuri, Douglas. *Five More Minutes*. Dev Community. dev.to/solidi/five-more-minutes-5b7d

2. ─────. *What is an Engineering Manager Anyway?* DEV Community. dev.to/solidi/what-is-an-engineering-manager-anyway-4and

3. ─────. *My Goal is to Ship*. Medium. medium.com/@solidi/my-goal-is-to-ship-c772f63c278d

4. ─────. *What is a Project Manager?* DEV Community. dev.to/solidi/what-is-a-project-manager-anyway-fbb

5. ─────. *Reply All Considered Harmful*. Medium. medium.com/@solidi/reply-all-considered-harmful-f895beb5eabc

6. ─────. *Do You Have a Forever Project?* DEV Community. dev.to/solidi/do-you-have-a-forever-project-kpk

7. ─────. *What is a Product Manager Anyway?* DEV Community. dev.to/solidi/what-is-a-product-manager-anyway-3pc4

8. ─────. In Software, *Philosophy Is Delegation*. Level Up Coding. levelup.gitconnected.com/in-software-philosophy-is-delegation-c786dd3a16cf

9. ─────. *The Manager Stew*. Medium. medium.com/hackernoon/the-manager-stew-dd59cd653728

14. The Not So Small Things of Developing Software

1. Arcuri, Douglas. *Rediscovering the .plan File*. DEV Community. dev.to/solidi/rediscovering-the-plan-file-4k1i

2. *LICECap*. Cockos Co. cockos.com/licecap

3. Arcuri, Douglas. *Short Circuiting Fantastical Debugging*. DEV Community. dev.to/solidi/short-circuiting-fantastical-debugging-ig3

4. ─────. *The Manager Stew*. HackerNoon. medium.com/hackernoon/the-manager-stew-dd59cd653728

5. Arcuri, Douglas. *Read These 5 Passionate Software Engineering Books*. Medium. medium.com/@solidi/read-these-5-passionate-software-engineering-books-this-holid ay-6c6ad8fbd211

6. —————. *Software is Unlike Construction*. HackerNoon. medium. com/hackernoon/software-is-unlike-construction-c0284ee4b723

7. Slimmon, Dan. *Do-nothing scripting: the key to gradual automation*. Scientific Incident Response. blog.danslimmon.com/2019/07/15/do-nothing-scripting-the-key-to-gradual-automation

8. Tietz-Sokolsaya, Nicole. *Names should be cute, not descriptive*. Technically a Blog. ntietz.com/blog/name-your-projects-cutesy-things

9. Arcuri, Douglas. *The Next Fantastic Software Project Code Name*. DEV Community. dev.to/solidi/the-next-fantastic-software-project-code-name-bbd

10. House, Cory. *Group by File Type vs Grouping by Concern Meme*. X. x.com/housecor/status/1603428432091701252

11. Arcuri, Douglas. *8 Observations on Test Driven Development*. freeCodeCamp. medium.com/free-code-camp/8-observations-on-test-driven-development-a9b5144f 868

12. Willisons, Simon. *PAGNIs: Probably Are Gonna Need Its*. Simon Willison's Weblog. simonwillison.net/2021/Jul/1/pagnis

13. Arcuri, Douglas. *Find Career Freedom with a Daily Code Workout*. DEV Community. dev.to/solidi/find-career-freedom-with-a-daily-code-workout-18e9

14. —————. *What is a Software Engineer Anyway?* DEV Community. dev.to/solidi/what-is-a-software-engineer-anyway-3fb2

15. —————. *Do Great at Remotely Working*. Medium. medium.com/ @solidi/do-great-at-working-remotely-adbfe4b7452b

16. —————. *The World I Worked into No Longer Exists*. Medium. medium.com/@solidi/the-world-i-worked-into-no-longer-exists-732659963058

17. —————. *My Goal is to Ship*. *Medium*. medium.com/@solidi/my-goal-is-to-ship-c772f63c278d

15. Do You Have a Forever Project?

1. Arcuri, Douglas. *Tell Me Your Childhood Without Telling Me Your Childhood*. X. x.com/dougarcuri/status/1516025802957242377

2. —————. *The One About Blogging*. Medium. medium.com/@solidi/ the-one-about-blogging-cd9e65a2055b

3. Arcuri, Douglas. *Building a Popular Half-Life Mod During the Rise of Counter-Strike.* SUPERJUMP Magazine. medium.com/super-jump/building-a-popular-half-life-mod-during-the-rise-of-counter-strike-fec6a5b9fd8f

4. ————. *What is a Software Engineer Anyway?* DEV Community. dev.to/solidi/what-is-a-software-engineer-anyway-3fb2

5. ————. *CQ: Personal Mastery Through Hobbies.* Medium. medium.com /@solidi/cq-personal-mastery-through-hobbies-f25aab2e49ad

6. ————. *My Goal is to Ship.* Medium. medium.com/@solidi/my-goal-is-to-ship-c772f63c278d

7. Ibid.

8. GunshipmarkII. *Presume I am Dead.* X. x.com/GunshipMarkII/status/15065636 31189745664

16. Video Gaming Concepts for the Uninitiated

1. Arcuri, Douglas. *Building a Popular Half-Life Mod During the Rise of Counter-Strike.* SUPERJUMP. medium.com/super-jump/building-a-popular-half-life-mod-during-the-rise-of-counter-strike-fec6a5b9fd8f

2. Grip, Thomas. *The Problem With Repetition.* Frictional Games. frictionalgames .com/2011-11-the-problem-of-repetition/

3. Arcuri, Douglas. *Read These 5 Passionate Software Engineering Books.* Medium. medium.com/@solidi/read-these-5-passionate-software-engineering-books-this-holid ay-6c6ad8fbd211

4. ————. *Five More Minutes.* Dev Community. dev.to/solidi/five-more-minutes-5b7d

5. Players testing their boundaries within a virtual environment is an introductory theme, discussed by Todd Howard.

17. Touch Typing Feels Good but Is It for Me?

1. Donelavicius, *Mantas Touch Typing: how long does it take to reach 100 WPM?* Medium. medium.com/@mantasd/touch-typing-how-long-does-it-take-to-reach-100 -wpm-129ba855d038

2. Sorrel, Charlie. *Touch Typing Is No Faster Than Pecking With A Few Fingers. Impact.* fastcompany.com/3056678/touch-typing-is-no-faster-than-pecking-with-a-few-fingers

18. Deception: Degenerate A/B Testing

1. Arcuri, Douglas. *What is a Product Manager Anyway?* DEV Community. dev.to/solidi/what-is-a-product-manager-anyway-3pc4
2. Gallo, Amy. *A Refresher on A/B Testing.* Harvard Business Review. hbr.org/2017/06/a-refresher-on-ab-testing
3. Constine, Josh. *The Morality Of A/B Testing.* TechCrunch. techcrunch.com/2014/06/29/ethics-in-a-data-driven-world
4. Benbunan-Fich, Raquel. *The ethics of online research with unsuspecting users: From A/B testing to C/D experimentation.* Research Ethics. journals.sagepub.com/doi/pdf/10.1177/1747016116680664

19. The Decision Hypothesis

In MM-M, Chapter 10: The Documentary Hypothesis is focused on the manager actor. Creative liberty was taken to refocus the conversation on the software team and their documents by combining thoughts on Chapter 6: Passing The Word and Chapter 15: The Other Face.

Fred's "The Documentary Hypothesis" discusses documents such as budget, organization charts, and schedule. For some software engineering teams, these documents are considered secret. However, these documents are data and decisions that control the variable inputs of all software projects—time, scope, developers, and quality.

> [From Chapter 3: The Surgical Team] . . . *Mills's concept in transformation of programming "from private art to public practice" and making all the computer runs visible to all team members and identifying all programs and data as team property, not private property.*

Since software development teams are under constraint, there are parallels drawn to code consistency, complexity, and why the organization constructed things the way they did. We should question why certain documents that drive software projects are hidden; instead, make them open so debate can flourish. However, this was not the goal of my contemplation. Thanks to Hazem Saleh [medium.com/u/ 8a8e3247b67] for pointing this out and providing summation of books which are written on this fascinating topic.

1. *Mythical Man-Month, The: Essays on Software Engineering, Anniversary Edition, 2nd edition*. Pearson. pearson.com/us/higher-education/program/Brooks-Mythical-Man-Month-The-Essays-on-Software-Engineering-Anniversary-Edition-2nd-Edition/PGM172844.html

2. Arcuri, Douglas. *Software is Unlike Construction*. HackerNoon. medium.com/hackernoon/software-is-unlike-construction-c0284ee4b723

3. Kazlou, Aliaksandr. *Every project should have a decisions making file*. Practice of Programming. https://web.archive.org/web/20200624143815/https://akazlou.com/posts-output/2015-11-09-every-project-should-have-decisions/

4. *Aliaksandr Kazlou*. Medium. medium.com/u/93bb84d49d5c

5. Graziotin, Daniel, Fagerholm, Fabian, Wang, Xiaofeng, and Abrahamsson, Pekka. *On the Unhappiness of Software Developers*. arxiv.org/pdf/1703.04993.pdf

6. Thanks to James Shvarts [medium.com/u/4e5a0d0c55e] for the inspiration of the write up. One thing that will never fade is overpriced sandwich shops.

20. Observations on the Culture of Test-Driven Development

1. *Extreme Programming Explained: Embrace Change, 2nd edition*. Pearson. pearson.com/us/higher-education/program/Beck-Extreme-Programming-Explained-Embrace-Change-2nd-Edition/PGM155384.html

2. *Jim Coplien and Bob Martin Debate TDD*. YouTube. youtu.be/KtHQGs3 zFAM

3. Arcuri, Douglas. *What is a Software Engineer Anyway?* DEV Community. dev.to/solidi/what-is-a-software-engineer-anyway-3fb2

4. *Companies, Teams, Coaches & Software Crafters*. WeDoTDD. wedotdd.com

5. Williams, Laurie, Kudrjavets, Gunnar, and Nagappan, Nachiappan. *On the Effectiveness of Unit Test Automation at Microsoft*. Microsoft Corporation. https://web.archive.org/web/20240422072206/https://collaboration.csc.ncsu.edu/laurie/Papers/Unit_testing_cameraReady.pdfhttps://web.archive.org/web/20240422072206/https://collaboration.csc.ncsu.edu/laurie/Papers/Unit_testing_cameraReady.pdf

6. Maximilien, E.M.; Williams, L. *Assessing test-driven development at IBM*. IEEE. ieeexplore.ieee.org/document/1201238

7. Mäkinen, Simo, *Effects of Test-Driven Development : A Comparative Analysis of Empirical Studies*. University of Helsinki. helda.helsinki.fi//bitstream/handle/10138/42741/2014_01_swqd_author_version.pdf

8. *Jim Coplien and Bob Martin,* op. cit.

9. Beck, Kent. *Test-Driven Development: By Example.* O'Reilly. oreilly.com/library/view/test-driven-development/0321146530/

10. MacIver, David R. *Welcome to Hypothesis!* hypothesis.readthedocs.io/en/latest

11. *Real world mutation testing.* pitest.org

12. Dominus, Marcus. *Testing for divisibility by 19.* The Universe of Disco. blog.plover.com/math/divisibility-by-19.html

13. Martin, Robert. *The Transformation Priority Premise.* The Clean Code Blog. 8thlight.com/blog/uncle-bob/2013/05/27/TheTransformationPriorityPremise.html

14. Ibid.

15. Asay, Matt. *Test-driven development may be more talked about than practiced.* Tech Republic. www.techrepublic.com/article/test-driven-development-talked

16. Meszaros, Gerard. *XUnit Test Patterns.* xunitpatterns.com

17. *Effective Unit Testing.* Manning. manning.com/books/effective-unit-testing

18. The inspiration for this essay was from Danny Preussler. As this author re-explores TDD, Danny has started running comprehensive Android TDD workshops. Check out his recent deck at speakerdeck.com/dpreussler/tdd-on-android-mobos-2018

19. Martin, Robert. *The Transformation Priority Premise.* The Clean Code Blog blog.cleancoder.com/uncle-bob/2013/05/27/TheTransformationPriorityPremise.html

21. No Description Provided

1. Harari, Yuval, *Sapiens: A Brief History of Humankind.* Amazon. amazon.com/Sapiens- Humankind-Yuval-Noah-Harari/dp/0062316095

2. Arcuri, Douglas. *Software is Unlike Construction.* HackerNoon. medium.com/hackernoon/software-is-unlike-construction-c0284ee4b723

3. *About pull requests,* GitHub Docs. help.github.com/articles/about-pull-requests

4. López-Mañas, Enrique. *A Comprehensive Introduction to Perform an Efficient Android Code Review.* Medium. medium.com/google-developer-experts/a-comprehensive-introduction-to-perform-an-efficient-android-code-review-75975ccaa20a

5. *Issue and Pull Request templates.* Github Blog. github.com/blog/2111-issue-and-pull-request-templates

6. Wharton, Jake. *Surfacing Hidden Change to Pull Requests.* Square Corner Blog. medium.com/square-corner-blog/surfacing-hidden-change-to-pull-requests-6a371266e479

7. Arcuri, Douglas. *PULL-REQUEST-TEMPLATE.md*. GitHub Gist. gist.github
.com/solidi/6be9d733b40fd1b40d5f2d7c745d731b

8. Geerling, Jeff. *Why I close PRs (OSS project maintainer notes)*. jeffgeerling.com/
blog/2016/why-i-close-prs-oss-project-maintainer-notes

9. J. David. *Git Commit Messages: 50/72 Formatting*. StackOverflow. stackoverflow
.com/questions/2290016/git-commit-messages-50-72-formatting

10. *The Magical Number Seven, Plus or Minus Two*. Wikipedia. en.wikipedia.org
/wiki/The_Magical_Number_Seven,_Plus_or_Minus_Two

11. Atwood, Jeff. *There are two hard things in computer science*. X. x.com/coding
horror/status/506010907021828096

12. Martin, Robert. *Uncle Bob Consulting LLC*. sites.google.com/site/unclebob
consultingllc

13. Martin, Robert. *The Programmer's Oath*. Clean Coder Blog. blog.cleancoder.
com/uncle-bob/2015/11/18/TheProgrammersOath.html

14. Arcuri, Douglas. *What is a Software Engineer Anyway?* DEV Community.
dev.to/solidi/what-is-a-software-engineer-anyway-3fb2

15. Preussler, Danny. *Find the right place*. Medium. medium.com/hackernoon/
find-the-right-place-1e3c9f0496a2

22. The Springboard Pattern

1. Arcuri, Douglas. *How to Crush Your Next Team Demo*. DEV Community.
dev.to/solidi/how-to-crush-your-next-team-demo-2bb5

2. —————. *What is a Product Manager Anyway?* DEV Community.
dev.to/solidi/what-is-a-product-manager-anyway-3pc4

3. *Google Play Instant*. Android Developer. developer.android.com/topic/google-
play-instant

4. Fowler, Martin. *Yagni*. martinFowler.com. martinfowler.com/bliki/Yagni.html

23. The Next Fantastic Software Project Code Name

Note: My mobile devices are named after moons of the Solar System. My favorite phone was Phobos, my Samsung Note 7. After I bought the device, the phone was banned from airplane flights due to its explosive internal battery. My replacement was called Demios, a smaller version of its cousin, the LG V20. Because of these names, I remembered them after they were long gone.

I wrote this essay on my machines—Tabulator and Hippocamp. Thanks to the podcast *Reconcilable Differences* for the inspiration to get this concept across the finish line. Their episode, #159: The Narrow Priesthood, [https://relay.fm/rd/159] inspired me. And the book, *Project Hail Mary* [https://andyweirauthor.com/books/project-hail-mary] by Andy Weir, reminded me that references to project names are crucial in human endeavors.

1. Libes, D. *Choosing a Name for Your Computer*. RFC 1178. datatracker.ietf.org/doc/html/rfc1178

2. Bias, Randy. *The History of Pets vs Cattle and How to Use the Analogy Properly*. cloudscaling. cloudscaling.com/blog/cloud-computing/the-history-of-pets-vs-cattle

3. *Nicktoons*. IMDB. imdb.com/title/tt5006214/

4. *Olmec*. Nickipedia. nickelodeon.fandom.com/wiki/Olmec

5. Dalek Warlord. *Every Dalek Exterminate From Doctor Who*. YouTube. youtu.be/RhEUBgu9j5Y

6. *BIF file creation using the Roku BIF tool*. Roku Developer. developer.roku.com/docs/developer-program/media-playback/trick-mode/bif-file-creation.md

7. Shubernetskiy, Miroslav. *Importanize*. GitHub. github.com/miki725/importanize

8. Aghion, Joey. *Why Projects Need Code Names*. Artsy Engineering Blog. artsy.github.io/blog/2019/05/10/why-projects-need-codenames

9. Hudlow, Gandalf. *You need Software Developers to believe in your project*. International Institute of Software Management. iism.org/article/you-need-software-developers-to-believe-in-your-project-45

24. The One About Blogging

1 A special thank you to Aida Issayeva on naming the method as "Blogging as a System." x.com/Aida_Isay/status/1486018778001555457

25. Deconstructing My Reading Habits

1. Arcuri, Douglas. *The One About Blogging*. Medium. medium.com/@solidi/the-one-about-blogging-cd9e65a2055b

2. ————. *The One About Software Engineering Interviewing*. The Startup.medium.com/swlh/the-one-about-software-engineering-interviewing-6f126e3a3171

3. Heaton, Robert. *How to read*. robertheaton.com/2018/06/25/how-to-read

4. Arcuri, Douglas. *CQ: Personal Mastery Through Hobbies*. Medium. medium.com/@solidi/cq-personal-mastery-through-hobbies-f25aab2e49ad

5. ——————. *The Meta Skills of a Software Engineer.* HackerNoon. medium.com/hackernoon/meta-skills-of-a-software-engineer-bed411f6685e

6. Kleppmann, Martin. *Writing a book: is it worth it?* martin.kleppmann.com/2020/09/29/is-book-writing-worth-it.html

7. *How to Read Fewer Books.* The School of Life. theschooloflife.com/thebookoflife/how-to-read-fewer-books

8. Frost, Brad. *Creative Exhaust.* My Name Is Brad Frost. bradfrost.com/blog/post/creative-exhaust

26. Rediscovering the .plan File

1. Arcuri, Douglas. *Building a Popular Half-Life Mod During the Rise of Counter-Strike.* SUPERJUMP Magazine. medium.com/super-jump/building-a-popular-half-life-mod-during-the-rise-of-counter-strike-fec6a5b9fd8f

2. *The Carmack Plan.* Robbie's Garage. garbagecollected.org/2017/10/24/the-carmack-plan

3. Arcuri, Douglas. *Masters of Doom Quote Summary.* Github. github.com/solidi/learning-notes/blob/main/books/masters-of-doom.md

4. Sanglard, Fabian. *Game Engine Black Book DOOM.* Fabian Sanglard's Website. fabiensanglard.net/gebbdoom

5. Arcuri, Douglas. *Learnings.md.* GitHub. github.com/solidi/hl-mods/blob/main/workspace/plan/learnings.md

6. Denic, Marko. *Google like a pro.* Marko. markodenic.com/use-google-like-a-pro

27. Technically Considered Writing

1. Shapiro, Julian, *Writing Better.* julian.com/guide/write/intro

2. Graham, Paul. *How to Write Usefully.* paulgraham.com/useful.html

3. Smith, Steph. *Writing is Thinking: Learning to Write with Confidence.* Steph | Smith. blog.stephsmith.io/learning-to-write-with-confidence

4. Faliq, Adam. *How to Write Well: 4 Steps to Improve Your Writing.* adamfaliq.wordpress.com/2020/10/28/write-well

5. Nath, Preetam. *Why You Should Write.* preetamnath.com/blog/why-you-should-write

6. *The Surprising Reason Writing Remains Essential in an AI-Driven World.* The Knowledge Project. fs.blog/why-write

7. Birming, Robert. *Just Write.* robert.bearblog.dev/just-write

8. Bukowski, Charles. *So you want to be a writer?* Poets.org. poets.org/poem/so-you-want-be-writer

28. How to Place on the Front Page of Hacker News

1. Arcuri, Douglas. *My Goal is to Ship.* Medium. medium.com/@solidi/my-goal-is-to-ship-c772f63c278d

2. *Touch-typing feels good but isn't for me (medium.freecodecamp.org).* Hacker News Rank. hnrankings.info/19672434

3. Arcuri, Douglas. *Touch Typing Feels Good But Isn't For Me.* freeCodeCamp. medium.freecodecamp.org/touch-typing-feels-good-but-isnt-for-me-2cfbafee2074

4. ————. *Touch Typing Feels Good But Isn't For Me.* Hacker News Thread. news.ycombinator.com/item?id=19672434

5. ————. *8 Observations on Test Driven Development.* freeCodeCamp. medium.com/free-code-camp/8-observations-on-test-driven-development-a9b5144f868

6. ————. *8 Observations on Test Driven Development.* Hacker News Thread. news.ycombinator.com/item?id=17756835

7. *Observations on Test Driven Development (medium.freecodecamp.org).* Hacker News Rank. hnrankings.info/17756835

8. Arcuri, Douglas. *In Software, When an Engineer Exits the Team.* Better Programming. medium.com/@solidi/in-software-when-an-engineer-exits-the-team-1e550303cff8

9. ————. *In Software, When an Engineer Exits the Team.* Hacker News Thread. news.ycombinator.com/item?id=28692059

10. ————. *In Software, When an Engineer Exits the Team.* Hacker News Rank. hnrankings.info/28692059

11. ————. *CQ: Personal Mastery Through Hobbies.* Medium. medium.com/@solidi/cq-personal-mastery-through-hobbies-f25aab2e49ad

12. ————. *Ham Radio – CQ: Personal Mastery Through Hobbies.* Hacker News Thread. news.ycombinator.com/item?id=18635362

13. ————. *CQ: Personal Mastery Through Hobbies.* Hacker News Rank. hnrankings.info/18635362

14. ————. *Writing Repo.* GitHub. github.com/solidi/writing

15. Issayeva, Aida. X Profile. x.com/Aida_Isay

16. Issayeva, Aida. *More on Writing.* X. x.com/Aida_Isay/status/1486018778001555457

17. *The Red Pen Process: How to Edit Your Content.* Palm Beach Content. web.archive.org/web/20220415000000*/palmbeachcontentco.com/blog/2017/9/7/how-to-edit-your-content

29. What is a Software Engineer Anyway?

1. Arcuri, Douglas. *The Many Senses of Software Engineering.* Level Up Coding. levelup.gitconnected.com/the-many-senses-of-software-engineering-aba9f289498c

2. ————. *In Software: Philosophy is Delegation.* Medium. medium.com /@solidi/in-software-philosophy-is-delegation-c786dd3a16cf

3. *Mise en Place.* Wikipedia. en.wikipedia.org/wiki/Mise_en_place

4. *Tools for better thinking.* Untools. untools.co

5. Arcuri, Douglas. *Software is Unlike Construction.* HackerNoon. medium.com /hackernoon/software-is-unlike-construction-c0284ee4b723

6. ————. *The Meta Skills of a Software Engineer.* HackerNoon. medium.com/hackernoon/meta-skills-of-a-software-engineer-bed411f6685e

7. ————. *How to Crush Your Next Team Demo.* DEV Community. dev.to/solidi/how-to-crush-your-next-team-demo-2bb5

8. ————. *What is a Tech Lead Anyway?* DEV Community. dev.to /solidi/what-is-a-tech-lead-anyway-483p

30. What is a Software Development Engineer in Test Anyway?

1. Arcuri, Douglas. *What is a Product Manager Anyway?* DEV Community. dev.to/solidi/what-is-a-product-manager-anyway-3pc4

2. ————. *What is a Software Engineer Anyway?* DEV Community. dev.to/solidi/what-is-a-software-engineer-anyway-3fb2

3. *Mutation Testing.* Google Testing Blog. testing.googleblog.com/2021/04/mutation-testing.html

4. Arcuri, Douglas. *On Kotlin: A Unit Test Conversion Guide.* Pro Android Dev. proandroiddev.com/on-kotlin-a-unit-test-conversion-guide-71e0597bb45d

5. Karmakar, Dipto. *A Practical Guide to Load Testing.* freeCodeCamp. freecodecamp.org/news/practical-guide-to-load-testing

6. *Test Flakiness - One of the main challenges of automated testing.* Google Testing Blog. testing.googleblog.com/2020/12/test-flakiness-one-of-main-challenges.html

7. Fowler, Martin. *The Practical Test Pyramid.* martinfowler.com/articles/practical-test-pyramid.html

8. Dodds, Kent C. *Write tests. Not too many. Mostly integration.* kentcdodds.com/blog/write-tests

31. What is a Tech Lead Anyway?

1. *Universal Viewer*. universalviewer.io
2. Santo, Jerod. *How to build a generative engineering culture.* changelog.com/posts/how-to-build-a-generative-engineering-culture
3. *TechLead.* YouTube Channel. youtube.com/channel/UC4xKdmAXFh4ACyhpiQ_3qBw

32. What is a Staff Engineer Anyway?

1. Lopp, Michael. *The single most productive engineer: Free Electron*. Rands in Repose. randsinrepose.com/archives/free-electron
2. Arcuri, Douglas. *The Many Senses of Software Engineering*. Level Up Coding. levelup.gitconnected.com/the-many-senses-of-software-engineering-aba9f289498c
3. —————. *What is a Product Manager Anyway?* DEV Community. dev.to/solidi/what-is-a-product-manager-anyway-3pc4
4. —————. *What is a Principal Engineer Anyway?* DEV Community. dev.to/solidi/what-is-a-principal-engineer-anyway-55n0
5. —————. *What is a Tech Lead Anyway?* DEV Community. dev.to/solidi/what-is-a-tech-lead-anyway-483p

33. What is a Principal Engineer Anyway?

1. Arcuri, Douglas. *In Software: Philosophy Is Delegation*. Medium. medium.com/@solidi/in-software-philosophy-is-delegation-c786dd3a16cf
2. —————. *How to Crush Your Next Team Demo*. DEV Community. dev.to/solidi/how-to-crush-your-next-team-demo-2bb5
3. —————. *Be Amazing in Your New Engineering Role*. DEV Community. dev.to/solidi/be-amazing-in-your-new-engineering-role-1klc
4. —————. *What is a Software Engineer Anyway?* DEV Community. dev.to/solidi/what-is-a-software-engineer-anyway-3fb2

34. What is a Project Manager Anyway?

1. Arcuri, Douglas. *What is a Product Manager Anyway?* DEV Community. dev.to/solidi/what-is-a-product-manager-anyway-3pc4
2. Fisher-Pricing was a term I learned from Steve Guyer, a TPM.

3. Arcuri, Douglas. *The Springboard Pattern*. HackerNoon. medium.com/hacker noon/the-springboard-pattern-340e00379404

4. *Project Management Triangle*. Wikipedia. en.wikipedia.org/wiki/Project_manage ment_triangle

5. Arcuri, Douglas. *What is an Engineering Manager Anyway?* DEV Community. dev.to/solidi/what-is-an-engineering-manager-anyway-4and

6. *Parkinson's Law*. Wikipedia. en.wikipedia.org/wiki/Parkinson%27s_law

7. *Po (Lateral Thinking)*. Wikipedia. en.wikipedia.org/wiki/Po_(lateral_thinking)

35. What is a Product Manager Anyway?

1. Arcuri, Douglas. *What is a Software Engineer Anyway?* DEV Community. dev.to/solidi/what-is-a-software-engineer-anyway-3fb2

2. As discussed at length by Patton, Jeff. X Profile. x.com/jeffpatton

3. Arcuri, Douglas. *The Springboard Pattern*. HackerNoon. medium.com/hacker noon/the-springboard-pattern-340e00379404

4. Recognized by Cagan, Marty. X Profile. x.com/cagan

36. What is an Engineering Manager Anyway?

1. Hogan, Lara. *Resilient Management*. resilient-management.com

2. Arcuri, Douglas. *What is a Tech Lead Anyway?* DEV Community. dev.to/solidi/what-is-a-tech-lead-anyway-483p

3. Beck, Kent. *Make It Work Make It Right Make It Fast*. WikiWikiWeb. wiki.c2.com/?MakeItWorkMakeItRightMakeItFast

4. Arcuri, Douglas. *The Manager Stew*. HackerNoon. medium.com/hackernoon/the-manager-stew-dd59cd653728

5. —————. *How to Crush Your Next Team Demo*. DEV Community. dev.to/solidi/how-to-crush-your-next-team-demo-2bb5

6. Curry, Jeff. *A new manager's guide to growing into your role*. Atlassian Work Life Blog. atlassian.com/blog/leadership/new-manager-tips

37. How to Organize Your Thoughts on the Whiteboard

1. Cook, John. *Organizational Skills Beat Algorithmic Wizardry*. Hacker News Thread. news.ycombinator.com/item?id=16703553

2. —————. *The most important skill in software development*. John D. Cook Consulting. johndcook.com/blog/2015/06/18/most-important-skill-in-software

3. Hague, James. *Organizational Skills Beat Algorithmic Wizardry*. Programming in the twenty-first century. prog21.dadgum.com/177.html

4. Arcuri, Douglas. *Hurry Up Culture*. X. x.com/dougarcuri/status/97463178345 4117889

5. ————. *No Description Provided*. HackerNoon. hackernoon.com/no-description-provided-8d9e0f3a3abb

6. ————. *The Decision Hypothesis*. HackerNoon. hackernoon.com/the-decision-hypothesis-aa512e0113

38. Find Career Freedom with a Daily Code Workout

1. Arcuri, Douglas. *What is a Software Engineer Anyway?* DEV Community. dev.to/solidi/what-is-a-software-engineer-anyway-3fb2

2. ————. *Interview Well for Your Next Incredible Engineering Role*. Level Up Coding. levelup.gitconnected.com/interview-well-for-your-next-incredible-engineering-role-a5513e6596ae

3. Thomas, Dave. *CodeKata*. https://web.archive.org/web/20240428075425/http://codekata.com/

4. *Rubber Duck Debugging*. Wikipedia. en.wikipedia.org/wiki/Rubber_duck_debugging

5. Sharma, Uma and Pagano, Alyssa. *How eating spicy food affects your brain and body*. Business Insider. businessinsider.com/eating-spicy-food-capsaicin-hot-pepper-side-effects-2017-10

6. *Fibonacci Sequence*. Math is Fun. mathsisfun.com/numbers/fibonacci-sequence.html

7. *Big O Notation*. Wikipedia. en.wikipedia.org/wiki/Big_O_notation

8. *Dijkstra's Algorithm*. Wikipedia. en.wikipedia.org/wiki/Dijkstra%27s_algorithm

9. *A Star Search Algorithm*. Wikipedia. en.wikipedia.org/wiki/A*_search_ algorithm

10. Laakmann McDowell, Gayle. *Cracking the Code Interview*. CareerCup. crackingthecodinginterview.com

11. Arcuri, Douglas. *How to Organize Your Thoughts on the Whiteboard and Crush Your Technical Interview*. freeCodeCamp. medium.com/free-code-camp/how-to-organize-your-thoughts-on-the-whiteboard-and-crush-your-technical-interview-b668 de4e6941

12. Young, Scott H. *Variability, Not Repetition, is the Key to Mastery*. scotthyoung.com/blog/2022/10/26/variable-mastery

13. Arcuri, Douglas. *What is a Tech Lead Anyway?* DEV Community. dev.to/solidi/what-is-a-tech-lead-anyway-483p

39. The One About Software Engineering Interviewing

1. Arcuri, Douglas. *How to Organize Your Thoughts on the Whiteboard and Crush Your Technical Interview.* freeCodeCamp. medium.com/free-code-camp/how-to-organize-your-thoughts-on-the-whiteboard-and-crush-your-technical-interview-b668 de4e6941

2. ———. *What is a Software Engineer Anyway?* DEV Community. dev.to/solidi/what-is-a-software-engineer-anyway-3fb2

3. ———. *The Many Senses of Software Engineering.* Level Up Coding. levelup.gitconnected.com/the-many-senses-of-software-engineering-aba9f289498c

40. Interview Well for Your Next Incredible Engineering Role

1. Arcuri, Douglas. *What is a Software Engineer Anyway?* DEV Community. dev.to/solidi/what-is-a-software-engineer-anyway-3fb22

2. ———. *How to Organize Your Thoughts on the Whiteboard and Crush Your Technical Interview.* freeCodeCamp. medium.com/free-code-camp/how-to-organize-your-thoughts-on-the-whiteboard-and-crush-your-technical-interview-b668 de4e6941

3. Kleppmann, Martin. *Designing Data-Intensive Applications.* dataintensive.net

4. Arcuri. Douglas. *Be Amazing in Your New Engineering Role.* DEV Community. dev.to/solidi/be-amazing-in-your-new-engineering-role-1klc

5. ———. *The One About Software Engineering Interviewing.* The Startup. medium.com/swlh/the-one-about-software-engineering-interviewing-6f126 e3a3171

41. Meta Skills of a Software Engineer

1. Correctness and pattern recognition has a strong association with practices around machine learning.

2. Arcuri, Douglas. *Software is Unlike Construction.* HackerNoon. medium.com/hackernoon/software-is-unlike-construction-c0284ee4b723

3. *Programming Pearls, 2nd edition.* Pearson. pearson.com/us/higher-education/program/Bentley-Programming-Pearls-2nd-Edition/PGM203056.html

4. Arcuri, Douglas. *What is a Software Engineer Anyway?* DEV Community. dev.to/solidi/what-is-a-software-engineer-anyway-3fb2

5. *The Pragmatic Programmer, 20th Anniversary Edition*. The Pragmatic Bookshelf. pragprog.com/titles/tpp20/the-pragmatic-programmer-20th-anniversary-edition

6. Arcuri, Douglas. *No Description Provided*. HackerNoon. medium.com/hackernoon/no-description-provided-8d9e0f3a3abb

7. —————. *The Decision Hypothesis*. HackerNoon. hackernoon.com/the-decision-hypothesis-aa512e0113

8. Ousterhout, John. *I'm excited to announce...* X. x.com/JohnOusterhout/status/989260683836506112

9. Ousterhout, John. *Creating Great Programmers with a Software Design Studio - John Ousterhout (Stanford)*. UC Berkeley Events (YouTube). youtu.be/ajFq31OV9Bk

10. Engineers should practice high levels of learning and communication. These concepts aren't unique to software, they have strong associations with the sciences.

42. Be Amazing in Your New Engineering Role

1. Arcuri, Douglas. *What is a Software Engineer Anyway?* DEV Community. dev.to/solidi/what-is-a-software-engineer-anyway-3fb2

2. —————. *Be a Rockstar at Pull Requests*. DEV Community. dev.to/solidi/be-a-rockstar-at-pull-requests-1e4f

3. —————. *How to Crush Your Next Team Demo*. DEV Community. dev.to/solidi/how-to-crush-your-next-team-demo-2bb5

4. *The First 90 Days, Updated and Expanded*. Harvard Business Review. hbr.org/books/watkins

5. Bourguignon, Tim; Arcuri, Douglas. *#98 Doug Arcuri is curious & learning, always!* Software Developers Journey Podcast. devjourney.info/Guests/98-DougArcuri.html

43. What's in a Career Promotion?

1. Bion, Wilfred R. *Experience in Groups*. Amazon. amazon.com/Experiences-Groups-Papers-W-R-Bion/dp/0415040205

2. Kahn, Zain. *11 soft skills to accelerate your career*. X. x.com/heykahn/status/1551556521628094465

3. Arcuri, Douglas. *How to Crush Your Next Team Demo*. DEV Community. dev.to/solidi/how-to-crush-your-next-team-demo-2bb5

4. Evans, Julia. *Get your work recognized: write a brag document*. Julia Evans. jvns.ca/blog/brag-documents

5. Hermansen, Erik. *Getting Promoted: The Boring Work You'll Need to Do.* Level up Coding. levelup.gitconnected.com/getting-promoted-the-boring-work-youll-need-to -do-398e0c9defb2

6. Arcuri, Douglas. *In Software, When an Engineer Exits the Team.* Better Programming. betterprogramming.pub/in-software-when-an-engineer-exits-the-te am-1e550303cff8

44. Onboard Effectively in an Engineer Manager Role

1. Arcuri, Douglas. *What is an Engineering Manager Anyway?* DEV Community. dev.to/solidi/what-is-an-engineering-manager-anyway-4and

2. *Are You Ready To Take Charge Of Your Career?* Manager Tools. manager-tools.com

3. Arcuri, Douglas. In Software, *Philosophy is Delegation.* Level Up Coding. levelup.gitconnected.com/in-software-philosophy-is-delegation-c786dd3a16cf

4. ——————. *The Meta Skills of a Software Engineer.* HackerNoon. medium.com/hackernoon/meta-skills-of-a-software-engineer-bed411f6685e

5. ——————. *The Decision Hypothesis.* HackerNoon. hackernoon.com/ the-decision-hypothesis-aa512e0113

6. ——————. *What is a Product Manager Anyway?* DEV Community. dev.to/solidi/what-is-a-product-manager-anyway-3pc4

7. ——————. *What is a Project Manager?* DEV Community. dev.to /solidi/what-is-a-project-manager-anyway-fbb

8. Doerr, John. *Measure What Matters: How Google, Bono, and the Gates Foundation Rock the World with OKRs.* Amazon. amazon.com/Measure-What-Matters-Google -Foundation/dp/0525536221

9. Grove, Andy. *High Output Management.* Amazon. amazon.com/High-Output -Management-Andrew-Grove/dp/0679762884

10. Arcuri, Douglas. *What is a Tech Lead Anyway?* DEV Community. dev.to/solidi/what-is-a-tech-lead-anyway-483p

11. Bourguignon, Tim; Arcuri, Douglas. *#98 Doug Arcuri is curious & learning, always!* Software Developers Journey Podcast. devjourney.info/Guests/98 -DougArcuri.html

12. Watkins, Michael D. *The First 90 Days: Proven Strategies for Getting Up to Speed Faster and Smarter, Updated and Expanded.* Amazon. amazon.com/First-90-Days -Strategies-Expanded/dp/1422188612

45. The Manager Stew

1. Lopp, Michael. *Rands in Repose*. randsinrepose.com
2. *Are You Ready To Take Charge Of Your Career?* Manager Tools. Manager -tools.com
3. Cahier Journals, *Moleskine*. us.moleskine.com/cahier-journal-black/p0411
4. In my experience, the morning is a time to make great decisions.

46. On Kotlin: a Reply From Management

1. *Google I/O*. Google. events.google.com/io
2. *Google Play Instant*. Android Developer. developer.android.com/topic/google-play-instant
3. *Animate movement using spring physics*. Android Developer. Google. developer.android.com/preview/features/spring-animation.html
4. Android Developers. *Android performance: An overview (Google I/O '17)*. YouTube. youtu.be/Qfo5fdoXrTU
5. Townsend, Tess. *Google Lens is Google's future*. Vox Media. vox.com/2017/5/19/15666704/google-lens-key-example-ai-first-computer-vision
6. Shafirov, Maxim. *Kotlin on Android. Now official*. Jetbrains Blog. blog.jetbrains.com/kotlin/2017/05/kotlin-on-android-now-official
7. Arcuri, Douglas. *What is a Principal Engineer Anyway?* DEV Community. dev.to/solidi/what-is-a-principal-engineer-anyway-55n0
8. Android Developers. *Introduction to Kotlin (Google I/O '17)*. YouTube. youtu.be/X1RVYt2QKQE
9. Arcuri, Douglas. *What is an Engineering Manager Anyway?* DEV Community. dev.to/solidi/what-is-an-engineering-manager-anyway-4and
10. *Experimental New Android Tool Chain - Jack and Jill*. Android Studio Site. web.archive.org/web/20170729223207/tools.android.com/tech-docs/jackandjill
11. Lopp, Michael. *Managing Humans: Biting and Humorous Tales of a Software Engineering Manager*. Amazon. amazon.com/gp/aw/d/1484221575
12. *Tony Hoare*, Wikipedia. en.wikipedia.org/wiki/Tony_Hoare
13. Oracle. *NullPointerException*. Java 7 Documentation. docs.oracle.com/javase/7/docs/api/java/lang/NullPointerException.html
14. Wharton, Jake. *The trillion dollar mistake: assuming the billion dollar mistake of null is its existence, and not the absence of support in the type system (Tweet was removed)*. Twitter. twitter.com/JakeWharton/status/863083342215950336

15. Arcuri, Douglas. In Software, *Philosophy Is Delegation.* Level Up Coding. levelup.gitconnected.com/in-software-philosophy-is-delegation-c786dd3a16cf

16. Wharton, Jake. *(Tweet was removed).* twitter.com/JakeWharton/status/86379118 2094241792

17. *Demand for a Kotlin Community Style Guide?* Reddit. reddit.com/r/androiddev /comments/6chi91/demand_for_a_kotlin_community_style_guide

18. *Laziness Impatience Hubris.* WikiWikiWeb. wiki.c2.com/ ?LazinessImpatience Hubris

19. *Voodoo Programming.* Wikipedia. en.wikipedia.org/wiki/Voodoo_programming

20. *Programming Pearls, 2nd edition.* Amazon. amazon.com/Programming-Pearls -2nd-Jon-Bentley/dp/0201657880

21. McConnell, Steve. *My Books.* stevemcconnell.com/books

22. *Kotlin Koans.* JetBrains. kotlinlang.org/docs/tutorials/koans.html

23. Brandom, Russell. *Google wins Oracle copyright fight over Android code.* Bloomberg. theverge.com/2016/5/26/11754002/oracle-google-verdict-copyright-inf ringement-ruling-api-fair-use

24. *Null safety.* JetBrains. kotlinlang.org/docs/reference/null-safety.html

47. In Software, Philosophy Is Delegation

1. Christian. *Single Level of Abstraction (SLA).* Principles Wiki. principles-wiki.net/principles:single_level_of_abstraction

2. Arcuri, Douglas. *Software is Unlike Construction.* HackerNoon. medium.com /hackernoon/software-is-unlike-construction-c0284ee4b723

3. —————. *What is a Product Manager Anyway?* DEV Community. dev.to/solidi/what-is-a-product-manager-anyway-3pc4

4. —————. *What is an Engineering Manager Anyway?* DEV Community. dev.to/solidi/what-is-an-engineering-manager-anyway-4and

5. *What is Delegation?* WikiWikiWeb. wiki.c2.com/?WhatIsDelegation

6. Storlie, Chad. *Manage Uncertainty with Commander's Intent.* Harvard Business Review. hbr.org/2010/11/dont-play-golf-in-a-football-g

7. Arcuri, Douglas. *Be a Rockstar at Pull Requests.* DEV Community. dev.to/ solidi/be-a-rockstar-at-pull-requests-1e4f

8. Sack, Warren. *The Software Arts.* The MIT Press. mitpress.mit.edu/books/ software-arts

9. Castle, Louis. *How Command & Conquer: Tiberian Sun Solved Pathfinding.* Ars Technica. youtu.be/S-VAL7Epn3o&t=412s

48. When a Software Engineer Exits the Team

1. Arcuri, Douglas. *What is an Engineering Manager Anyway?* DEV Community. dev.to/solidi/what-is-an-engineering-manager-anyway-4and
2. Responders to the post said leaving their software job was mainly about money. This author agrees.
3. Arcuri, Douglas. *What is a Software Engineer Anyway?* DEV Community. dev.to/solidi/what-is-a-software-engineer-anyway-3fb2
4. —————. *Software is Unlike Construction.* HackerNoon. medium.com /hackernoon/software-is-unlike-construction-c0284ee4b723
5. —————. *The Manager Stew.* HackerNoon. medium.com/hackernoon/ the-manager-stew-dd59cd653728
6. *The Evolution of Cooperation.* Wikipedia. en.wikipedia.org/wiki/The_Evolution_ of_Cooperation

49. CQ: Personal Mastery Through Hobbies

1. Readers learn fundamentals from old magazines and books too.

50. The Zen of Motorcycling and Programming

1. Amolat, Capt. Carl. *Safety Third – An Army Context.* U.S. Army. www.army.mil/ article/266448/safety_third_an_army_context

51. Driven to Optimize for Nice

1. Arcuri, Douglas. *10 Self-Care Tips for a Great Vacation.* DEV Community. dev.to/solidi/10-self-care-tips-for-a-great-vacation-2jgp
2. —————. *The Zen of Motorcycling and Programming.* Hacker Noon. medium.com/hackernoon/the-zen-of-motorcycling-and-programming-620907dbab
3. —————. *Apps Doing Sh*t.* Medium. medium.com/@solidi/apps-doing-sh-t-f5ffa72140db
4. Anderson, Dex. *had an incident while driving to pick up dinner that reminded me that "be predictable, not nice" should be taught in every driver's ed course ever.* X. x.com/diannaeanderson/status/1557155725796941830

5. Atwood, Jeff. *The 2030 Self-Driving Car Bet.* Coding Horror. blog.coding horror.com/the-2030-self-driving-car-bet

6. Edmondson, Laurence. *Lewis Hamilton 'lost a little bit of faith' in F1 at Abu Dhabi GP.* ESPN. espn.com/f1/story/_/id/33319352/lewis-hamilton-lost-little-bit -faith-f1-abu-dhabi-gp

7. Genter, Ethan. *Route 6 exit signs' days are numbered on Cape Cod.* Cape Cod Times. capecodtimes.com/story/news/2020/11/27/route-6-exit-signs-days-numbered /6410312002

8. Bordonaro, Lori. *Nassau Shuts Down Controversial School Zone Speed Cameras.* NBC New York. nbcnewyork.com/news/local/nassau-county-shuts-down-school-zone-speed-cameras/2015385

9. *Third rail (politics).* Wikipedia. en.wikipedia.org/wiki/Third_rail_ %28politics%29

10. *Newly Released Estimates Show Traffic Fatalities Reached a 16-Year High in 2021.* NHTSA. nhtsa.gov/press-releases/early-estimate-2021-traffic-fatalities

11. *Red Barchetta.* Wikipedia. en.wikipedia.org/wiki/Red_Barchetta

12. *Alignment (Dungeons & Dragons) - Lawful Good.* Wikipedia. en.wikipedia. org/wiki/Alignment_%28Dungeons_%26_Dragons%29#Lawful_good

13. *Speed limits in thickly settled or business districts.* Commonwealth of Massachusetts. mass.gov/info-details/speed-limits-in-thickly-settled-or-business-distr icts

14. Kuta, Sarah. *Driverless Taxis Are Coming to San Francisco.* Smithsonian Magazine. smithsonianmag.com/smart-news/driverless-taxis-are-coming-to-san-fran cisco-180980202

15. Geller, Avi. *Artificial Intelligence: The Trucking Industry's Biggest Asset.* Global Trade Magazine. globaltrademag.com/artificial-intelligence-the-trucking-industrys -biggest-asset

16. *Automated Vehicles for Safety.* NHTSA. nhtsa.gov/technology-innovation/ automated-vehicles-safety

17. *Death of Elaine Herzberg.* Wikipedia. en.wikipedia.org/wiki/Death_of_Elaine _Herzberg

18. *Flying car.* Wikipedia. en.wikipedia.org/wiki/Flying_car

52. Listening Alone on the Internet

1. Andrea Ribeca and Giuseppe Ottaviani made up Nu NRG.

2. *Nu NRG - Dreamland (Original Mix) (HD).* YouTube. youtu.be/d8Ee59Y d1lI&t=180s

3. The original flier to Nu NRG in 2003, their coming to America tour. madeevent.com/082303.php

4. Before Internet saturation, this author openly spoke to others about the music in person. This is no longer the case.

5. *Xennials*. Wikipedia. en.wikipedia.org/wiki/Xennials

6. *Napster*. Wikipedia. en.wikipedia.org/wiki/Napster

7. *Wave Music*. Wikipedia. en.wikipedia.org/wiki/Wave_music

8. After Internet music sharing, contiguity is present globally.

53. A Love Letter to My YouTube Subscriptions

1. Bonifacic, Igor. *Disney is bringing the first episode of 'The Mandalorian' to broadcast TV.* Engadget. engadget.com/disney-is-bringing-the-first-episode-of-the-mandalorian-to-broadcast-tv-231407016.html

2. Ranallo, Nathan. *Nate the Hoof Guy.* YouTube Channel. youtube.com/@NatetheHoofGuy

3. Kulakov. Taras. *Crazy Russian Hacker.* YouTube Channel. youtube.com/@CrazyRussianHacker

4. Smith, Arieh. *Xiaoma.* YouTube Channel. youtube.com/@xiaomanyc

5. Willett, Tom. *Featureman.* YouTube Channel. youtube.com/@Featureman

6. Henn, Jürgen. *11foot8.* YouTube Channel. youtube.com/@11foot8plus8

7. Henn, Jürgen. *11foot8. FAQ.* 11foot8.com/11foot8-faq

8. *Mr. Heang Update.* YouTube Channel. youtube.com/@MrHeangUpdate

9. Beschizza, Rob. "Primitive building" videos deemed fraudulent. Boing Boing. boingboing.net/2022/07/08/primitive-building-videos-deemed-fraudulent.html

10. Thoms, Steven. *Steve1989MREInfo.* YouTube Channel. youtube.com/@Steve1989MRE

11. *SBMoving.* YouTube Channel. youtube.com/@SBMowing

12. Vuohensilta, Lauri. *Hydraulic Press Channel (HPC).* YouTube Channel. youtube.com/@HydraulicPressChannel

13. Strahle, Kevin Thomas. *LABeast.* YouTube Channel. youtube.com/@LABEAST

14. Strahle, Kevin Thomas. *Enjoying A 20 Year Old CRYSTAL PEPSI.* YouTube. youtu.be/CGwibPdEOVk

15. *RailCowGirl.* YouTube Channel. youtube.com/@RailCowGirl

16. Mitchell, Ralfy. *The Whisky Bothy.* YouTube Channel. youtube.com/@thewhiskybothy

17. *RoyalJordanian.* YouTube Channel. youtube.com/@royaljordanian

18. Jurasek, John. *ReportOfTheWeek*. YouTube Channel. youtube.com/@The ReportOfTheWeek

19. *Hydraulic Press Channel*. Wikipedia. en.wikipedia.org/wiki/Hydraulic_Pres s_Channel

54. The Many Senses of Software Engineering

1. Arcuri, Douglas. *Software is Unlike Construction*. HackerNoon. medium.com /hackernoon/software-is-unlike-construction-c0284ee4b723

2. —————. *What is a Software Engineer Anyway?* DEV Community. dev.to/solidi/what-is-a-software-engineer-anyway-3fb2

3. —————. *What is a Principal Engineer Anyway?* DEV Community. dev.to/solidi/what-is-a-principal-engineer-anyway-55n0

4. —————. *In Software: Philosophy is Delegation*. Medium. medium.com /@solidi/in-software-philosophy-is-delegation-c786dd3a16cf

55. Recognizing Remote Romantic Bibliophilia

1. Arcuri. Douglas. *Deconstructing My Reading Habits*. The Innovation. medium .com/the-innovation/deconstructing-my-reading-habits-cef9e7d82bad

2. —————. *Do Great at Working Remotely*. DEV Community. dev.to /solidi/do-great-at-working-remotely-1oh9

3. —————. *What is an Engineering Manager Anyway?* DEV Community. dev.to/solidi/what-is-an-engineering-manager-anyway-4and

4. —————. *The Decision Hypothesis*. HackerNoon. hackernoon.com/ the-decision-hypothesis-aa512e0113

5. —————. *Learning Notes*. Github. github.com/solidi/learning-notes/ blob/main/books/reading-list.md

56. Short Circuiting Fantastical Debugging

1. Arcuri, Douglas. *Secret of Mana: An Oral History of Playing the JRPG in the 1990s*. SUPERJUMP Magazine. medium.com/super-jump/secret-of-mana-an-oral -history-of-playing-the-jrpg-in-the-1990s-39029a28584f

2. —————. *The Meta Skills of a Software Engineer*. HackerNoon. medium.com/hackernoon/meta-skills-of-a-software-engineer-bed411f6685e

3. —————. *Software is Unlike Construction*. HackerNoon. medium.com /hackernoon/software-is-unlike-construction-c0284ee4b723

57. Five More Minutes

1. Arcuri, Douglas. *What is a Software Engineer Anyway?* DEV Community. dev.to/solidi/what-is-a-software-engineer-anyway-3fb2

2. Woo, Michelle. *What to Tell Your Kid Instead of 'Five More Minutes.'* LifeHacker. lifehacker.com/what-to-tell-your-kid-instead-of-five-more-minutes-1836058634

3. Arcuri, Douglas. *Building a Popular Half-Life Mod During the Rise of Counter-Strike.* SUPERJUMP Magazine. medium.com/super-jump/building-a-popular-half-life-mod-during-the-rise-of-counter-strike-fec6a5b9fd8f

4. ————. *What is an Engineering Manager Anyway?* DEV Community. dev.to/solidi/what-is-an-engineering-manager-anyway-4and

5. ————. *The Joy of Collecting Timeless Engineering Posts.* DEV Community. dev.to/solidi/the-joy-of-collecting-timeless-engineering-posts-5el3

6. ————. *Short Circuiting Fantastical Debugging.* DEV Community. dev.to/solidi/short-circuiting-fantastical-debugging-ig3

7. ————. *The One About Blogging.* Medium. medium.com/@solidi/the-one-about-blogging-cd9e65a2055b

58. Learning from Structures Around Us

1. Arcuri, Douglas. *Software is Unlike Construction.* HackerNoon. medium.com/hackernoon/software-is-unlike-construction-c0284ee4b723

2. ————. *What is a Software Engineer Anyway?* DEV Community. dev.to/solidi/what-is-a-software-engineer-anyway-3fb2

59. Software Development Is Unlike Construction

1. Arcuri, Douglas. *The Springboard Pattern.* HackerNoon. medium.com/hackernoon/the-springboard-pattern-340e00379404

2. Brooks, Frederick P. *No Silver Bullet: Essence and Accidents of Software Engineering.* IEEE Computer, Vol. 20, No. 4 (April 1987) pp. 10-19. cgl.ucsf.edu/Outreach/pc204/NoSilverBullet.html

3. Arcuri, Douglas. *How to Crush Your Next Team Demo.* DEV Community. dev.to/solidi/how-to-crush-your-next-team-demo-2bb5

4. *Tracer Bullets.* WikiWikiWeb. wiki.c2.com/?TracerBullets

5. Arcuri, Douglas. *In Software: Philosophy Is Delegation.* Medium. medium.com/@solidi/in-software-philosophy-is-delegation-c786dd3a16cf

6. Arcuri, Douglas. *8 Observations on Test Driven Development.* freeCodeCamp. medium.com/free-code-camp/8-observations-on-test-driven-development-a9b5144f 868

7. ――――. *What is a Software Engineer Anyway?* DEV Community. dev.to/solidi/what-is-a-software-engineer-anyway-3fb2

8. ――――. *The Decision Hypothesis.* HackerNoon. hackernoon.com /the-decision-hypothesis-aa512e0113

9. ――――. *The Zen of Motorcycling and Programming.* Hacker Noon. medium.com/hackernoon/the-zen-of-motorcycling-and-programming-620907dbab

10. Enden, Tom. *Software Engineering - A philosophical activity.* YouTube. youtu.be/JJ7UgLpgkzc

60. On Names: A Brief Encounter with Guido van Rossum

1. Arcuri, Douglas. *The Meta Skills of a Software Engineer.* HackerNoon. medium.com/hackernoon/meta-skills-of-a-software-engineer-bed411f6685e

2. *About PyCon 2019.* Python Software Foundation. us.pycon.org/2019/about

3. Arcuri, Douglas. *The Zen of Motorcycling and Programming.* Hacker Noon. medium.com/hackernoon/the-zen-of-motorcycling-and-programming-620907dbab

4. Guido, van Rossum. *Guido van Rossum - Personal Home Page.* gvanrossum .github.io

61. When to Take a Vacation

1. Arcuri, Douglas. *The World I Worked into No Longer Exists.* Medium. medium.com/@solidi/the-world-i-worked-into-no-longer-exists-732659963058

2. ――――. *10 Self-Care Tips for a Great Vacation.* DEV Community. dev.to/solidi/10-self-care-tips-for-a-great-vacation-2jgp

62. Building a Popular Half-Life Mod During the Rise of Counter-Strike

1. *Half-Life SDK.* Blues News. bluesnews.com/s/1239/half-life-sdk

2. *Stalkyard,* Combine Overwiki. combineoverwiki.net/wiki/Stalkyard

3. *Video game modding.* Wikipedia. en.wikipedia.org/wiki/Mod_%28video _games %29

4. *Cold-Ice.* ModDB. moddb.com/mods/cold-ice

5. *Cold Ice Mod Review*. members.tripod.com/~Half_Life_Page/Cold_ice.htm

6. Overholt, Jeff. Kent, Jeff. *Video Game Subcultures: Mods*. transcriptions-2008. english.ucsb.edu/curriculum/lci/magazine/s_02/eric/mod.htm

7. *Valve Hammer*. Wikipedia. developer.valvesoftware.com/wiki/Valve_Hammer_ Editor

8. *BSP (Source)*. Valve Developer Wiki. developer.valvesoftware.com/wiki/Source_ BSP_File_Format

9. articles.thewavelength.net

10. *Wasteland Half-Life Screenshots*. web.archive.org/web/20220727202600/waste landhalflife.com/screenshots.shtml

11. Birdwell, Ken. *The Cabal: Valve's Design Process For Creating Half-Life*. Gamasutra. web.archive.org/web/20200926184656/gamasutra.com/view/feature /3408/the_cabal_valves_design_process_.php

12. *Mod of the Week - Cold Ice*. Planet Half-Life. web.archive.org/web/ 20000816001652/http://planethalflife.com:80/community/motw/coldice2.shtm

13. Wofford, Taylor. *Fuck You And Die: An Oral History of Something Awful*. Vice. vice.com/en/article/nzg4yw/fuck-you-and-die-an-oral-history-of-something-awful

14. *Half-Life Mod Expo*. Combine Overwiki. combineoverwiki.net/wiki/Half-Life_Mod_Expo

15. *2001-09-15 Mailbag*. Planet Half-Life. planethalflife.gamespy.com/View555b .html?view=Mailbag.Detail&id=414

16. *Poll Results*. angelfire.com/hi2/tfclassic/poll.html

17. *Half-Life Pro*. Planet Half-Life. web.archive.org/web/20000815070305/http:// planethalflife.com/hlpro

18. *Half-Life OZ Deathmatch*. Steam. steamcommunity.com/groups/halflife-ozdm

19. *Cold-Ice SDK*. ModDB. moddb.com/downloads/cold-ice-sdk

20. *Action Half-Life*. Wikipedia. en.wikipedia.org/wiki/Action_Half-Life

21. Abrash, Michael. *Quake's 3-D Engine: The Big Picture*. BluesNews. bluesnews .com/abrash/chap70.shtml

22. *Day of Defeat: Source*. dayofdefeat.com

23. Arcuri, Douglas. *What is a Software Engineer Anyway?* DEV Community. dev.to/solidi/what-is-a-software-engineer-anyway-3fb2

24. *Valve Corporation - Valve Time*. Wikipedia. en.wikipedia.org/wiki/Valve_Corp oration#%22Valve_Time%22

25. quakewiki.net/archives/features/polls/poll991110.shtml

26. *Half-Life Advanced Readme.txt*. Github. github.com/solidi/hl-mods/blob/ main/hla/redist/readme.txt

27. *Adrenaline Gamer*. ModDB. moddb.com/mods/adrenaline-gamer

28. *Half-Life Advanced: Arena*. Github. github.com/solidi/hl-mods/blob/main/hla/src/dlls/multiplay_gamerules.cpp#L502

29. *Half-Life Pong: Update Pong Ball*. Github. github.com/solidi/hl-mods/blob/main/pong/src/dlls/multiplay_gamerules.cpp#L180

30. *Cold-Ice Beta 2.5*. ModDB. moddb.com/mods/cold-ice/downloads/cold-ice-v-beta-25

31. *Cold Ice - a Hot Half-Life mod*. Tom's Hardware Forum. Forums.tomshardware.com/threads/cold-ice-a-hot-half-life-mod.137751

32. *[Does] Anyone still play the COLD ICE mod?* Steam Forums. steamcommunity.com/app/70/discussions/0/1489992713697672376

33. *Half-Life Mods*. Github. github.com/solidi/hl-mods

63. The World I Worked into No Longer Exists

1. Arcuri, Douglas. *My Goal is to Ship*. Medium. medium.com/@solidi/my-goal-is-to-ship-c772f63c278d

2. —————. *In Software, When an Engineer Exits the Team*. Better Programming. medium.com/@solidi/in-software-when-an-engineer-exits-the-team-1e550303cff8

3. *"Your parents raised you for a world that no longer exists."* Reddit. reddit.com/r/Millennials/comments/ps3r69/your_parents_raised_you_for_a_world_that_no

64. My Goal Is to Ship

1. Arcuri, Douglas. *The Next Fantastic Software Project Code Name*. DEV Community. dev.to/solidi/the-next-fantastic-software-project-code-name-bbd

2. Graham, Paul. *Great Hackers*. paulgraham.com/gh.html

3. Arcuri, Douglas. *Software is Unlike Construction*. HackerNoon. medium.com/hackernoon/software-is-unlike-construction-c0284ee4b723

4. Grant, Adam. *Give and Take*. adamgrant.net/book/give-and-take

5. Arcuri, Douglas. *What is an Engineering Manager Anyway?* DEV Community. dev.to/solidi/what-is-an-engineering-manager-anyway-4and

6. —————. *The Meta Skills of a Software Engineer*. HackerNoon. medium.com/hackernoon/meta-skills-of-a-software-engineer-bed411f6685e

7. —————. *CQ: Personal Mastery Through Hobbies*. Medium. medium.com/@solidi/cq-personal-mastery-through-hobbies-f25aab2e49ad

8. *Hackers*. O'Reilly Media. oreilly.com/library/view/hackers/9781449390259

9. Arcuri, Douglas. *The Decision Hypothesis.* HackerNoon. hackernoon.com/the-decision-hypothesis-aa512e0113

10. Spolsky, Joel. *Picking a Ship Date.* Joel on Software. joelonsoftware.com/2002/04/09/picking-a-ship-date

11. Arcuri, Douglas. *In Software, When an Engineer Exits the Team.* Better Programming. betterprogramming.pub/in-software-when-an-engineer-exits-the-team-1e550303cff8

12. —————. *Recognizing Remote Bibliophilia.* DEV Community. dev.to/solidi/recognizing-remote-romantic-bibliophilia-255f

Selected Bibliography

Beck, Kent; Andres, Cynthia. *Extreme Programming Explained: Embrace Change, 2nd Edition (The XP Series)*. Addison-Wesley, 2004.

Beck, Kent. *Test-Driven Development: By Example*. Addison-Wesley Professional, 2002.

Bently, Jon. *Programming Pearls (2nd Edition)*. Addison-Wesley Professional, 1999.

Bion, Wilfred R. *Experiences in Groups: and Other Papers*. Routledge, 1968.

Brooks, Frederick P. *The Mythical Man-Month and Other Essays On Software Engineering*. Dept. of Computer Science, University of North Carolina at Chapel Hill, 1974.

Cagan, Marty. *Inspired: How to Create Tech Products Customers Love*. Wiley, 2017.

DeMarco, Tom. *Slack: Getting Past Burnout, Busywork, and the Myth of Total Efficiency*. Currency, 2002.

DeMarco, Tom; Lister, Tim. *Peopleware: Productive Projects and Teams*. Addison-Wesley Professional, 2013.

Doerr, John. *Measure What Matters: How Google, Bono, and the Gates Foundation Rock the World with OKRs*. Portfolio, 2018.

Fisher, Roger; Ury, William L. *Getting to Yes: Negotiating Agreement Without Giving In.* Penguin Books, 1983.

Fournier, Camille. *The Manager's Path: A Guide for Tech Leaders Navigating Growth and Change.* Shroff/O'Reilly, 2017.

Graham, Paul. *Hackers & Painters: Big Ideas from the Computer Age.* O'Reilly Media, 2010.

Grant, Adam. *Give and Take: Why Helping Others Drives Our Success.* Penguin Books, 2014.

Grove, Andrew S. *High Output Management.* Vintage, 1995

Harari, Yuval. *Sapiens: A Brief History of Humankind.* Harper Perennial, 2015.

Haugeland, John. *Artificial Intelligence: The Very Idea.* Bradford books, 1985.

Hogan, Lara. *Resilient Management.* Independently Published. 2019.

Jemerov, Dmitry; Isakova, Svetlana. *Kotlin In Action.* Manning, 2017.

Kahneman, Daniel. *Thinking Fast and Slow.* Farrar, Straus and Giroux, 2013.

Kidder, Tracy. *The Soul of A New Machine.* Back Bay Books, 2001.

Kleppmann, Martin. *Designing Data-Intensive Applications: The Big Ideas Behind Reliable, Scalable, and Maintainable Systems.* O'Reilly Media, 2017.

Koskela, Lasse. *Effective Unit Testing.* Manning Publications Company, 2013.

Kushner, David. *Masters of Doom: How Two Guys Created an Empire and Transformed Pop Culture.* Random House Trade Paperbacks, 2004.

Larson, Will. *An Elegant Puzzle: Systems of Engineering Management.* Stripe Press, 2019.

Levy, Steven. *Hackers: Heroes of the Computer Revolution - 25th Anniversary Edition.* O'Reilly Media, 2010.

Lopp, Michael. *Managing Humans: Biting and Humorous Tales of a Software Engineering Manager.* Apress, 2016.

Ousterhout, John. *A Philosophy of Software Design.* Yaknyam Press, 2018.

Martin, Robert C. *Clean Code: A Handbook of Agile Software Craftsmanship.* Pearson, 2008.

McDowell, Gayle Laakmann. *Cracking the Coding Interview: 189 Programming Questions and Solutions.* CareerCup, 2015.

Meszaros, Gerard. *xUnit Test Patterns: Refactoring Test Code.* Addison-Wesley, 2007.

Petzold, Charles. *Code: The Hidden Language of Computer Hardware and Software.* Microsoft Press, 1999.

Pirsig, Robert M. *Zen and the Art of Motorcycle Maintenance: An Inquiry into Values.* Bantam New Age Books, 1974.

Raymond, Eric S. *The Cathedral & the Bazaar: Musings on Linux and Open Source by an Accidental Revolutionary.* O'Reilly Media, 1999.

Sack, Warren. The Software Arts. The MIT Press, 2019.

Sanglard, Fabien. *Game Engine Black Book: DOOM: v1.2.* Independently Published, 2022.

Scott, Kim. *Radical Candor: How to Get What You Want by Saying What You Mean.* Pan Macmillan UK, 2017.

Thomas, David, Hunt, Andrew. *The Pragmatic Programmer: Your Journey To Mastery, 20th Anniversary Edition (2nd Edition).* Addison-Wesley Professional, 2019.

Watkins, Michael D. *The First 90 Days: Proven Strategies for Getting Up to Speed Faster and Smarter, Updated and Expanded.* Harvard Business Review Press, 2013.

DSR

Index

INDEX

About the Author

DOUGLAS W. ARCURI resides with his family on Long Island, New York. Throughout his career, he has worked for media companies developing mobile video streaming applications.

Now, as a long-running engineering manager at tech software corporations, he manages SaaS solutions.

In his spare time, he writes business history and rides motorcycles. He enjoys crafting and painting plastic auto models, and developing retro game modifications.

The author and his father in front of a Kenwood TS-530S transceiver in 1985.

DSR

Even More Praise for the Author

"Medium won't let me read the story without signing into Medium."

—A reader

"I feel like I had a stroke while attempting to read this."

—A reader

"Your submission was automatically removed in violation of Rule #2."

—An admin

"This whole 'turn yourself into a brand' movement and then aggressively market yourself everywhere pisses me off [to] no end."

—A reader

"I honestly never thought of cross posting dev.to to niche Reddits."

—A reader

"Interesting topic but the blog doesn't have much substance."

—A reader

"Your submission has been removed, it is a 'Change My View' post."

—An admin

"Personal essays by people who aren't traditionally essayists are something I always enjoy. Thanks for sharing!"

—A reader